PROBLEMS OF POPULATION

PROBLEMS OF POPULATION

BEING THE

REPORT OF THE PROCEEDINGS

OF THE SECOND GENERAL
ASSEMBLY

OF

THE INTERNATIONAL UNION FOR THE
SCIENTIFIC INVESTIGATION OF
POPULATION PROBLEMS

Held at the Royal Society of Arts, London, June 15–18, 1931

Published under the direction of the Executive Committee

EDITED BY

G. H. L. F. PITT-RIVERS, B.Sc.(OXON)

Hon. General Secretary

KENNIKAT PRESS
Port Washington, N. Y./London

PROBLEMS OF POPULATION

First published in 1932
Reissued in 1971 by Kennikat Press
Library of Congress Catalog Card No: 74-115327
ISBN 0-8046-1118-1

Manufactured by Taylor Publishing Company   Dallas, Texas

INVENTORY SLIP

_____ No inventory card

_____ Check classification

__✓__ Check cutter number

_____ Check spine

_____ Check book card

_____ Verify accession number

_____ No book card

_____ Repair

_____ Other

EDITOR'S PREFACE

THIS volume of Proceedings is the first to be published under the auspices of the International Union for the Scientific Investigation of Population Problems since it was inaugurated in 1928. It contains the full text of all scientific papers read at the London Meeting of the Second General Assembly in June 1931. Communications made in the French and German languages are preceded by abstracts in English. All discussions are in English. Titles of addresses or communications; the principal topics dealt with; authors; the names of the officers of the Union, of the officials of adhering countries, and of those taking part in discussions, will be found in the Index, as well as listed in their appropriate sections. The Official Business of the Union was conducted at three morning sessions of the delegates to the Assembly, June 15th to 17th. The business proceedings are reported in the official *Bulletin* of the Union, and are therefore not included. The Revised Statutes are also published separately.

The first World Population Congress, which led to the formation of the International Union, was held at Geneva from August 29th to September 3rd in 1927. Its proceedings were published and the volume was edited by Mrs. Margaret Sanger (Edward Arnold & Co., London, 1927), whose work in preliminary organization made possible the co-operation of international scientists leading to the first World Congress at which twenty-seven countries were represented.

The world-wide interest shown on that occasion, the increasing attention that has since been paid to the many pressing problems that in one form or another are directly related to the study of population, and the recent inauguration in England of a British Population Society, as well as similar societies in other countries, may have prepared for this volume of scientific papers a circle of readers wider than that confined to those who approach the study from any specialized technical aspect.

This non-specialist and wider public may not, however, appreciate how differently the many-sided study of population presents itself to the student of to-day, since the work of Malthus first provoked such lively controversy.

The older Malthusian controversy appeared to present the problem almost exclusively in terms of density in relation to food supply; whereas to-day the question whether any geographical area or country exceeds or falls short of the most favourable or optimum density has to be decided on many other grounds than the actual or possible food supply. Furthermore, it is now better appreciated that the effects of over-population and of under-population or depopulation may co-exist among communities in close contact or in adjoining areas, and these opposite effects may even be detected, by various criteria, among different strata of society within the same area.

The Malthusian conception of an actual or proximate shortage of food resulting in famine, war, or pestilence, is seldom the first harbinger of an encroach by a rapidly increasing population upon the resources of a people striving to accommodate its numbers successfully. Some workers see the first consequences of an expansion beyond optimum density in a gradual breakdown in organization, with reactions upon the control of society and, in the economic sphere, upon its distributive capacity. They show in various ways that an economically unabsorbed or unabsorbable population can co-exist with over-production, and in a world producing a food surplus.

Another factor affecting the birth-rate unevenly in different groups of a modern population that has gradually come into prominence is the influence of the spread of contraceptive practices; while in some populations a falling birth-rate accompanying a falling death-rate and an increasing longevity brings about changes in the age distribution, with important social and other consequences.

The problem of the economic absorption of population without damage to an acceptable quantum of health and happiness is therefore approached from many different angles; the qualitative and the quantitative distribution of population being interdependent and equally important.

It remains almost inevitable that experts, approaching these intricate and complex problems in their different aspects under widely different conditions in all different parts of the world, should occasionally arrive at different, or even contrasted, conclusions. A circumstance which in no way detracts from the value to be gained by a careful study of all the researches.

The arrangements in connection with the preparation and accommodation of the International Congress on Population and the Second General Assembly of the International Union in London were in the hands of the British National Committee, the composition of which is given on p. 25. Mr. Eldon Moore, who also acted as Secretary to the British Committee, was entrusted with the task of carrying out all preliminary local arrangements.

Among the social functions at which kind hospitality was shown to the visiting delegates must be recorded the reception given by Mrs. Anstruther at Rutland House, Knightsbridge, on Monday evening, June 15th, and also the Garden Party at Douglas House, Petersham, on Wednesday, June 17th, given by Sir Bernard and Lady Mallet.

NOTE.—*After the termination of the Second General Assembly a Central Office for the General Headquarters of the Union was established in London. All inquiries may therefore be addressed to the Hon. General Secretary, International Population Union, c/o The Royal Geographical Society, Kensington Gore, London, S.W.7.*

PRÉFACE DE L'ÉDITEUR

Ce volume de comptes-rendus de travaux est le premier qui soit publié sous les auspices de l'Union Internationale pour l'Étude Scientifique des Problèmes de Population depuis son inauguration en 1928. Il contient le texte complet de tous les rapports scientifiques lus à Londres, lors de la Deuxième Assemblée Générale, en juin 1931. Les communications faites en français et en allemand sont précédées de résumés en anglais. Toutes les discussions sont reproduites en anglais. Les titres des discours et communications, les principaux sujets traités, les noms des auteurs, les noms des membres de l'Union y exerçant des fonctions administratives, ceux des fonctionnaires des pays adhérents et des personnes ayant pris part aux discussions seront trouvés à l'Index, en plus de leur inclusion dans les sections appropriées. Les Affaires Officielles de l'Union ont été traitées au cours de trois séances du matin tenues par les délégués à l'Assemblée, les 15, 16 et 17 juin. Les travaux de ces séances ont été publiés dans le *Bulletin* officiel de l'Union, et sont, par suite, exclus du présent recueil. Les Statuts Modifiés sont également publiés séparément.

Le premier Congrès Mondial de la Population, qui conduisit à la formation de l'Union Internationale, fut tenu à Genève du 29 août au 3 septembre 1927. Ses travaux furent publiés, et le volume fut édité par Mrs. Margaret Sanger (Edward Arnold et Cie., Londres, 1927), dont l'œuvre d'organisation préliminaire avait rendue possible la collaboration internationale de savants qui aboutit au premier Congrès Mondial, où 27 pays étaient représentés.

L'intérêt universel témoigné à cette occasion, l'attention croissante portée depuis aux nombreux problèmes urgents liés directement, sous une forme ou sous une autre, à l'étude de la population, et l'inauguration récente en Angleterre d'une *British Population Society*, ainsi que d'associations similaires dans d'autres pays, ont dû préparer au présent recueil de rapports scientifiques un cercle de lecteurs plus vaste que celui que forment les spécialistes qui abordent ces études d'un point de vue purement technique.

Ce public non spécialiste, ce public plus étendu, ne voit peut-être pas clairement sous quels angles très différents l'étude de la population, étude aux aspects si divers, se présente au chercheur d'aujourd'hui, depuis l'époque où l'œuvre de Malthus provoqua des controverses si vives.

La polémique malthusienne d'autrefois semblait faire consister le problème presque exclusivement dans la considération de la densité par rapport aux ressources alimentaires, tandis qu'aujourd'hui la question de savoir si un territoire géographique ou un pays donnés dépassent ou n'atteignent pas la densité la plus favorable, ou *optimum*, doit être résolue en tenant compte de beaucoup d'autres facteurs en plus de celui des ressources alimentaires existantes ou possibles. En outre, on voit mieux maintenant que les effets de la sur-population et de la sous-population ou de la dépopulation peuvent même être révélés, à l'aide de divers critères, chez différentes couches sociales à l'intérieur du même territoire.

La conception malthusienne d'une disette, réelle ou approximative, aboutissant à la famine, à la guerre ou à la pestilence, est rarement le premier signe avant-coureur de la main-mise par une population rapidement croissante sur les ressources d'un peuple s'efforçant de satisfaire au mieux les besoins des individus qui le composent. Certains savants voient, comme premières conséquences d'une expansion dépassant la densité optima, une dislocation graduelle du système, avec des contre-coups sur la discipline sociale, et, dans l'ordre économique, sur sa capacité distributive. Ils montrent, de différentes façons, qu'une population économiquement inabsorbée ou inabsorbable peut coexister avec de la sur-production, et cela dans un monde produisant un surplus de denrées alimentaires.

Un autre facteur qui affecte la natalité inégalement dans divers groupes sociaux d'une population moderne, et qui a graduellement acquis une grande importance, c'est l'influence de la diffusion des pratiques anticonceptionnelles; d'autre part, dans certaines populations, une natalité en baisse, accompagnée d'une mortalité également en baisse et d'une longévité croissante, amène des changements dans la répartition des âges, ce qui a des conséquences importantes, sociales et autres.

Le problème de l'absorption économique de la population sans dommage pour un *quantum* acceptable de santé et de bonheur se trouve donc abordé sous bien des angles différents, la distribution qualitative et quantitative de la population étant interdépendantes et également importantes.

Il devient donc presque inévitable que les experts qui abordent ces problèmes ardus et complexes sous leurs différents aspects et dans des conditions qui varient énormément selon les différentes régions du monde, arrivent parfois à des conclusions différentes ou même opposées, —fait qui n'enlève rien au profit à retirer d'une étude soigneuse de toutes les recherches.

Les mesures pour la préparation et l'hospitalisation du Congrès International de la Population et de la Deuxième Assemblée Générale de l'Union Internationale à Londres ont été prises par le Comité National Britannique, dont la composition est indiquée page 25. À Mr. Eldon Moore, qui remplissait aussi les fonctions de Secrétaire du Comité Britannique, a été confiée la tâche d'exécuter sur place toutes les mesures préliminairement fixées.

Parmi les fonctions mondaines où une bienveillante hospitalité fut accordée aux délégués, il faut mentionner la réception donnée par Mrs. Anstruther à Rutland House, Knightsbridge, le lundi soir 15 juin, et la Garden-party à Douglas House, Petersham, le mercredi 17 juin, donnée par Sir Bernard et Lady Mallet.

N.B.—*A l'issue de la Deuxième Assemblée Générale, un Bureau Central pour le Siège Social de l'Union a été établi à Londres. Par suite, toutes les demandes de renseignements peuvent être adressées à The Hon. General Secretary, International Population Union, c/o The Royal Geographical Society, Kensington Gore, Londres, S.W.7.*

CONTENTS

FIRST SESSION

SECOND SESSION

THIRD SESSION

FOURTH SESSION

FIFTH SESSION

GENERAL POPULATION

DIAGRAMS

OFFICERS OF THE UNION

EXECUTIVE COMMITTEE

PRESIDENT:

Col. Sir CHARLES CLOSE, K.B.E., F.R.S.

VICE-PRESIDENTS:

Professor RAYMOND PEARL, *Ex-President* (U.S.A.)
Professor E. MAHAIM (Belgium)
Professor LÉON BERNARD (France)
Professor Dr. EUGEN FISCHER (Germany)
Sir BERNARD MALLET (Great Britain)
Dr. H. W. METHORST (Holland)
Professor CORRADO GINI (Italy)

HON. GENERAL SECRETARY AND TREASURER
Captain G. H. L. F. PITT-RIVERS (*Ex officio*)

CHAIRMEN OF INTERNATIONAL COMMISSIONS

COMMISSION I
Population and Food Supply
Chairman: Professor J. D. BLACK (U.S.A.)

COMMISSION II
Fertility, Fecundity, and Sterility
Chairman: Professor F. A. E. CREW (Great Britain)

COMMISSION III
Vital Statistics of Primitive Races
Chairman: Professor C. GINI (Italy)

LIST OF ADHERING COUNTRIES IN 1931

The following countries are represented in the International Population Union by fully constituted National Committees:

Country	Chairman
AMERICA	Dr. LOUIS I. DUBLIN, Metropolitan Life Insurance Company, New York City, U.S.A.
ARGENTINE	Dr. TOMAS AMADEO, Museo Social Argentino, Buenos Aires, Argentine, South America
BELGIUM	Professor E. MAHAIM, Institut de Sociologie Solvay, Parc Leopold, Brussels, Belgium
CZECHOSLOVAKIA	Dr. ANTONIN BOHAC, Office de Statistique de la République Tchécoslovaque, 2, Belskeho tr. 2, Prague VII, Czechoslovakia
DENMARK	Dr. SOREN HANSEN, Danish Anthropological Committee, Kristiansgade 12B, Copenhagen, Denmark
FRANCE	Dr. LÉON BERNARD, 166, Faubourg St.-Honoré, Paris, France
GERMANY	Professor Dr. EUGEN FISCHER, Kaiser Wilhelm Institute, Ihnestrasse 22/24, Berlin-Dahlem, Germany
GREAT BRITAIN (British Population Society).	Sir BERNARD MALLET, K.C.B., 8, Eccleston Square, London, S.W.1
HOLLAND	Dr. H. W. METHORST, Comité National Néerlandais de l'Union Internationale pour l'Étude Scientifique des Problèmes de Population, La Haye, Holland
ITALY	Professor C. GINI, 10, Via delle Terme di Diocleziane, Rome, Italy
SPAIN	Dr. Severino Aznar, University of Madrid, Madrid, Spain
SWEDEN	Dr. ALFRED PETTERSSON, University of Stockholm, Stockholm, Sweden

Besides these countries, National Committees are in process of organization in the following countries:

Brazil	Hungary
Canada	Switzerland
Greece	

OFFICERS AND STEWARDS OF
THE GENERAL ASSEMBLY IN LONDON

BRITISH NATIONAL COMMITTEE

(*British Population Society*)

*†Sir BERNARD MALLET, K.C.B., *Chairman*
Sir WILLIAM BEVERIDGE, K.C.B.
*Miss M. C. BUER, Sc.D. Econ.
*Professor A. L. BOWLEY, Sc.D.
*†Colonel Sir CHARLES CLOSE, K.B.E., C.B., D.Sc., F.R.S.
Professor F. A. E. CREW, D.Sc.
Professor A. M. CARR-SAUNDERS
*Professor C. B. FAWCETT
Mr. R. A. FISHER, Sc.D., F.R.S.
Professor J. W. GREGORY, F.R.S.
Mr. DAVID HERON, Sc.D.
Professor JULIAN S. HUXLEY
The Very Rev. W. R. INGE, K.C.V.O., D.D., Dean of St. Paul's
Sir ARTHUR KEITH, F.R.S.
Mr. J. MAYNARD KEYNES, C.B.
Professor B. MALINOWSKI
Mr. MICHAEL PEASE
*†Captain G. H. PITT-RIVERS
Miss GLADYS POTT
Sir HUMPHREY ROLLESTON, Bart., G.C.V.O., K.C.B., M.D.
Sir JOSIAH STAMP, G.B.E.
Mr. ELDON MOORE, *Arrangements Secretary*

---

* *Executive Committee, appointed November 6, 1931.*
† *Stewards of the Assembly.*

DELEGATES AND VISITORS TO ASSEMBLY

Those marked with an asterisk were not members of the Union, but read papers.

Professor F. BAUDHUIN, Professeur de science financière et d'économie politique, Université de Louvain, Belgium.

M. le Dr. LÉON BERNARD, Président du Conseil Supérieur d'Hygiène Publique de France. Professeur à la Faculté de Médecine de Paris, France.

Sir WILLIAM BEVERIDGE, K.C.B., D.Sc., Director of London School of Economics, England.

Professor J. D. BLACK, Harvard University, Cambridge, Mass., U.S.A.

Professor A. L. BOWLEY, Sc.D., Professor of Statistics, University of London, England.

Dr. H. D. BRACKENBURY, LL.D., England.

Miss M. C. BUER, D.Sc.Econ., Reading University, England.

Professor A. M. CARR-SAUNDERS, M.A., Professor of Social Science, Liverpool University, England.

Professor R. E. CHADDOCK, Columbia University, New York, U.S.A.

Colonel Sir CHARLES CLOSE, K.B.E., F.R.S., President International Population Union, England.

Professor F. A. E. CREW, M.D., D.Sc., Professor of Animal Genetics, University of Edinburgh, Great Britain.

Dr. L. I. DUBLIN, M.D., Statistician Metropolitan Life Insurance Co., New York, U.S.A.

M. EUGÈNE DUPRÉEL, Professeur de philosophie à l'Université de Bruxelles, Belgium.

Dr. KARL ARVID EDIN, Stockholm, Sweden.

*CHARLES ELTON, Department of Zoology, University Museum, Oxford.

Professor H. P. FAIRCHILD, New York University, New York, U.S.A.

Professor C. B. FAWCETT, D.Sc., Professor of Economic Geography, University of London, England.

Professor C. R. FAY, D.Sc., Professor of Economic History, University of Toronto; also reader in Economic History, Cambridge University, England.

Professor Dr. EUGEN FISCHER, Direktor des Kaiser Wilhelm Instituts für Anthropologie, Berlin-Dahlem, Germany.

Dr. G. P. FRETS, Poortugaal, Rotterdam, Holland.

Professor J. W. GLOVER, President Teachers' Insurance and Annuity Association, New York, U.S.A.

The late Professor J. W. GREGORY, D.Sc., F.R.S., Professor of Geology, University of Glasgow, Great Britain.

Professor F. H. Hankins, Smith College, Northampton, Mass., U.S.A.

Dr. David Heron, D.Sc., Secretary London Guarantee and Accident Co. Ltd., London, England.

Professor Julian S. Huxley, M.A., Professor of Physiology in the Royal Institution, London, England.

*Dr. I-Chin Yuan, China.

The Very Rev. Inge, K.C.V.O., Dean of St. Paul's, England.

Sir Arthur Keith, F.R.S., Hunterian Professor Royal College of Surgeons, England.

Dr. Tage Kemp, Institute for General Pathology, University of Copenhagen, Denmark.

Dr. G. W. Kosmak, Editor *American Journal of Obstetrics and Gynæcology*, New York, U.S.A.

R. Legendre, Chef du laboratoire de Physiologie au Collège de France, Paris, France.

Dr. A. J. Lotka, Metropolitan Life Insurance Co., New York.

Professor B. Malinowski, Professor of Anthropology, University of London, England.

Sir Bernard Mallet, K.C.B., former Registrar-General, England.

Dr. H. W. Methorst, The Hague, Holland.

Eldon Moore, Editor *Eugenics Review*, England.

*Dr. F. W. Notestein, Division of Research, Milbank Memorial Fund, New York City, U.S.A.

Professor Raymond Pearl, Director of the Institute for Biological Research, Johns Hopkins University, Baltimore, U.S.A.

Michael Pease, Biologist, University of Cambridge, England.

Captain G. H. Pitt-Rivers, Anthropologist; General Secretary of the International Population Union, England.

Miss Gladys Pott, Chairman, Society for the Overseas Settlement of British Women, England.

Professor L. J. Reed, Biostatistician, Johns Hopkins University, Baltimore, Maryland, U.S.A.

*J. A. Fraser Roberts, Department of Animal Genetics, Edinburgh University, Great Britain.

Dr. Richelet, Argentine Embassy, London.

Sir Humphrey Rolleston, Bart., G.C.V.O., D.Sc., M.D., President, Institute of Radiology; Vice-President, St. George's Hospital, England.

Sir Josiah Stamp, G.B.E., President Royal Statistical Society.

Professor Jens Warming, Professor of National Economics, Copenhagen University, Denmark.

Professor P. K. Whelpton, Scripps Foundation for Research in Population Problems, Miami University, Oxford, Ohio, U.S.A.

Dr. S. D. Wicksell, Professor of Statistics, University of Lund, Sweden.

*Captain J. G. Withycombe, R.E., Ordnance Survey, Southampton, England.

INTRODUCTION

By COLONEL SIR CHARLES CLOSE, K.B.E., C.B., Sc.D., F.R.S.,
President of the Union

THE International Union for the Scientific Investigation of Population Problems—briefly entitled The International Population Union—owes its origin to the World Population Conference, which assembled at Geneva in August and September 1927. The hope was expressed by the organizers of the Geneva Conference that one of the results of the Conference would be the formation of a "Permanent International Union on Population," and the Executive Committee of the Conference, under the chairmanship of Professor Raymond Pearl, Director of the Institute for Biological Research, Johns Hopkins University, resolved that "A permanent international organization be set up to consider in a purely scientific spirit the problems of population."

The Union was formed in 1928, Professor Pearl being elected its first President. Statutes for the new Union were drawn up and approved, and these were published in the first number of the *Bulletin* of the Union, which appeared in October 1929. In 1931 Professor Pearl was able to report that the Union had made excellent progress and was well supported by eminent scientific workers in both hemispheres. The always difficult matter of finance, a matter especially difficult in these post-War times, had been most satisfactorily dealt with by means of large benefactions from American sources; namely, the Milbank Memorial Fund, which contributed no less than $25,000 during the first three years of the Union's existence, and the Rockefeller Foundation, which gave $5,000; other, much smaller, amounts came from the statutory subscriptions of the various National Committees. The Population Union as a body, and all those who are interested in population questions, are deeply indebted to the generosity of the above-named institutions.

It is laid down in the Statutes of the Union that there shall be held an ordinary meeting of the General Assembly once every three years, and, in accordance with that regulation, the meeting of the Second General Assembly was held in London from June 15 to 18, 1931. It was attended by the officially appointed delegates of the National

Committees of nine of the adhering countries. It is, perhaps, permissible to remark that the proceedings were very harmonious, and that the meeting of the Assembly constituted a valuable stage in the history of the development of the Union. In addition to the official delegates, the Union was glad to welcome other scientific workers, some of whom contributed papers and joined in the discussions.

The Union takes a broad view of its functions and desires to include in its organization all those who can contribute anything of value to the clear enunciation and discussion of the difficult but immensely important inquiries with which it is concerned. It does not desire to limit its activities to any one aspect of these inquiries, but wishes to discuss the science of population from every helpful point of view. Amongst these points of view we naturally include that of Biology, so intimately concerned with the study of humanity in its physical development and relationships. The Union was fortunate in having, as its first President, an eminent biologist, and is glad to reckon amongst its supporters many others distinguished in the same science. But the Union also requires the help of Sociology. Social problems—that is, problems dealing with the structure of human society, and the fitness and happiness of the units that compose that society—are matters that intimately concern the Union. And we must also seek for the assistance of Anthropology. The anthropologist, as a student of mankind, can guide the discussion of cultural evolution, and explain manners and customs which bear directly upon population questions. And the Statistician, also, has his important share in the work of the Union. Statistics is a branch of political science which is indispensable to the student of human affairs in the mass. The *Oxford Dictionary* quotes, in this connection, an interesting remark by Sir J. Sinclair, who said in 1798, "The idea I annex to the term (Statistics), is an inquiry for the purpose of ascertaining the quantum of happiness enjoyed by the inhabitants of a country, and the means of its future improvement." We also seek the help of the science of Economics, dealing with such matters as trade, industry, and finance, and the effect of economic phenomena upon the populations of the world. And though the above list may, by some, be thought long enough, we are bound to add the scientific study of that fundamental occupation, Agriculture. The discussion of the relation between agricultural production and the standards of life of the various countries of the world is of first-class importance, and it is a discussion which can only be adequately undertaken by the agricultural economist.

The International Population Union therefore invites, for the efficient prosecution of its task, the co-operation of biologists, sociologists, anthropologists, statisticians, economists, students of agricultural economics, and, it must be added, geographers and historians. In fact, the Union desires the assistance of all those men and women of science, all over the world, who are disposed, by joining its counsels, to help in the work of the scientific examination of the many difficult and pressing problems of population. We may thus, we hope, arrive one day at a better knowledge, in each country, of the "quantum of happiness," and so, in due time, provide the means of increasing it.

INTRODUCTION

Par le Colonel Sir Charles Close, K.B.E., C.B., Sc.D., F.R.S.,
Président de l'Union

L'Union Internationale pour l'Étude Scientifique des Problèmes de Population,—connue plus brièvement sous le nom d'Union Internationale de la Population,—doit son origine à la Conférence Mondiale sur la Population, qui se tint à Genève en août-septembre 1927. Les promoteurs de la Conférence de Genève avaient exprimé l'espoir que l'un des résultats de la Conférence serait la formation d'une "Union Internationale Permanente pour l'Étude de la Population," et le Comité Exécutif de la Conférence, sous la présidence du professeur Raymond Pearl, directeur de l'Institut de Recherches Biologiques de l'Université Johns Hopkins, décida qu' "une organisation internationale permanente serait fondée pour considérer dans un esprit purement scientifique les problèmes de population."

L'Union fut formée en 1928, et le professeur Pearl en fut élu le premier président. Les statuts de la nouvelle Union furent rédigés et approuvés; ils furent publiés dans le premier numéro du *Bulletin* de l'Union, qui parut en octobre 1929. En 1931 le professeur Pearl était en mesure de faire connaître que l'Union avait fait d'excellents progrès et jouissait de l'appui d'éminents savants dans les deux hémisphères. La question, toujours épineuse, des finances, question particulièrement difficile en cette époque d'après-guerre, avait été résolue de la manière la plus satisfaisante aux moyens d'importantes donations provenant de sources américaines, à savoir le Milbank Memorial Fund, qui n'attribua pas moins de 25.000 dollars pendant les trois premières années de l'existence de l'Union, et la Rockefeller Foundation, qui a donné 5.000 dollars; d'autres sommes, beaucoup moindres, sont venues des cotisations statutaires des différents Comités Nationaux. L'Union de la Population en tant que corps collectif et tous ceux qui s'intéressent aux questions de population, sont profondément reconnaissants de la générosité de ces institutions.

Il est stipulé dans les Statuts de l'Union qu'il sera tenu une réunion ordinaire de l'Assemblée Générale une fois tous les trois ans, et, conformément à cette règle, la réunion de la Deuxième Assemblée Générale a eu lieu à Londres du 15 au 18 juin 1931. A cette réunion assistaient les délégués officiellement désignés par les Comités Nationaux de neuf des pays adhérents. Il est peut-être loisible de faire observer que les travaux de l'Assemblée furent remplis d'harmonie et que cette réunion a constitué une étape précieuse dans l'histoire du développement de l'Union. Outre les délégués officiels, l'Union a eu le plaisir d'accueillir d'autres savants, dont quelques-uns ont apporté des rapports et ont pris part aux discussions.

L'Union envisage ses fonctions avec une vue large, et désire inclure dans son organisation tous ceux qui peuvent contribuer un apport précieux à l'énonciation claire et à la discussion des investigations difficiles, mais immensément importantes, dont elle s'occupe. Elle ne souhaite pas voir ses activités limitées à l'un quelconque des aspects de ces investigations, mais désire poursuivre l'étude de la population de tous les points de vue utiles. Parmi ces points de vue nous comprenons naturellement celui de la Biologie, science si profondément intéressée à l'étude de l'humanité dans son développement et ses rapports physiques. L'Union a eu le bonheur d'avoir pour premier président un biologiste éminent et est heureuse de compter parmi ses appuis beaucoup d'autres personnes distinguées dans cette même science. Mais l'Union a aussi besoin de l'aide de la Sociologie. Les problèmes sociaux, c'est-à-dire les problèmes portant sur la structure de la société humaine et sur l'aptitude et le bonheur des individus qui composent cette société, sont des sujets qui intéressent l'Union au plus haut point. Et de plus nous devons solliciter le concours de l'Anthropologie. L'anthropologiste, en tant que savant s'occupant de l'humanité, peut guider les discussions sur l'évolution culturelle, et expliquer des mœurs et des coutumes qui affectent directement les questions de population. Et le Statisticien, lui aussi, a sa part importante dans la tâche de l'Union. La statistique est une branche des sciences politiques qui est indispensable à celui qui étudie les affaires humaines selon la masse. Le Dictionnaire d'Oxford cite à cet égard une remarque intéressante de Sir J. Sinclair, qui disait en 1798 : "L'idée que j'annexe à ce terme (statistique), c'est une investigation ayant pour objet de déterminer le quantum de bonheur dont jouissent les habitants d'un pays, et les moyens de l'accroître dans l'avenir." Nous accueillons aussi l'aide de l'Économie Politique qui traite de sujets tels que le commerce, l'industrie et les finances, et de l'effet des phénomènes économiques sur les populations du monde. Et, quoique la liste ci-dessus puisse à certains paraître assez longue, il nous faut encore ajouter l'étude scientifique de cette occupation fondamentale qu'est l'Agriculture. La discussion du rapport entre la production agricole et le niveau de vie des divers pays du monde est d'une importance primordiale, qui ne saurait être convenablement entreprise que par le spécialiste de l'économie agricole.

L'Union Internationale de la Population invite donc, en vue de la poursuite efficace de son œuvre, la collaboration des biologistes, des sociologues, des anthropologues, des statisticiens, des économistes, des spécialistes de l'économie agricole, et, il faut l'ajouter, des géographes et des historiens. En effet, l'Union sollicite le concours de tous les savants, dans le monde entier, qui sont disposés, en se joignant à elle, à contribuer à l'œuvre de l'étude scientifique des nombreux, difficiles, et urgents problèmes de population. On peut, donc, espérer qu'il arrivera enfin un jour où une connaissance plus exacte du quantum de bonheur dans chaque pays pourra contribuer aux moyens de son accroissement.

First Session

POPULATION AND FOOD SUPPLY

Chairman: Professor J. D. BLACK

Papers read:

1. SCHEME FOR A POPULATION MAP OF GREAT BRITAIN. By Captain J. G. WITHYCOMBE.

2. ECONOMIC ASPECTS OF THE TENDENCY OF POPULATION IN GREAT BRITAIN. By Professor A. L. BOWLEY.

3. TRENDS IN AGRICULTURAL PRODUCTION IN DENMARK. By Professor JENS WARMING.

4. TIME CHANGES IN THE NUMBER OF GAINFULLY EMPLOYED MEN AND WOMEN IN THE UNITED STATES IN RELATION TO POPULATION GROWTH. By Professor LOWELL J. REED.

5. THE FUTURE GROWTH OF THE POPULATION OF THE UNITED STATES. By Professor P. K. WHELPTON.

PAPER No. 1

SCHEME FOR A POPULATION MAP OF GREAT BRITAIN

By Captain J. G. WITHYCOMBE
(*Great Britain*)

SCHEME FOR A POPULATION MAP OF GREAT BRITAIN

FOR the study of population in many of its aspects the presentation of the distribution of population upon the map is a necessity. Thus the cartographic question is one of primary importance, and the best means of constructing Population Maps one of the first subjects to be investigated when approaching the study of population.

I cannot enter into the general question, as I am only here to show you the beginning of an attempt the Ordnance Survey is making to produce a Population Map of Great Britain, but I am sure you all recognize the desirability of building up a series of National Population Maps for every country uniform in scale, style, and symbol, so that they may be readily compared. The difficulties are great. There is only one world map at the present time, the International Carte du Monde on the scale of 1/1,000,000, and this is far from complete, but such as it is it might possibly be used for those countries for which it is available.

I must apologize for the incomplete way in which I have been obliged to present my drawings, but I have had very short notice. They are being prepared by direction of Brigadier Winterbotham, Director-General of the Ordnance Survey, for submission to a Committee of the British Association.

Turning to the scheme, I would point out that it is designed for this country, and could only be used in a country divided as Great Britain is, into comparatively small administrative areas such as the parish, and which issues Census Reports based upon those areas, and of course possesses topographical maps which portrayed the boundaries. Given these conditions, I submit that it is easy and economical to compile and reproduce; that it gives a good view of the distribution of the population, and that it can be easily generalized and brought down to a smaller scale.

A geometrical progression has been adopted upon which to base the scale of densities for the rural areas—25, 100, 400, 1,600, and 6,400 per square mile. The interval for urban areas is closer—6,400, 12,800, 25,600, and 51,200, and closer still for very congested districts where the increase shown is 12,800. The reason these densities per square mile are not given in round figures is that they are based on acreages—the Census Reports for Great Britain give population per acre.

Outside the large boroughs the parish is the unit which has been coloured. For the boroughs we have taken advantage of the figures given in the Census Reports of this country for the population of wards, and, as you will see, these can be satisfactorily shown and distinctly coloured on the scale of 4 miles to 1 inch, as there are few wards of less than 80 acres. Thus the whole range of densities is portrayed on the map, from the sparsely inhabited pastoral districts to the congested slums of the large cities. All the areas are shown correctly to scale.

The adoption of a prismatic scale of colouring based on the spectrum helps to make the map intelligible at a glance. Beginning with violet and blue for the thinly populated districts, we get a range of greens for the rural areas leading up to yellows and oranges for the semi-urban and open urban densities, and reds and deep reddish tints for thickly populated and congested wards. This scale of colours can be shown by three printings only, the red, blue, and yellow being combined in various degrees of intensity to give the violets, greens, and oranges in the scale; thus it is economical besides being scientific and effective.

There is one obvious defect. In some of the large rural parishes, the population is concentrated in one village or small town, whilst the greater part of the area of the parish is uninhabited. The colouring, of course, gives the impression of an even distribution. To remedy this we propose to overprint upon the coloured parish map a dot distribution showing the position of habitations. Upon the small scale used it is impossible to make each dot represent one house, but these dots do represent the position of habitations (although one may perhaps indicate three or four houses), and thus they show the actual dissemination of the inhabitants with the parish itself.

As to how much detail should be shown on the map other than the bare population symbols and colouring, is a difficult matter to decide. Personally I think that it is best to study the relation of density of population to relief, geology, hydrography, means of transport, and so forth, by comparing the Population Map with physical and topographical sheets.

If each class of information is abstracted and drawn or printed on tracing paper so that it may be superimposed over the Population Map, all sorts of correspondence become apparent which are hidden if it is attempted to show everything at once. This scheme is only tentative and put forward as a basis for discussion.

In designing a Population Map it is necessary to remember that it must be upon practical lines, and that it should be such as may be easily and economically compiled from available data; that it should be cheap to reproduce, and also, if possible, that it should be so arranged that the plates can be revised, so that when a new Census becomes available the work that has already been done can be readily utilized for bringing out a new map.

PAPER No. 2

ECONOMIC ASPECTS OF THE TENDENCY OF POPULATION IN GREAT BRITAIN

By PROFESSOR A. L. BOWLEY
(*London School of Economics*)

ECONOMIC ASPECTS OF THE TENDENCY OF POPULATION IN GREAT BRITAIN

IT may be relevant to the purpose of the International Population Union to consider the interaction of the changes in the economic position of various classes of the population and the changes of the constitution of the population itself. In this paper I cannot present any hitherto unknown facts or conclusions, but hope to indicate some lines of investigation, for which material is becoming available.

The data I have in mind relate to working-class families, and it is a matter of importance to define such a family in terms practical for use in investigation. The Census private family is arbitrarily defined, officially, in separating a family from a boarding establishment, unofficially in that a lodger may be merged in a family or constitute a "family" by himself as he prefers. If we are considering the adequacy of house room, we should merge in one unit all who board together and sleep in the same house; if our subject is the economic position of a family, lodgers should be excluded except as contributing to the income, and absent earning members (e.g. at sea) should be included.

The families in the New London Survey are considered from both points of view, though in fact the numbers of lodgers and absentees are inconsiderable. A more difficult question is the extent to which the incomes of different members of a family can be regarded as pooled. The general practice is that earning children, except the youngest, and other earning members of the family, pay arranged sums to the house-keeper. Where the family is fairly well-to-do these may only cover bare expenses, but in other cases there is a more definite contribution to the common purse. In respect to the well-being of the children, the important thing to know is how much cash the housekeeper has for feeding and clothing and otherwise providing for the family; but from the point of view of the adequacy of wages, we should rather look only at the income of the parent in relation to the persons for whom he is legally responsible or whom he actually supports. The only numerically important classes are children under 14, 15, or 16, and parents past working age. As regards the minor group of relatives incapable of self-support owing to bodily or mental infirmity, it is probable that institutional relief is diminishing the burden.

During the past twenty years in this country, on the one side, real wages have increased and payments in cases of old age, sickness, and unemployment have been developed; on the other side there are progressive changes in the constitution of the family.

As regards the increase in real wages, though there was a definite increase for skilled work since 1914, even before the recent fall in prices, this increase was in many cases trifling, the net effect of the movements between 1914 and 1924 being principally a reduction of hours of work. But the real wages of nearly all grades of unskilled town labour have increased markedly. Thus in Warrington—to take a typical industrial provincial town—the ordinary unskilled wage was 22s. in 1913 and 44s. in 1924. In 1924 this wage met the standard of bare sufficiency for man, wife, and four children; in 1913 it hardly sufficed for three children. Though information is incomplete, it may be affirmed with some confidence that a town labourer in regular work in 1929 had a wage sufficient to cover bare necessaries for a family of four children under 14 years, unless his rental expense was unusually heavy, with of course a margin if the dependent family was smaller. Receipts during times of illness and unemployment are insufficient to preserve this standard, but in many cases income is supplemented by earnings of other members of the family.

I cannot speak with any confidence of the corresponding position of the agricultural labourer, but it is certain that his real income has not increased since 1913 as much as that of town labourers.

Poverty in the towns is now due to illness, age, unemployment, incapacity, death, or absence of the natural breadwinner, or faulty expenditure, not to lowness of wages-rates, except where the number of children is abnormally great, or where there are other ineffectives to support.

Now we may turn to the changes in constitution of the family, but must begin with those in the population as a whole. The fifth column (c) of the table on p. 49 shows the distribution by age and sex that would result if there were an unchanged number of births every year indefinitely, and the death-rates were continually as in the English Life Table No. 9, based on the experience of 1920–22.* The earlier columns show some progress towards this distribution in the decade 1911 to 1921.

* This differs, but only slightly, from that based on an earlier Life Table and published in the *Economic Journal*, 1924, p. 189.

But if we now consider the birth-rate, it becomes evident that this distribution will not be reached during the next half century. The number of births per annum per 1,000 women aged 15 to 45 that is necessary to preserve a stationary population with death-rates as in 1920–22 is 84·7. Actually this rate was 99·3 in 1911, which led to a growing population, but had fallen to about 67·3 in 1930.

POPULATION OF GREAT BRITAIN
PER 100 MEN AGED 15 TO 65

Age	Sex	(a) 1911	(b) 1921	(c) Life Table	(d) 1951 (approx.)
Under 15	M	50·3	45·2	35·5	30
	F	50·1	44·6	34·5	30
15–65	M	100	100	100	100
15–45	F	81	80	64	66
45–65	F	27	31	36	40
Over 65	M	7	8	16	13½
	F	10	11	19	18½
Total	—	325	320	305	298

If the present *number* of births (viz. 748,000 per annum) continued, it would lead to a stationary population of 42,000,000, death-rates assumed constant and no migration, and its distribution by age and sex would be that of column (c). But in fact this number will not be reached with the existing birth-rate (per women 15 to 45), and the population will dwindle, if these hypotheses of birth- and death-rates are realized; in fact, the population in 1951 would be very little greater than that about to be announced for 1931.

I have worked out the 1951 population in detail, attending to the diminishing number of women of child-bearing age, which will very soon result from the falling number of births since 1914. With the same birth-rate (per women 15 to 45) the number of births in 1950 would be 675,000. The resulting distribution is shown in column (d). The relative number of persons aged over 65 is considerable; but the number of children under 15 is only 60 per 100 men aged 15 to 65, whereas it was over 100 in 1911, and would be 70 in a stationary population. It had already fallen to 90 in 1921 and (pending the results of the Census) may be computed roughly at 73 this year, or rather more, since allowance has not been made for the recent fall in infant mortality.

This reduction is, of course, only possible because the diminution in the number of births per marriage has extended to the working class. The only definite evidence I have in this direction is based on inquiries in five towns in 1913 and 1924, which covered by sample the whole working-class population in them. The number of children under 14 years per family was reduced from 1·50 to 1·30; the number per 100 males aged 15 to 65 fell from about 113 to 93. These figures are not quite comparable in date or age or region with those just given, but they are not inconsistent with them.

The reduction in this average is connected with a marked falling off in the number of families with many children. In 1913 of 100 families with children, 19 had 4 or more living; in 1924 the number was 14. The proportion of all children in such families is, of course, greater, but the percentage had fallen from 40 to 33. It is highly probable that this process has been accelerated since 1924.

With the rise in real wages of unskilled labourers, where the larger families are commonly found, and the reduction in the number of children, together with all the social and official care now taken of children, the rising generation is in an environment continually more and more favourable for satisfactory development. Even the housing conditions are improving, since the families are smaller. After school-age (apart from the present condition of acute unemployment), the smaller supply of boys and girls competing for employment, while the adult working population is continuing to increase, leads to higher juvenile wages, and may easily lead to better conditions of work.

We have still to consider the effect on the economy of a household of small means of the increasing number of the aged (over 65), which has risen from 17 per 100 males (aged 15 to 65) to about 22 now, and will increase to about 32 in 1951, and to 35 in a stationary population. In fact, however, these old people, if they have not accumulated means of their own, are a burden on the community rather than on individual poor households. The New London Survey will lead to definite information on this question, together with the allied questions of the number of other non-effectives, and the distribution of the burden among two or more earners. But it should also be remembered that the age of retirement may rise, as the vitality of elderly people becomes greater.

The broad result of this analysis is that (apart from unemployment) the earning strength of the population is increasing rapidly in relation to the number of dependent children, and that therefore some of the main causes of poverty and mal-development and insufficient training are being removed. But it is evident that these general averages need interpretation by detailed study of separate classes. How far does number of children vary inversely as income? In what proportion of cases is the natural breadwinner dead, incapable, or neglectful of his duties? Though in the towns investigated in 1924 there were only about 90 children under 14 years to 100 males of working age, in fact 11 per cent. of these children were in a condition of poverty in the week of inquiry. Though remedial measures can be taken as and where needs are evident, further definite investigation is needed to determine the magnitude of the problem of how to make the best of the generation that is actually growing up, with the knowledge that the productive power of the nation is becoming continually more adequate for the task.

DISCUSSION

Professor BOWLEY, replying to questions, stated that in his estimates of fertility no special allowance had been made for the number of women unmarried as a consequence of the deaths of men in the War. He had noticed, however, that in the 1921 Census there were 111 women to 100 men in the particular age group affected.

In his calculations he had taken the birth-rate to be constant. On figures worked out for Sweden it was a justifiable assumption.

Dr. L. I. DUBLIN asked what the birth-rate would be in England in 1951. He realized that Professor BOWLEY had assumed a constant fertility rate, but with the constitution of the population changing the rate itself would become modified, and it would be interesting to know what that would be between now and 1951.

Professor BOWLEY replied that it would be 2·98.

In reply to a further question he said there was reason to believe that the age at which people retired from work would tend to increase with increasing longevity. There were no comparative figures of how long people used to work which could be compared with the age to which people worked to-day, neither could it be discovered from the London Survey.

PAPER No. 3

TRENDS IN AGRICULTURAL PRODUCTION IN DENMARK

By PROFESSOR JENS WARMING

(University of Copenhagen)

TRENDS IN AGRICULTURAL PRODUCTION IN DENMARK

WHEN the chairman of Commission I asked me to prepare a discussion on Trends in Agricultural Production of Denmark, I supposed it was not because this small country with 3½ million inhabitants had any direct interest, but because the same problems, which we have met, have arisen or will arise in other countries. However, Denmark is not a typical country with respect to the problem of population and food supply; it is neither a regular exporting nor a regular importing country, but we have an enormous import of grain and oilcakes, not for our own consumption, but as raw materials for production of butter, bacon, and eggs for export; no other country in the world has so great an import of oilcakes as Denmark, even in absolute figures. This shows that the problem of population and food supply cannot be considered for a single country; we must take the world in its entirety.

From the Danish Statistics we learn that it is important to have statistics not only for the production of grain, but for *all crops*, including coarse fodders, as beets and grass; we can reach much more optimistic conclusions when we take all crops (see the Addendum). While the *per capita* increase in the production of grain culminated in 1880, all crops, counted as grain, have since then increased more than 25 per cent. *per capita*; this means *wealth*, not only because the figure is greater, but because it shows that we do not want much more grain, but more animal food or fodder. This development has probably been stronger in Denmark than in most other countries, but there is no doubt that the world in its entirety has the same tendency.

For the whole world, the statistics, however, can already be supplemented in another direction, by including most *other raw materials*, such as minerals, oilseed, cotton, etc. (see the Memorandum on Production and Trade, Geneva, 1930). This is important also for the problem of population and food supply, as there is competition between the production of food and other raw materials; the same area holds good for food, cotton, wood, etc. Also these statistics for the whole production of raw materials show faster increase in production than in population, and this is also to be expected, when the world has an agrarian crisis and very low prices for most raw materials.

However, there exist countries where they actually have difficulties with the population and food-supply problem, namely, in years of *failure of crop*. Great districts of Russia and Asia have so dense a population, and are so near the maximum population which the food supply allows, that a bad harvest must often cause famine.

In Denmark we have a very *stable food supply*, which is due to the following three facts: (1) The harvest is very stable on account of the climate and the civilization; in the forty years before the War we had only six years where the total harvest of grain, beet, etc., was more than 10 per cent. greater or smaller than the average of the nearest five years. (2) It is very easy to get quickly and cheaply supplies from other countries; all parts of the country are in the neighbourhood of seaports, and the freights are now very low. We can buy grain from the Baltic, from the Black Sea, from North or South America, etc., wherever prices are lowest. (3) We use 87 per cent. of the grain, oilcakes, and bran for cattle; when the supply of grain is small, as it was during the World War, we can easily reduce the quantity given to the cattle and thus get sufficient for men. In over-populated countries like China this elasticity is small; the men do the work of horses (ploughing and transport), and accordingly get their grain; they have very few cows and pigs, and consume the vegetation directly. This means that the animal fodder is not a reserve, from which the men can get food in case of bad harvest or over-population.

We may ask, whether countries, where crop failure is frequent, can learn something from Denmark. Our stability depends in part on our climate, in which respect many lands are less fortunate; and also our maritime situation is an advantage. These countries could improve their position by developing roads, railways, canals, harbours, etc. But the most essential thing is to make the crop itself more stable, and in that respect civilization has a good effect, as, for instance, on drainage, while the use of fertilizers and improved varieties makes for increased stability of crop.

However, we must say that for the world as a whole statistics do not support any theory of over-population. But in the last ten years we often meet another argument, namely, that the widespread *unemployment* in most countries shows that the world is over-populated. But this argument is wrong; the natural effect of over-population on the conditions of the workers is not unemployment, but low wages, according to the theory of marginal productivity. Society can adjust itself to a greater population, and employ all the workers, only on a basis of lower wages, and that adjustment requires time and initiative; therefore, if the rate of the growth of the population suddenly increases—for instance, on account of restrictions on immigration to other countries—there may come intermittent unemployment until there has been sufficient initiative to expand the trades, and sufficient understanding of what the unemployed will buy, if they get work (as this is the right field for expansion). However, in most countries the wages have increased fast for many years, giving no support to the theory of over-population.

The pessimism of Robert Malthus is thus not supported by the statistics of crop or wages. Certainly the Danish periods of doubling the harvest are much longer than his twenty-five years, but the increase is at least much faster than of the population. The same is probably true for the other Western European countries and for America, while a real over-population sometimes is felt in the mentioned districts of Asia, etc.

But the fact that we have been able until now to increase our control over the instability of crops, and even to meet the danger of chronic over-population by a correspondingly greater production, gives no guarantee that this can *continue* indefinitely. If the world population continues to increase at an annual rate of 1 per cent., in 1,000 years there would only be one square metre of land area *per capita*. At present we have enormous reserves of food in the fodder of cattle; but this cannot suffice if the population continues to grow. Still more rapidly the exhaustion of the world's supply of coal, oil, etc., will limit population growth unless quite new methods and inventions are introduced.

When we read Malthus and Darwin, we get the impression that the majority of *men and animals* are constantly living on the margin of subsistence. But this is not so under natural conditions. I have asked some foresters whether wild animals in the forest were generally weak and lacked nourishment. Not at all; the animals have plenty of food and live healthily until the moment when their enemies kill them or until a great famine occurs, or a severe winter, etc. One of these foresters concluded that the number of animals is not determined by the quantity of food, but by several other factors, such as their natural enemies (beast of prey, parasites), the snow which prevents them (especially the weaker) from getting food, lack of water, the weather in the breeding-time (both for mammals, birds, and insects), etc.

This means that Nature has a margin for the density *below* the normal food supply, a margin which is felt now and then, but not at all times, and therefore a much more tolerable margin than a chronic state of under-nourishment. But probably there is a certain ratio between the absolute margin of the food supply and the lower margin from enemies and weather. Where a hundred animals can live on the margin of subsistence, natural enemies may reduce the number to, say, sixty, and then a certain proportion of enemies will subsist on the surplus of births, which the sixty could have. Thus we have a state of equilibrium with ample food supply for the sixty; if the number became greater, they would begin to be weaker and be too easily devoured by their enemies. The smaller the distance is between the two margins, the more often will under-nourishment appear.

These discontinuous checks to the population, from enemies, weather, and famine, *civilization* has taught us to control to a certain degree; and therefore the danger of coming in the neighbourhood of the absolute margin would be expected to become greater. Two hundred years ago the great cities of Europe had a great epidemic about every twenty years, killing about one-fifth of the population; but now the death-rate is only one-half of the old figure. However, this problem of over-population, which civilization has created by lowering the death-rate, civilization also seems able to control, both by increasing production to such a degree that an agrarian crisis has resulted, and by *birth control*, which has altered the situation completely.

This birth control belongs rather to the field of Commission II. Therefore, in conclusion, I only wish to mention briefly the most important of its economic *effects*. (1) Progress of all kinds will become slower. (2) The rate of interest will become lower; the supply of capital will be greater and the demand smaller. (3) The land rent will not increase. (4) A smaller proportion of the population will be engaged in the trades, producing capital goods. (5) When we install plant, build factories, schools, etc., we should be very careful not to build them on too great a scale, or they will tend not to be used to full capacity. (6) Adjustment to new structural conditions will be more difficult and expensive, when relative decrease for a certain trade also means absolute decrease. (7) But the periodic depressions will be milder; when the towns do not grow, their growth cannot be discontinuous. (8) Migrations will be fewer. (9) A greater proportion of the population will be in the older age groups supported by old age pensions.

Generally conditions will become so altered that we elder economists and statisticians, familiar with constant conditions in the growth of population, will have much difficulty in understanding the new age.

ADDENDUM

The average Danish crop of grain at different times in the past is seen from the following table, whose older figures, of course, partly are estimated.

Year				Population	Millions Deciton of Grain	Grain *per capita*
						kg.
1750	..	..	..	750,000	5	670
1800	..	..	..	925,000	7	760
1850	..	..	..	1,415,000	10	710
1880	..	..	..	1,970,000	18	910
1900	..	..	..	2,440,000	20	820
1910	..	..	..	2,750,000	23	840
1924–30 {	without Sleswick			3,300,000	28	850
	with Sleswick ..			3,475,000	30	860

The table shows that the crop doubled in the century 1750–1850, and again in the next fifty years. Also in proportion to the population the crop increased fast until 1880; but later it decreased somewhat. From 1750 to 1880 the *per capita* production increased from 670 kg. to 910 kg., but now it is only 860, and dropped to an even lower level during the previous decades (1880–1930). This, however, simply means that the production has turned in another direction, namely, to fodder (beets, grass). When this production of fodder became more important, the statistics were gradually improved, until it now is *nearly complete*; the last and most difficult step was to include the grass, eaten in the fields; this is done by reports from a number of farmers, namely, the members of testing societies, about the number of grass-days for the cows, etc. It must be hoped that all countries will develop their statistics in the same direction.

The total harvest in Denmark, including roots, potatoes, straw, hay, and grass in pastures, etc., is given in the following table, where all the different kinds of plants are counted in according to their value as fodder, expressed in grain (barley).

		Millions Deciton
1879–1883	.. ..	41
1899–1903	.. ..	51
1909–1913	.. ..	67
1924–1930 { without Sleswick..	..	85
{ with Sleswick	.. ..	93

When we calculate the whole harvest in this way, we find even in the last fifty years a faster increase than in the population, namely, from 2,080 kg. *per capita*, about 1,880 to 2,680 kg. in the last years. It may be objected that it is unfortunate that the grain, which can be consumed directly and sold directly, has decreased from 41 per cent. of the whole harvest to 30 per cent.; but in reality this is an expression of wealth; we do not want more grain for direct consumption, but we want more animal food and therefore more *fodder*. (It has been possible to buy grain cheaper from other countries. Until 1880 Denmark exported grain; now we give the cattle so much grain, oilcake, and bran, that our own production of this is only 60 per cent. of the consumption. From this imported fodder we produce butter, bacon, etc., for export.)

Perhaps also it may be regarded as unfortunate that the last table shows a smaller increase in total harvest now than before the War, namely, 1·5 per cent. yearly since 1913, 1·6 per cent. before that time. The difference, however, is small and may be occasional; and further, it simply shows that we do not want more. Also the statistics of the whole world show a small increase for grain (see the Geneva Memorandum on Production and Trade); and nevertheless we have an agrarian crisis.

In proportion to the *number of farmers*, the harvest is still faster increasing; but as this is partly due to the fact that the farmer of our days is nearly 100 per cent. farmer, while the farmer of the past spent much of his time in other kinds of production (house economy), I shall not go more deeply into this matter. As to the *crop per hectare*, in about 1750 we had only seven deciton grain for the peasants, while landowners, clergy, and citizens (who cultivated the neighbourhood of the towns) had a good deal more; the peasants, however, had the greatest area. In about 1840 we had a total of about 10 deciton grain per hectare, and now 23 deciton. Professor O. H. Larsen has for the last thirty years before the War calculated that of the total increase in harvest 20 per cent. was due to the greater total area, 30 per cent. to a more intensive rotation (beets), and 50 per cent. to other kinds of intensity and to progress.

PAPER No. 4

TIME CHANGES IN THE NUMBER OF GAINFULLY EMPLOYED MEN AND WOMEN IN THE UNITED STATES IN RELATION TO POPULATION GROWTH

By Professor LOWELL J. REED
(*Johns Hopkins University, U.S.A.*)

TIME CHANGES IN THE NUMBER OF GAINFULLY EMPLOYED MEN AND WOMEN IN THE UNITED STATES IN RELATION TO POPULATION GROWTH*

HUMAN population in its various aspects is in such a constant state of flux that practically all of our population questions resolve themselves into problems dealing with time changes. We may at the start of a problem survey the condition of the population with respect to certain characteristics at a particular time, but eventually we find ourselves making comparisons between populations at one instant of time and another. This fact has in recent years led to the development of a field of treatment of the population problem which might be embraced under the word dynamics. The application of the logistic curve to the time changes in population number by Pearl and Reed,† Lotka's‡ work in the field of physical biology, Volterra's§ treatment of population from the mathematical point of view, are all instances of this tendency. In the present paper it is proposed to discuss the changes that have been taking place with regard to the proportion of people in the United States gainfully employed, with particular attention to the question of infiltration of women into industry. This problem is treated as a form of saturation process, employing a technique which may be found useful for other studies of this type.

The details of this technique have been brought out in a previous paper,‖ but it will be well to review its underlying philosophy in connection with the present application. It has been shown that the logistic curve fits with considerable accuracy the time changes in the population of many places, and gives us, therefore, a start toward a satisfactory

---

* Papers from the Department of Biostatistics, School of Hygiene and Public Health, The Johns Hopkins University, Baltimore, Maryland, No. 159.

† "On the Rate of Growth of the Population of the United States since 1790 and its Mathematical Representation." *Proc. Nat. Acad. Sci.*, Vol. 6, No. 6, pp. 275–288, June 1920.

‡ *Elements of Physical Biology.* Williams and Wilkins Press, Baltimore, Md. 1925.

§ *Leçons sur la théorie mathématique de la lutte pour la vie.* Gauthier-Villars et Cie., Paris. 1931.

‖ "A Form of Saturation Curve." *Jour. Amer. Stat. Assoc.* September 1925.

rationalization of the process of population growth. The equation of the curve may be expressed in the form

$$y = \frac{K}{1 + e^{a_1 + b_1 x}} \quad \cdot \quad \cdot \quad \cdot \quad \cdot \quad \cdot \quad (1)$$

in which y is population, x is time, K represents the limiting value of the population, and b the intrinsic growth rate. The derivative equation for this function is

$$\frac{dy}{dx} = -\frac{b_1}{K} y (K - y) \quad \cdot \quad \cdot \quad \cdot \quad \cdot \quad \cdot \quad (2)$$

and from this we see that the rate of change of population with time is proportional to the population present at that time, and to the remaining possible population, as determined by the limiting value K. Thus, this process may be viewed as an instance of the saturation with population of a universe capable of maintaining K units of population.

A population, however, that is growing in such a fashion may have subordinate populations that are so developing that they are inherently limited at any given time to some fractional part of the population present at that time. If we let z represent such a subordinate population and take m as the limiting fractional amount of the total population that will fall into this subordinate class, and assume that z, the subordinate population, may be expressed by the same law as that which governs y, the total population, we shall have for the derivative equation expressing the time-rate of change of z

$$\frac{dz}{dx} = -\frac{b_2}{my} z (my - z) \quad \cdot \quad \cdot \quad \cdot \quad \cdot \quad \cdot \quad (3)$$

If we substitute in this equation the value of y as given by (1), and integrate, we find that the progress of the subordinate population with time is represented by the equation

$$z = \frac{mK}{1 + e^{a_2 + b_2 x} + \dfrac{b_2}{b_2 - b_1} e^{a_1 + b_1 x}} \quad \cdot \quad \cdot \quad \cdot \quad (4)$$

Thus we have an expression for the representation of a population that is forcing its way into and becoming constantly a greater part of a total population that is itself growing on a logistic. The constant m represents the ultimate proportion of the total population that will be of this specified character, and b_2 indicates the intrinsic rate of infiltration of this subordinate population into the total population.

If now we consider the people classified as gainfully employed in the United States Census, we encounter the general phenomenon of industrialization of society. We find a constantly increasing proportion of population, both male and female, turning from occupations so closely allied to home activity that formerly they were not counted as gainfully employed, and now appearing in forms of occupation so related to our industrial fabric that we are classifying them as gainfully employed. We might expect to find an increasing proportion of women turning to industrial pursuits, but it would be generally considered that this is not true of the men. Examination of the records, however, shows that the proportion of men gainfully employed has been on the increase as well as the proportion of women. The difference between the sexes is indicated by the fact that the proportion of women gainfully employed is increasing faster than the proportion of men. The question of greatest interest in this situation is perhaps as to the ultimate proportion of men and women that will enter such classes, for we would like to foresee the equilibrium toward which we are moving. Since the population of the United States is following a logistic curve so consistently, it would seem possible to apply the theory just outlined to a study of this question. For this purpose, logistic curves were derived to represent the total male and total female populations. These curves were obtained by using the curve

$$y = \frac{197 \cdot 274}{1 + e^{3 \cdot 26930 - 0 \cdot 31340x}}. \quad \cdot \quad \cdot \quad \cdot \quad \cdot \quad \cdot \quad (5)$$

previously* fitted to the total population of the United States. In this equation and all the equations in this paper x is in decades and the origin at 1810. The asymptote for this total curve is $197 \cdot 274$ millions of people, and the assumption was made that the asymptote for the male and female populations should satisfy the relationship

$$K_m + K_f = 197 \cdot 274 \quad \cdot \quad \cdot \quad \cdot \quad \cdot \quad \cdot \quad (6)$$

---

* "On the Rate of Growth of the Population of the United States since 1790 and its Mathematical Representation." Loc. cit.

where K_m and K_f are the asymptotes for the male and female curves respectively.

With this conditional equation, the male and female population counts between the years 1820 and 1920 were fitted by the method of least squares. This resulted in equations for total male and female populations that were as follows:

$$y_m = \frac{99 \cdot 532}{1 + e^{3 \cdot 25635 - 0 \cdot 31314x}} \quad \cdots \quad \cdots \quad (7)$$

$$y_f = \frac{97 \cdot 742}{1 + e^{3 \cdot 24790 - 0 \cdot 30702x}} \quad \cdots \quad \cdots \quad (8)$$

The raw material used in fitting these curves together with the calculated population values will be found in Table I. A graphical comparison of observed and calculated values is shown in Figs. 1, 2, and 3.

With these logistic curves to represent growth of total population and population of each sex, the numbers of gainfully employed individuals in total and for each sex were fitted by the saturation curve previously derived [equation (4)], using the method of least squares. This resulted in the following set of equations for representing time changes in gainfully employed:

Total gainfully employed:

$$z_t = \frac{89 \cdot 369}{1 + e^{7 \cdot 02733 - 1 \cdot 14139x} + 1 \cdot 37851 e^{3 \cdot 26930 - 0 \cdot 31340x}} \quad \cdot \quad (9)$$

Male gainfully employed:

$$z_m = \frac{66 \cdot 719}{1 + e^{9 \cdot 40154 - 1 \cdot 62074x} + 1 \cdot 23948 e^{3 \cdot 25635 - 0 \cdot 31314x}} \quad \cdot \quad (10)$$

Female gainfully employed:

$$z_f = \frac{21 \cdot 104}{1 + e^{6 \cdot 99422 - 0 \cdot 84418x} + 1 \cdot 57156 e^{3 \cdot 24790 - 0 \cdot 30702x}} \quad \cdot \quad (11)$$

The observed and calculated numbers of gainfully employed are given in Table II, and are brought into graphical comparison in Figs. 1, 2, and 3.

These equations might have been fitted by making use of an assumption that the asymptotes for male and female should add to the total asymptote, but because the series of observed data on this subject run

TABLE I

GROWTH OF POPULATION IN THE UNITED STATES

POPULATION IN MILLIONS OF PERSONS

Year	Total		Male		Female	
	Observed	Calculated	Observed	Calculated	Observed	Calculated
1820	9·638	9·757	4·897	4·982	4·742	4·904
1830	12·866	13·110	6·532	6·691	6·334	6·548
1840	17·069	17·507	8·689	8·931	8·381	8·692
1850	23·192	23·193	11·838	11·825	11·354	11·449
1860	31·443	30·413	16·085	15·496	15·358	14·935
1870	38·558	39·373	19·494	20·047	19·065	19·245
1880	50·156	50·179	25·519	25·528	24·637	24·433
1890	62·948	62·771	32·237	31·906	30·711	30·475
1900	75·995	76·872	38·816	39·037	37·178	37·253
1910	91·972	91·975	47·332	46·661	44·640	44·540
1920	105·711	107·398	53·900	54·435	51·810	52·027
1930	—	122·401	—	61·986	—	59·367
1940	—	136·321	—	68·981	—	66·243
1950	—	148·681	—	75·186	—	72·412
1960	—	159·233	—	80·479	—	77·738
1970	—	167·947	—	84·845	—	82·184
1980	—	174·944	—	88·350	—	85·795
1990	—	180·439	—	91·102	—	88·660
2000	—	184·679	—	93·225	—	90·892

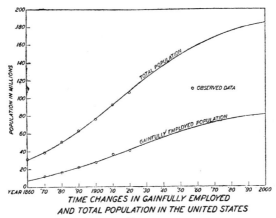

TIME CHANGES IN GAINFULLY EMPLOYED
AND TOTAL POPULATION IN THE UNITED STATES

FIG. 1

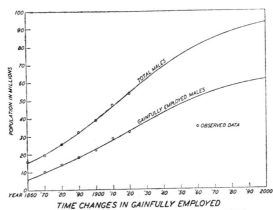

TIME CHANGES IN GAINFULLY EMPLOYED
AND TOTAL MALE POPULATION IN THE UNITED STATES

FIG. 2

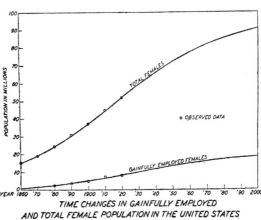

TIME CHANGES IN GAINFULLY EMPLOYED
AND TOTAL FEMALE POPULATION IN THE UNITED STATES

FIG. 3

TABLE II

GROWTH OF POPULATION GAINFULLY EMPLOYED IN THE UNITED STATES

POPULATION IN MILLIONS OF PERSONS

Year	Total		Male		Female	
	Observed	Calculated	Observed	Calculated	Observed	Calculated
1850	—	3·8734	—	2·3240	—	0·4213
1860	—	7·2611	—	5·8613	—	0·8203
1870	11·7668	11·5698	10·1216	10·0501	1·6452	1·4764
1880	16·2737	16·4798	13·9198	14·0862	2·3540	2·4327
1890	21·8144	21·9269	18·2178	18·2515	3·5966	3·6759
1900	27·3231	27·9449	22·4894	22·7983	4·8336	5·1488
1910	36·1771	34·4969	28·7384	27·7353	7·4387	6·7806
1920	40·5534	41·4212	32·3505	32·9138	8·2029	8·5026
1930	—	48·4517	—	38·1069	—	10·2478
1940	—	55·2763	—	43·0736	—	11·9500
1950	—	61·6054	—	47·6101	—	13·5472
1960	—	67·2272	—	51·5821	—	14·9897
1970	—	72·0294	—	54·9326	—	16·2462
1980	—	75·9967	—	57·6717	—	17·3052
1990	—	79·1844	—	59·8538	—	18·1728
2000	—	81·6892	—	61·5568	—	18·8668

only from 1870 to 1920 inclusive, it was thought that it would be better to use this conditional equation as a type of check on the approximation involved in the fitting process. When we examine the equations for this fact, we find that the limiting number of males gainfully employed is 66·719 millions and of females is 21·104 millions, making a total of 87·823 millions. The asymptote for the curve fitted to the totals is 89·369 millions, giving us an agreement that is within 1·8 per cent., which is certainly as satisfactory as could be expected from Census material of this character.

The other important constant of these fitted curves is the constant m, which indicates the proportion of gainfully employed persons toward which we are tending. For the males the value of m is 0·670, indicating that the percentage of males gainfully employed, which has been on the increase for the past fifty years, is approaching the equilibrium position of 67 per cent. The age distribution of the population for the year 1920 shows that we had 67 per cent. of the male population over 16 years of age, but we must remember that the age distribution of the population has been changing in the direction of that encountered in a stationary population; and if we examine the life tables for the United States, we find that in the stationary life-table populations approximately 73 per cent. of the male population is over 16 years of age. Thus we may say that the present trends seem to indicate an ultimate population in which 73 per cent. of the male population will be over 16 years of age and 67 per cent. of the male population will be gainfully employed.

For the females, the corresponding figures are 74 per cent. of the stationary population over 16 years of age, and 21·6 per cent. of the female population gainfully employed.

A comparison of the male and female constants shows that the trend is toward approximately 3 gainfully employed males for every gainfully employed female. The 1920 figures indicate a ratio of approximately 4 to 1 in the gainfully employed of the two sexes. Thus we may conclude that although in recent times women have been moving into the gainfully employed class at a fairly rapid rate, the movement is not directed toward an end that will result in the number of gainfully employed women even approximating the number of men, but rather toward a situation in which the employed men outnumber the women 3 to 1.

It should be remembered that the equations and constants discussed in this paper have been derived from an observed series that is not as long as we might desire, and the conclusions therefore must be taken with a degree of caution. We may, however, form some judgment of their validity by the agreement of the asymptotes of male, female, and total curves as previously indicated in this paper. This agreement is such as to suggest that the general proportions stated are not wide of the mark. The entire approach to the question assumes, of course, that future changes will be such as might be considered as growth processes rather than as changes revolutionary in character.

SUMMARY

The theory for the saturation curve as developed in this paper would seem to express with a reasonable degree of accuracy the changes that are taking place in the number of gainfully employed persons in the United States.

The results of the application of these curves to the observed figures for the United States indicate that we are tending toward a position where we shall have one gainfully employed female for every three gainfully employed males.

DISCUSSION

Professor BLACK asked whether a larger number of women and children in 1910 were counted as gainfully employed? And whether, in the curve of gainfully employed, the women and children had been separated out?

Professor REED maintained that the effect of 1910 was not sufficient to make an adjustment such as would change the curve to any marked extent, or seriously change the end result. It was obvious that in any approach based on such a theory as the applicability of the logistic curve to population, certain assumptions were necessarily made which could only be tested by the future. It could be said that the explanation represented population changes over a short time.

Professor BLACK said it was easy to pick out some important changes which had taken place rather suddenly. The introduction of the motor-car had certainly introduced some important changes touching economic phenomena. There were a rapid set of changes in evolution that were likely to show up in population figures during the 10–20 year period in which they had taken place. There was a parallel in the field of agricultural production. Was not the logistic curve likely to be the correlation of a lot of influences, and could not a given period within a time range be selected in the development of population to illustrate it?

Professor REED agreed with Professor BLACK. He thought the logistic curve was best considered as a statistical curve. Given a set of S-shaped curves, not themselves necessarily logistic, nor necessarily symmetrical, the sum of these curves would tend to smooth out into a curve similar to the logistic.

Professor FAIRCHILD asked whether, with the available data on the population curve, any conceivable set of curves could be taken which would give the population history of the nineteenth century?

Professor REED said the question begged speculative treatment. The answer was conceivably Yes. Too widely changing conditions could not be predicted in any way.

Professor GLOVER said that the logistic curve furnished an example of the growth of the population very clearly, and he had no doubt that it could be fitted to a population of any kind for some time.

Dr. B. DUNLOP, referring to the activities of Commission I (Population and Food Supply), hoped the Commission would be able to state the rate at which the food supply increased per annum. It seemed far more important if this could be expressed as an annual rate than in the form "some day the food supply will be increased." What would be of practical interest would be to know what the income would be next year and the year after. Was it possible to have a statement of the rate at which the food supply of the world—not only cereals—increased?

Professor BLACK said that that would be difficult, as the composition of the foodstuffs is shifting from cereals to dairy produce and meat, and the tonnage is quite different. An attempt had been made to put it on a caloric basis; that was better, but some difficulties still arose.

PAPER No. 5

THE FUTURE GROWTH OF THE POPULATION
OF THE UNITED STATES

By P. K. WHELPTON

(*Scripps Foundation for Research in Population Problems,*
Miami University, Oxford, Ohio)

THE FUTURE GROWTH OF THE POPULATION OF
THE UNITED STATES

POPULATION growth in the United States has been slowing up rapidly of late, more so than most people realize, even many who have studied the returns of the last Census. A decline in the rate of growth is not a new thing for the nation, since the decennial percentage increase, which fluctuated between 32 and 36 per cent. from 1790 to 1860, has declined rather steadily during the past seventy years. Nevertheless, each decade up to the World War showed a larger numerical increase than the preceding; and the fact that the post-War decade surpasses them all tends to obscure the speed at which population gains have been dwindling recently.

It is only when the years between the last two Censuses are studied separately that it is possible to see just what has actually happened. To obtain the annual increase in population, it is necessary to calculate the excess of births over deaths, and of aliens entering over those leaving the country. This cannot be done with absolute accuracy because of deficiencies in the available data on births, deaths, and immigration; but the results presented in Table I should be approximately correct. They indicate a gain in population of 1,948,000 in 1920, rising to a peak of 2,133,000 in 1923, and then declining steadily to 1,110,000 in 1930. The annual rate of population increase has declined still more rapidly, that for 1930 being 9·1 per thousand as compared with 18·4 per thousand in 1920 and 19·0 in 1923.

With a brief examination of certain factors, it may be possible to show why population growth in the United States has been decreasing so rapidly and what its future course may be. The birth-rate, which apparently started downward over a century ago, fell abruptly during the World War, took an upward trend in the first post-War years, since 1921 has again been falling rapidly, and probably will continue to do so, though at a decreasing rate. This does not mean that child-bearing will stop altogether (barring accidents in the practice of birth control), but the probability is that it will be stabilized around one- to three-child families throughout a large proportion of the population.

Mankind is somewhat more handicapped in its efforts to prolong life than to prevent births. A perfect application of the best-known methods of contraception would accomplish the latter end, but science has not yet indicated how all the present inhabitants of this earth may secure ever-lasting life. Nevertheless, death-rates at the younger ages have been lowered greatly in the United States, particularly the infant mortality-rate; and the future trend should be downward, though less rapid.

TABLE I

ANNUAL INCREASE OF POPULATION IN THE UNITED STATES

(*In Thousands*)

Year	Population January 1	Births *	Deaths †	Net Immigration ‡	Increase of Population §
1920	105,711‖	2,848	1,390	495	1,948
1921	107,659	2,946	1,255	280	1,966
1922	109,625	2,772	1,291	277	1,753
1923	111,378	2,795	1,361	707	2,133
1924	113,511	2,851	1,326	295	1,815
1925	115,326	2,790	1,364	252	1,672
1926	117,008	2,725	1,432	304	1,592
1927	118,590	2,625	1,355	252	1,519
1928	120,119	2,491	1,445	216	1,258
1929	121,377	2,399	1,449	222	1,168
1930	122,536¶	2,410**	1,390**	90	1,110**
1931	123,645**	—	—	—	—

Until recent years, death-rates at ages over 40 have also been decreased, but the present trend is upward. Although certain diseases, such as tuberculosis and typhoid fever, have been controlled or almost

* Estimated by Scripps Foundation from current numbers of *Birth Statistics*. Cf. P. K. Whelpton, "Population of the United States 1925 to 1975," *The American Journal of Sociology*, September 1928.

† Estimated from current numbers of *Mortality Statistics* on the assumption that the crude death-rate in the United States is the same as in the registration area.

‡ United States Department of Labour: *Annual Report of the Commissioner-General of Immigration*.

§ Births plus net immigration, minus deaths, decreased by 0·3 per cent. each year, so that the total gain for 10 years and 3 months agrees with that shown by the Census enumerations of January 1, 1920 and April 1, 1930.

‖ Census of January 1, 1920.

¶ Census of April 1, 1930, minus estimated population increase during first three months of 1930.

** Preliminary estimates.

eradicated, there have been noticeable increases in specific death-rates
from cancer and the so-called degenerative diseases (chronic infectious
in part), such as nephritis, cerebral hemorrhage, and diseases of the
heart, which are exceedingly important among the causes of death
after 40 years of age. It may be that death-rates after 40 in future years
will continue at about the present level, though possibly this is too
optimistic in view of the recent upward trend and the increased herding
of the population in large cities where the pace is rapid and the strain
on vitality is great.

Compared with birth-rates and death-rates, the future trend of
immigration is hard to forecast for the United States, since the laws
may be changed by Congress, and the Commissioner of Immigration
may alter radically the regulations under which the laws are admin-
istered. At present, immigrants with a job or the promise of a job are
prohibited from entering by the contract labour law, and most of those
without jobs are refused admission on the ground that they are liable
to become public charges. Entrance is thus limited almost exclusively
to those with independent means, but probably will be less restricted
after the end of the present business depression. That the net admission
of aliens during the next few decades will amount to about 200,000 per
year may be a fair estimate, and will be used here.

On the basis of the projected trends in specific birth- and death-rates
and in net immigration, which have just been roughly indicated, the
Scripps Foundation has computed the population that would result
during the next fifty years. Starting with 122,536,000 persons on
January 1, 1930, the results of our calculations presented in Table II
show the population increasing at a slower and slower rate up to a maximum of 144,600,000 in 1970, and declining thereafter. The probability
is, of course, that the actual increase of population will not coincide
with these estimates. They are simply presented to show what will
happen if recent downward trends in birth-rates and in death-rates at
ages under 40 continue at a diminishing rate, and if death-rates at
ages over 40 and immigration remain about as at present.

A set of estimates prepared in 1927 by the Scripps Foundation indicated that a population of 175,000,000 might be reached by 1975, but
at that time it appeared as though the annual number of births, which
increased in the years following the World War, would decline at a
slow rate instead of the rapid pace followed since 1926. The fact that

the present estimates indicate a population for 1975, which is about 31,000,000 below that indicated by the estimates prepared four years ago, serves to illustrate the cumulative effect during a 45-year period of the acceleration in the decline in the birth-rate from 1927 to 1931, since the same method of estimating was followed in both cases and little change was made in the trends of death-rates and immigration. Perhaps the actual course of population growth will lie between the two extremes, although at present it appears as though the lower estimates are the more probable, and that the maximum during the century will not exceed 150,000,000, even though surpassing the

TABLE II

POSSIBLE FUTURE INCREASE OF POPULATION IN THE
UNITED STATES*

(*In Thousands*)

Year	Population January 1	Decennial Increase	
		Numbers	Per Cent.
1920	105,711†	16,825	15·9
1930	122,536†	9,964	8·1
1940	132,500	7,300	5·5
1950	139,800	4,100	2·9
1960	143,900	700	0·5
1970	144,600	— 1,700	— 1·2
1980	142,900	—	—

142,600,000 mark resulting from our present calculations. Further revisions of the Scripps Foundation estimates will be published from time to time as new data for births, deaths, and immigration become available. A detailed description of the method followed together with the various specific birth- and death-rates used for future years will appear in a few months, shortly after data on age distribution for 1930 are received from the Bureau of the Census.

The slowing up of population growth in the United States will be accompanied by important changes in the composition of the population. Among other things, the Scripps Foundation estimates show the

* According to assumptions discussed in text.
† See Table I, notes ‖ and ¶.

white population gaining slightly relative to the Negro population, the proportion of whites who are foreign-born declining considerably with restricted immigration, the present excess of males among whites decreasing somewhat for the same reason, and the age constitution quite different from what it is now.

Of these trends in composition of the population probably the most important, though less obvious as to causes, is that of age. Due largely to the decline in the birth-rate, the proportion of younger persons in the population has declined for several decades. This last decade, however, is the first to witness a decline in the actual number of children under 5 years of age. Calculations of our Foundation indicate that there were about 1,000,000 fewer children under 5 on January 1, 1930, than on January 1, 1925, and public-school enrolment shows a decrease in the number of children in the first grade during recent years. This downward trend in the number of children under 5 is likely to continue and to extend into older age groups as time goes on. Fifty years from now persons under 20 probably will constitute about 26 per cent. of the population instead of 39·1 per cent. as in 1930.

The age group 20 to 49, which includes the best period for physical work, will show little relative change, amounting to about 43 per cent. of the estimated 1980 population, as it now does in 1930. Immigration will not add to this age period to the same extent as in the past, but the number of births will be fairly high and infant and child mortality low from 1930 to 1960, so that survivors from these births, who will be 20 to 50 in 1980, will constitute a large group. More outstanding changes will occur in the older age periods as is shown in Table III. Persons 50 to 69 will amount to about 24 per cent. in 1980 against 13·9 per cent. in 1930, and those 70 or over to nearly 7 per cent. instead of 3·1 per cent. It will be as though one-third of the children and adolescents of to-day were transformed overnight into men and women all past middle-age—some in their dotage.

The future trend of population growth and composition in itself is of interest mainly to demographers. The probable consequences of changed conditions as to growth and composition, however, should be of much more general interest because of their relation to the entire economic and social structure. Some of these consequences will be briefly mentioned.

The slowing up of population growth, and the possibility of even a decline in numbers, will be hard on the extreme optimists and professional boosters, of which we have perhaps more than our share in the United States. Even among a large proportion of our citizens the idea of rapid population growth as being the normal thing is so firmly ingrained that it will be a shock to learn that times have changed in this respect as well as in others. A spirit of optimism, engendered by our rapid and continuous population growth, has been suggested as partially responsible for the efficiency of our industrial development. If this disappears it may lead to a greater caution in many ways. For example, there may be less readiness to allot funds to install up-to-the-minute equipment in place of highly serviceable but slightly obsolete models.

TABLE III

AGE COMPOSITION OF THE POPULATION
OF THE UNITED STATES

(*In Thousands*)

Age Period	Numbers		Percentage	
	1920 *	1980 †	1920	1980
0–19	48,229	37,300	39·1	26·1
20–49	54,106	61,600	43·9	43·1
50–69	17,158	34,500	13·9	24·1
70 and over	3,866	9,500	3·1	6·7
Totals	123,359	142,900	100·0	100·0

The slower growth of population is likely to make competition increasingly keen in industry and commerce unless executives chart their course in accordance with the new signs. That they will do so in the near future seems unlikely, however, since estimates of 142,000,000 persons in 1940 and of 250,000,000 in 2000 are typical of those recently made by such men. Expecting that the rapid growth of population will continue, they are planning additions to the stores, factories, and offices of

* *Fifteenth Census of the United States.* The number of persons aged 0–4 has been increased to allow for under-enumeration. Cf. Elbertie Foudray, *Abridged Life Tables, 1919–1920.*
† Obtained according to assumptions discussed in text.

their organizations in a year or two, by which time they hope the present business depression will have ended. Certain few men whose judgment carries weight believe that an important cause of the present depression is that production facilities have been increased too rapidly in past years and have outstripped too far the capacity of the public to consume the finished products. This situation will become worse unless expansion programmes in commerce and industry are planned carefully in relation to future population trends.

It is conceivable that a few executives may soon be found doing all in their power to combat the spread of birth control, because of an appreciation of its long-time effect on the market for the products of their companies. That such efforts would be futile would seem a foregone conclusion. A more promising programme for offsetting a decrease in the number of new customers added to the nation each year will be to make better customers of those already here. This will mean increasing the purchasing power of the great bulk of the population through a more even distribution of income—a goal toward which progress seems quite slow and laborious in the present capitalistic structure. Another possible course open to executives to offset the slower growth of the home market will be increased efforts in the foreign field. This will bring the United States into keener competition with other exporting nations, and may make it more difficult to prevent strained international relations from developing, unless the machinery for handling such problems between nations is further improved.

In certain respects a decline in population growth will be a blessing for the United States. School facilities will have a much better chance than formerly to catch up with the number of children for whom they are supposed to provide. Perhaps it will be possible to pay more attention to the quality of education when demands for enlarging the physical plant are not so pressing. Cities, too, may be able to give more thought to improvements and less to extensions. If there are fewer claims on the Treasury to pave streets and build sewers in the new residential or industrial additions, it may be possible to devote more attention to beautifying the city within present boundaries, and to develop civic auditoriums, parks, art galleries, and other institutions that add to the amenities of life. With slower growth of cities and less frequent changes in their physical layout, such as the spread of business sections into residential sections, and the replacement of twenty-story buildings with fifty-story skyscrapers, it may be more possible to build for permanence. Just at present one of the qualifications for a successful building in New York City seems to be the ease with which it may be torn down. Think what a blow it must be to the owners of a moderate-sized building, who are striving for a new record in height and size, if they have to pay the wreckers for tearing down the existing structure instead of being able to sell it to a salvage company.

The changes in age composition that will accompany this slowing up in population growth will have innumerable effects on social and economic life. For one thing, the ageing of the population is likely to make for greater conservatism. In business and industry this may mean a continuation of older men in positions of control and a check on the rapid rise of youngsters. In countries with a slowly increasing population and a large proportion of elders complaints are frequent from young men that they have no opportunity to show what they can do, since the older generation continues at the helm. Quite likely this is one phase of the ancient conflict between youth and age, but there seems to be a basis for it. No doubt part of the rapid progress in certain countries has been due to the larger proportion of younger men and the chances that they have had. Care should be taken to see that a shift of control from youth to age is not accompanied by too much stagnation of methods.

While there are evils to be avoided in connection with control becoming too much centred in the hands of older executives, it is vital that a change take place in the attitude of industry and business in general toward wage-earners who are middle-aged or older. At present many concerns have an absolute dead-line at 40 years of age, while 50 is more common, and applicants who are above these limits will not be hired. If the age of those in control becomes higher, this problem may work out gradually of itself, since older executives may have different ideas than younger ones have as to the qualifications of older workers. If some way is not found to prolong the working life of unskilled and skilled wage-earners, the burden on the productive forces of the nation is going to be heavy when the elders become so much more numerous in the population. Persons in the prime of life for physical work—20 to 49—were over three times as numerous in 1930 as those 50 to 69; but by 1980 the ratio will be less than two to one.

If older workers are kept profitably employed in the future, the change in age composition of the population may work to increase economic prosperity. The main shifts in the age groups will be a decrease in children and an increase in elders. If persons 15 to 19 and 50 to 69 are counted as half-workers and added to the 20 to 49 group on this basis, and those under 15 and 70 or over are classed as dependents, the ratio of dependents to workers will fall from about 60 to 100 in 1930 to 44 to 100 in 1980. Even though persons 50 to 69 cannot earn as much as they did between 20 and 49, it should be possible for them to contribute more toward their support than can persons under 15, the group which they will be replacing in the population. The extent to which they are profitably employed, and hence not dependent on younger adults, will have, therefore, an important bearing on the problem of offsetting the decrease in the addition of new customers by making better customers of the existing population.

Regardless of any change in individual buying capacity, this ageing of the population will have a marked effect on the consumption of various products. With fewer children and more old people, there will be less need for baby carriages and more for wheel chairs, less for toys and more for golf equipment and knitting-needles; while the profession of mortician will grow faster than that of obstetrician. Younger people care more for automobiles and older ones for radios. Styles for youngsters are different from those of their parents, even though grandmother often does look like her flapper granddaughter from a distance. In fact, a long list can be made of consumption habits which are affected in greater or lesser extent by the age of the consumer.

The ageing process of the population may have its effect on the system of taxation. As older people become more numerous among those living, so will they be more numerous among those dying. Since older people have had a longer opportunity to accumulate property, the average value of estates may rise. The decrease in birth-rates and size of families will mean fewer heirs among whom to divide the property, and may lessen the opposition to extending the scope of inheritance taxes and to raising the rates. The net result may be a greater reliance by the State on this source of revenue in the future than in the past.

The effects on political life of the coming age composition should not be overlooked. Older persons usually are more conservative in politics, so we may expect our main political parties to adhere more closely to the *status quo* as time goes on. Such action may force the formation of a more radical party, but this may come so late that the younger element will be hopelessly outnumbered and unable to attain control.

Other important effects of the slower growth and increasing age of the population could be mentioned if there were time. Indeed, their ramifications offer an almost unlimited field for speculation. But now it is more important to sum up what has been said than to go further. In brief, population growth is slowing up rapidly in the United States, and may cease within four decades; the number of youngsters will decrease, while elders will increase rapidly; business and industry will be disturbed by the smaller additions to the home market and by changes in consumption habits due to shifts in age groups; and conservatism may become more dominant in the economic, social, and political life as elders increase in relative numbers and power.

Second Session

DIFFERENTIAL FERTILITY

Chairman: Professor F. A. E. CREW

Papers read:

6. THE FERTILITY OF THE SOCIAL CLASSES IN STOCKHOLM IN THE YEARS 1919–29. By Dr. KARL ARVID EDIN.

7. REPORT ON MUCKERMANN'S STUDIES OF THE DIFFERENTIAL FERTILITY WITHIN CERTAIN SOCIAL GROUPS IN GERMANY. By Professor Dr. EUGEN FISCHER.
UNTERSUCHUNGEN ÜBER DIE DIFFERENZIERTE FORTPFLANZUNG AM DEUTSCHEN VOLK NACH HERMANN MUCKERMANN. Von Professor Dr. EUGEN FISCHER.

8. THE OUTLOOK FOR THE AMERICAN BIRTH-RATE. By Dr. LOUIS I. DUBLIN.

9. FIRST FINDINGS OF THE BELGIAN INVESTIGATION OF THE CONDITIONS OF LIFE IN LARGE FAMILIES. By M. EUGÈNE DUPRÉEL.
PREMIERS RÉSULTATS DE L'ENQUÊTE BELGE SUR LES CONDITIONS DE VIE DES FAMILLIES NOMBREUSES. Par M. EUGÈNE DUPRÉEL.

10. RESEARCH ON INCOME, NATALITY, AND INFANT MORTALITY IN HOLLAND. By Dr. H. W. METHORST.

THE FERTILITY OF THE SOCIAL CLASSES IN STOCKHOLM IN THE YEARS 1919–29

By Dr. KARL ARVID EDIN

(Sweden)

THE FERTILITY OF THE SOCIAL CLASSES IN STOCKHOLM
IN THE YEARS 1919–29

IN a paper published two years ago in the *Eugenics Review*, Vol. XX, under the title "The Birth-Rate Changes," I reported some results of an investigation I made on the fertility of the social classes in Greater Stockholm in the years 1919–22. The results of this investigation may be summed up as follows:

The number of wives who were not legally separated from their husbands and were living in Stockholm (including suburbs) at the date of the Census, December 31, 1920, aged then below 40 years, was 40,000. Of these, 900, or 2·2 per cent., did not live with their husbands. They belonged on the whole to a lower social class than the other 39,000, and were, as one would expect, to a much greater extent engaged in their own occupations. Of course, the fertility of these 900, who for the most part were abandoned by their husbands, was very low. For the 39,000 wives who were living with their husbands, I have calculated their period of potential fertility in the years 1919–22 as 150,000 years in marriage. Throughout I have dealt with the period when these wives first came under observation in Stockholm to the time they left. During this period the wives have had nearly 18,000 confinements with children born alive.

I have split up this material into many sub-groups, according to the duration of marriage—i.e. four chronological groups: marriages contracted before 1911 and between the years 1911–15, 1916–18, and 1919–20—each subdivided according to the ages of wives and husbands into four subsidiary age groups; and also according to the occupations, incomes, and birth-places of both couples, into many sub-groups. I have found that a classification by duration of marriage into four groups, and a classification according to the income of the husband, in the three groups, i.e. an income below 6,000 Swedish crowns, between 6,000–10,000 crowns and a minimum of 10,000 crowns, and a classification according to employment or non-employment of the wife, are the divisions which give the most important results. As regards occupation, the principal division (according to fertility) is into industrial workers and other people. The former group seldom earned as much as 6,000 crowns. In the group of people earning the lowest class of income (below 6,000 crowns) there is no significant difference in fertility between industrial workers and others. If the fertility rates of this class of lowest income for each of the four marriage-duration groups are calculated on the basis of the wife, population of the corresponding groups with higher incomes (minimum 6,000 crowns), the actual number of confinements will be 24 per cent. higher for this higher income class than is expected—29 per cent.—of *all* families belonging to this higher class. If a division into four wife age groups (below 25, 25–29, 30–34, and 35–39 years) is combined with the marriage duration, the standardized fertility rate for the higher income class will rise to 25 per cent.; with *only* this wife age-division the fertility rate will decline to 21 per cent. The difference in fertility between the two income classes is only 14 per cent. These differences are, of course, derived from the fact that the higher income class is more strongly represented in the higher marriage-duration groups than the higher age groups, with their lower fertility. Hence I draw the conclusion that the strength of the *negative* correlation between social standard and fertility, which appears from former investigations in wealthier and poorer districts of great towns—where the differences of the fertility rates are not computed—is slightly overrated. The very important distinction of marriage duration is very seldom made at any Census—as far as I know it has only been done in France on the Census of 1911, and then into very unsatisfactory groups. For a period of very remarkable transition, like the present, as regards the fertility in different social and occupational classes in different parts of the country, and in towns and rural districts, it would be of great benefit to make it possible to split up the Census material *and* the birth register material according to duration of marriage in many groups, in combination with as many other divisions as possible, so that one can obtain as many "pure types" as possible. The most important point is, of course, that the confinements for each sub-group (and space of time) can be set *exactly* in relation to the corresponding groups from which they are derived, and which are being observed. This is possible only if individual births in the birth registers can be identified in the Census material.

Such arrangements for obtaining a reliable conformity between the returns, for instance, of occupation on the birth, death, and marriage registers for the years 1931–32, and on the schedules for the Census, December 31, 1930, have now been taken in Sweden. Thus the figures in the pages of the parish registers (from which the Census returns are in part derived) are copied from both these sources for the parishes where the persons were living at the date of the Census. In the case of persons who have been parents, or have married or died during the time from that date to the end of the year 1932, or have migrated from another parish during this time, copies of the birth, marriage, and death registers can be sent over to the parish where they are living at the Census. Thus one can state how many confinements took place in the whole country during these two years in families whose marriages were contracted in a specified year, in which the couples were living together in Stockholm at the Census, and had then a specified age, occupation, and income (in the year 1930, according to special declaration). From the new Census returns one is also informed of the last year of migration (and from which parish), of the occupation in the year 1925, of the degree of education (last examinations), and of permanent occupational disability and causes thereof.—From the Census material for 1920 one can, of course, also obtain the income and occupational returns for this year.—And finally one is also informed of the exact dates of birth of all children born alive in marriages continuing at the date of the Census. Thus one can make a very reliable calculation of the fertility rates during the years 1924–32 for young couples according to their occupations, for the year 1925 as well as for 1930, and with sub-groups for those who have improved or fallen in occupational situation during that time, and for those who have migrated during the same time. There is some reason to suggest, for instance, that people who migrate from rural districts to great towns marry on the whole more frequently and earlier, but are more liable to practise birth control than their former neighbours who remain in their native districts. Thus the natives of Stockholm are more likely to have a higher (standardized) fertility in marriage than those who have migrated to this town. *Such special calculations can also be made, for instance, for couples with higher degrees of education, for specified calendar years of marriage,* or for couples suffering from illnesses which have caused permanent disability. We have in Sweden in one of our Civil Service Departments returns on their incomes for each year from 1921 for nearly all persons between 15 and 60 years of age, on the same cards for each individual (not for persons who are State functionaries, or have an income of at least 10,000 crowns).

Thus the Swedish Census Material for 1930 and the returns from the birth, marriage, and death registers for the years 1931–32, which will be inserted in this material, *should be a most excellent laboratory material, especially for investigations on differential fertility*; and all the more because the Swedish population is very homogeneous in race and religion, and because the modern birth-control movement is now obviously widely spread among the masses of the great towns. I should like to emphasize especially the possibility which this material offers of deciding the question, *whether a very low fertility in a group where the birth-control movement is of late introduction* (for instance, in the lower social classes with longer marriage duration) *can to any great extent be due to this factor*. If one knows exactly all the calendar years of child-bearing in (and before) marriage, one can study the trend of the spacing between child-births for specified time intervals according to social standard, and state the rates of sterility, of one-child frequency, and so on.

Thus I should find good use for a large sum of money to be spent on a temporary institute for making representative investigations on the differential fertility in Sweden, established on the material here described, and I should be very glad if our Union would take steps to examine the possibilities thereof. Perhaps investigations of the influence of higher education on fertility would be of special interest.

In this connection I think Professor Warren S. Thompson is correct when he writes, in referring to my paper in the *Eugenics Review*, in his book *Population Problems* (New York, 1930): "These facts indicate new tendencies in population growth which are not unlikely to become general, as the knowledge and practice of birth control become universal among urbanized and industrialized populations."

I am sorry that I know very little of post-War investigations on the social class fertility for foreign countries. I do not think that the English occupational fertility investigation for 1921 is of decisive importance in this connection, and for many reasons, firstly because the first post-War years were very abnormal. From figures I have picked up from official German statistics (*Einkommen- und Körperschaft-Steuerveranlagung für 1925*, Vol. 348, Berlin, 1929) I have worked out percentages which prove that the average numbers of minors per married men who are entitled to deduction of taxes for having a wife and children to support decrease as the income rises, for rural districts and for towns with less than 50,000 inhabitants, and are the same with rising income for towns with 50,000–100,000 inhabitants, but rise with rising income for greater towns. Thus, if the averages for minors having incomes respectively of 3,000–5,000, 5,000–8,000, 8,000–12,000, and over 12,000 Rm. are set in percentages of the averages for incomes of 1,500–3,000 Rm., the percentages for rural districts and smaller towns would be respectively 4, 10, 14, and 17 per cent. *lower*, but for towns with 100,000–500,000 inhabitants respectively, 4, 7, 11, and 12 per cent. *higher*, and for the two greatest towns, Berlin and Hamburg together, respectively 3, 9, 24, and 30 per cent. *higher*. It is possible in the case of Hamburg to make a division for each district for the Census of 1925, according to the ages of the wives in five-year groups, and for the whole town according to the child-bearing wives too. Thus I found that while the fertility in marriage in the years 1900–01 was rising on the whole, from district to district with rising percentage of industrial workers (all men with a stated occupation), this correlation had quite disappeared in the year 1925. Taking the three wealthiest districts together, the fertility had declined from 1900–01 by only 44 per cent., as against 60 per cent. for the other districts, and the actual number of confinements in marriage was in 1925 in these districts 7 per cent. higher than that expected (if the fertility rates for each age group of the whole town are calculated on the corresponding wife population groups for the districts). As wealthier and poorer classes are largely mixed with one another in most districts, the positive correlation between fertility and social standard appears to be too low, judging from such figures as these.

For Gothenburg (the second Swedish town) a Census is taken for the individual parishes on the date January 1, 1925, when the wives were classified in age groups at intervals of five years. For the years 1925–26 I have also classified the married mothers into the same groups (from the birth registers). I have summed up the five parishes with an average income per employed person for the year 1920 of more than 3,000 Swedish crowns as wealthier districts (from 2,300 to 5,500 crowns), and the other four parishes (with from 2,500 to 2,800 crowns) as poorer districts, with respectively 9,500 and 9,800 wives aged below 45 years. The fertility of the wealthier group was respectively 19, 13, and 10 per cent. *higher* than of the poorer in the ages below 25, 25–30, and 30–35 years, but 20 per cent. *lower* in the senior ages, from which figures I suggest that the new type of differential fertility (produced by easier access to birth control in the lower classes) is advancing, especially for the younger families. The age-standardized fertility in marriage in Gothenburg was, for the years 1910–11, 12 per cent. *lower* (— 12) for the five wealthier parishes than for the four poorer, but in 1925–26, was 5 per cent. *higher* (+ 5), which represents a change of place of the differential fertility to + 17 per cent. For a wealthy and a poor district (or rather groups of districts) of Stockholm at the same time, the same percentages have been calculated to — 7, + 14, and + 21 per cent.

I have made a similar investigation for Greater Gothenburg for the same years as in that made for Greater Stockholm, and I have found that the standardized fertility for the years 1919–22 in marriages where the husband's income for the year 1920 was at least 6,000 crowns, was 10 per cent. lower than in the lower income class (in Greater Stockholm 25 per cent. higher). Plainly, the new type of differential social class fertility has not yet advanced in Gothenburg, where the mentality of the population is much more conservative in many ways (especially concerning religion) than in Stockholm. It is rather interesting to note that a similar investigation for the same years for Borås—a town with 30,000 inhabitants at the Census of 1920, situated close to Gothenburg, and which specializes particularly in the textile industry—has proved that the under-fertility of the higher income classes is yet more prominent in this town than in Gothenburg, in spite of the much greater employment of the wives and of low wages (in the lower classes); at the same time the fertility in marriage is higher than for Gothenburg; and for Gothenburg it is much higher than for Stockholm. In the whole district where Borås is situated the textile industry predominates, but the fertility is comparatively high, which feature I ascribe to the maintenance of a tradition of large families. From what I have said it follows, of course, that the difference of fertility between the three towns is much smaller for the higher classes than for the lower, and also that the fertility altogether is lower (for a town) the higher the (positive) differential fertility of the higher classes. Concerning the other results of these investigations I shall now confine myself to the following statements.

For wives whose marriages were contracted in the years respectively before 1911, 1911–15, and 1916–18, the standardized differential fertility rates for the years 1919–22, where the husband's income was at least 6,000 crowns, were, for Greater Stockholm, respectively + 4, + 40, and + 36 per cent. (higher than where the income was lower), but for Greater Gothenburg, were respectively, − 28, −16, and + 9 per cent., from which figures I suggest that the older type of differential social class fertility in the years 1919–22 was on the point of disappearing for the longest marriages, and had already disappeared for all shorter ones for Stockholm, but that it yet had a stronghold in Gothenburg for marriages which had lasted more than, say, 5 to 10 years; and thereafter it had changed to the new type—for marriages contracted in the years 1919–20 the fertility of the lower classes is very much influenced by prenuptial pregnancies.

In marriages where the husband's income in 1920 was below 6,000 crowns, the standardized fertility rate for employed wives (with an income of at least 300 crowns) was in Greater Stockholm 50 per cent. lower than for the unemployed in the same income class. The underfertility of this whole lower income class (below the fertility of the higher income class), which is 25 per cent., is one-third (8 per cent.) due to their working out of doors. For wives who are full industrial labourers (and have full earnings), the fertility is, of course, still lower. In the higher income classes (according to the husband's income), the wives are, of course, more seldom employed, and seldom as labourers, and their work does not influence their fertility so much. A rational investigation of the influence on the child-bearing from the employment of wives is one of the most important tasks for any investigation on differential fertility, and cannot be fulfilled without using the *method of identification* as described above.

My investigations for Gothenburg, as well as for Stockholm, have proved that a division of the higher income class into two classes, with husband's income being 6,000–10,000 crowns and a minimum of 10,000 crowns, throws still more light on this most important transition of the differential fertility. The higher one of these new groups is the leader of the two. For Stockholm, the standardized fertility was 28 per cent. higher for the higher group (minimum income, 10,000 crowns) than for the lower group (income, 6,000–10,000 crowns), and 41 per cent. higher than for the group where the husband's income was below 6,000 crowns. For the middle group the fertility was 12 per cent. higher than for the lowest group.

As I have already emphasized, it would be of very great interest, especially in this time of transition, to follow some specified late calendar year marriage groups some years (not too few) after marriage, and observe all births during the whole time, for people of different income, and of different social classes. I have made such an investigation for all marriages contracted in the year 1919, where the couples were living together in Stockholm at the beginning of the year 1921, and also of the year 1930, and where the wives were aged below 35 years at the wedding. All together these families numbered 1,778. All their confinements have been observed in the birth and population registers for ten years, and the numbers of the preceding confinements have for the most part been tested in the registers of the maternity hospitals. One can also find out from these registers whether the wives have had any miscarriages (and their dates), and whether they have had any confinements before marriage. Only for those wives in whom I have not observed *any* pregnancies during marriage, from 1919 to the beginning of 1930, *or* any confinement before the wedding (the child living after the same), I have not as yet had any opportunity to test their complete childlessness (in the maternity hospital registers) *if* they have been out of Stockholm for some longer part of the period of observation. On my family cards I have returns of the occupations and the incomes of both husband and wife for the years 1920 (the first whole year of marriage) and 1929. Thus I can not only study the influence of the husband's income (and of the wife's employment), during the first ten years of the marriage on the frequency of pregnancy, but also of the rising or falling of his income to the end of the period.

From the following Table I one can see that the fertility in marriage rises during the first ten years with rising income of the husband; in the year 1920 from 118 per 1,000 years of marriage (or 1·18 per couple), and where their income was below 4,000 Swedish crowns, to 125 per 1,000. Where the income was 4,000–6,000 crowns, the rise is 6 per cent., and rises to 149 per 1,000 where the income was at least 6,000 crowns; or an increase of 19 per cent. from the middle income group, and 22 per cent. from the lowest income group. The fertility also rises with rising income from 1920 to 1929, at least in the middle income group, which is the largest. Out of a total of all the 784 couples in this group, the income has risen from 1920 to 1929 for 225 couples, and

TABLE I

SOCIAL CLASS FERTILITY OF 1,778 MARRIAGES CONTRACTED IN THE YEAR 1919 AND FOLLOWED IN STOCKHOLM DURING TEN YEARS, FOR SEVEN INCOME GROUPS

Social Classes	Number of Wives aged below 35 Years at the Wedding	Aged below 25 Years in Percentage thereof	Wives employed in 1920 or 1929, or both Years, in Percentage of Column 1	Number of Child-bearings in Ten Years (Born Alive or Stillborn)	Fertility Rate Column 4 Percentage of Column 1	Sterility in Percentage of Column 1
	1	2	3		5	6
A. Husband's income. In the year 1920 below 4,000 Swedish crowns	570	42·5	31·4	674	118	33·8
(a) Income 1929 at least 10 per cent. lower than 1920	171	38·6	36·8	201	118	39·2
(b) Income 1929 from 10 per cent. lower to 40 per cent. higher	226	42·9	34·5	266	‑117	34·1
(c) Income 1929 at least 40 per cent. higher	173	45·7	22·0	207	120	28·3
B. Husband's income 1920, 4,000–6,000 crowns	784	43·5	23·6	977	125	28·3
(a) Income 1929 at least 30 per cent. lower than 1920	191	39·8	27·7	222	117	33·5
(b) Income 1929 below 30 per cent. lower	368	45·1	26·4	444	120	27·2
(c) Income 1929 higher than 1920	225	44·0	15·6	311	138	24·4
C. Husband's income 1920 at least 6,000 crowns ..	424	42·5	17·7	631	149	23·1
A + Ba + Bb Lower social class	1,129	42·8	29·1	1,340	119	31·6
Bc + C Higher social class ..	649	43·0	16·9	942	145	23·5
A + B + C	1,778	42·9	24·7	2,282	128	28·6

their fertility rate in marriage was 138 per 1,000, but was below the 120 per 1,000 for the rest of the group.

Especially important is the statement that sterility in marriage (children born during the last half-year before the wedding are in the table included as born *in* wedlock) fell decidedly with rising income from 1920 to 1929. In the three groups, A, B, and C, where the husband's income during 1920 was below 4,000 crowns, 4,000–6,000 crowns, and at least 6,000 crowns, the percentages of sterile marriages were respectively 34, 28, and 23 per cent. For the lowest income group the incidence of sterility where the income from 1920 to 1929 has fallen at least 10 per cent. (Aa), has fallen at most 10 per cent., or has risen at most 40 per cent., and has risen at least 40 per cent. (Bb, and Bc), are 39, 34, and 28 per cent. For the middle group, with an income for 1920 of 4,000–6,000 crowns, the incidence of sterility, where the income from 1920 to 1929 has fallen at least 30 per cent. (Ba), at most 30 per cent. (Bb), and has risen (Bc), respectively, 34, 27, and 24 per cent. All these percentages of sterility are very well (positively) correlated with the percentages of employed wives (in Column 3).

That the sterility percentage has risen from group Ac to group Ba, as well as also the percentage of employed wives, can be explained, I think, partly by the lower percentage of wives who have married before 25 years of age in the latter group (Ba), an indication that this group on the whole (the ten-year period taken as a whole) represents a lower social standard than the former group (Ac), where the income at the start was higher. This explanation is supported by the fact that the fertility is falling from group Ac to Ba especially during the latter part of the ten-year period (and the percentage of employed wives rises especially high for the year 1929).

Clearly, childless marriages are now very much commoner among the lower classes in Stockholm than among the higher classes; so much so that they influenced the differential fertility in a very high degree, and perhaps suggest a new phase of the birth-control movement.

I have also calculated the fertility and sterility rates inclusive of the wife's confinements before and after marriage. If the period under observation is calculated as exactly ten years from the date of marriage, or, if any child was born before the marriage, from the birth of the first child, the fertility rates for the groups A, B, and C would be 141, 143, and 154 per 1,000, the sterility percentages would be 27, 22, and 20 per 1,000.

Finally, I have made a low-class group (1) from groups A*a* and A*b*, a high-class group (4) from those families in group C where the husband in the year 1920 had an income of at least 10,000 crowns, or of 6,000–10,000 crowns, with a rise in 1929 of at least 10 per cent.; a lower middle-class group (2) from groups A*c*, B*a*, and B*b*, and a higher-middle-class group (3) from the remaining families. The fertility and sterility rates for these four new groups are exhibited in the following Table II:

TABLE II

FOUR SOCIAL CLASSES

Social Classes	Number of Wives	Number of Child-bearings	Fertility Rates	Sterility
1. Low class..	397	467	117	36·3
2. Lower middle class ..	732	873	119	29·1
3. Higher middle class ..	424	575	136	25·7
4. High class	225	367	163	19·6

The fertility rate for the highest class, 4, is 20 per cent. higher than for class 3, and for this class 15 per cent. higher than for classes 1 and 2 together. For those two lowest classes the fertility rate for the employed wives is 40 per cent. lower than for the unemployed. The sterility percentage for class 4 is 24 per cent. lower than for class 3, and for this class is 12 per cent. lower than for class 2, and for class 2 is 20 per cent. lower than for class 1.

REPORT ON MUCKERMANN'S STUDIES OF THE DIFFERENTIAL FERTILITY WITHIN CERTAIN SOCIAL GROUPS IN GERMANY

By Professor Dr. EUGEN FISCHER
(Germany)

REPORT ON MUCKERMANN'S STUDIES OF THE DIFFERENTIAL FERTILITY WITHIN CERTAIN SOCIAL GROUPS IN GERMANY

(Abstract)

THE Kaiser Wilhelm Institute for Anthropology, Human Heredity, and Eugenics, has in the last three years undertaken investigations into the fertility of some important social groups of the German people. "It is scarcely necessary to point out the extraordinary inequality existing between one social group and another, not only as regards economic condition, numerical proportion, and their relative importance within the body politic (nation as a whole), but also in the inherent quality and biological value of its individual members. One group (e.g. the peasants) is recruited from its own natural increase, and even by its surplus contributes to other groups; another—the artisan and factory operative—increases by unselected recruitment from other classes in addition to its own natural increase. And yet another—the academic and commercial employer—base recruitment on tests of personal aptitude and a system of selection; the natural increase of this class is to-day questionable.

"Between one social group and another there will exist great differences in intellectual endowment, the hereditary transmission of which is in most particulars now well established.

"This is not to say that one can state baldly the biological superiority of one class over others, for each is indispensable; each can have its own absolute value, but at the same time there may arise within a group (or a section thereof) a stratum of degeneration, caused by some specific cultural or biological circumstance contaminating the entire community. Thus at all times the proportional contribution of each group to the whole is a question of importance. It is a question of supreme moment in a period of diminishing fertility in a people. The present catastrophic fall, exceeding anything known in history, will, by comparison with periods of growth, reduce considerably the number of stocks which carry on to posterity the national heritage. The quality of the future depends now much more than in normal times on single lines. If the fall in the birth-rate occurred in the same ratio in all classes, it would only be a matter of counting heads from generation to generation, leaving the qualitative make-up unchanged."

Demographical surveys are apt to classify by distribution (urban, rural, etc.) or economic condition. Our investigations are related to individuals of selected social groups—questionnaires are used where the educational status permits (medical men, ministers of religion, etc.). Seven studies are in hand. Projected and in preparation are surveys of the whole of the teaching personnel and the evangelical ministers of Prussia (should financial support enable the prosecution of these). The first completed series consisting of High School Teachers has been published by Hermann Muckermann (*Archiv für Rassen- u. Gesellschafts-biologie*, Bd. 24, 1930). Their fertility is compared with that of 250 peasant families:

AVERAGE NUMBER OF CHILDREN

	Children
Professors of Universities	2·8
Professors of Technical, etc., High Schools	2·4
Peasants	6·5

AVERAGE NUMBER OF CHILDREN WHO REPRODUCE

	Children
Professors of Universities	1·8
Professors of Technical, etc., High Schools	1·6
Peasants	4·2

Thus this highly selected group of High School Teachers is not maintaining its numbers in two generations.

A spotlight is thrown in the reproductive habit by the following comparison of small and large families:

AVERAGE

Number of Children	Professor	Peasant
	Per Cent.	Per Cent.
1–2	31	3·6
3–4	36	14
5–6	5·7	17
7–8	2·7	27
9	0·7	34

The same result appears taking fertility in—

	Professor	Peasant
	Per Cent.	Per Cent.
First five years of marriage ..	1·65	2·3
Second five years of marriage ..	0·65	2·0
Later	0·3	1·8

Finally, an interesting review of the period of the establishment of this low fertility:

AVERAGE FOR COMPLETED FAMILIES

	Children
1879–1866	3·37
1887–1890	2·9
1891–1894	2·96
1895–1898	2·65
1899–1902	2·62
1903–1906	2·70
1907–1910	2·65

These few figures clearly indicate the condition of our people. It is that of a moribund community.

DISCUSSION

Dr. EDIN said, with reference to abortions, that in Stockholm he had good registers of miscarriages for the lower classes, as returns of these were made from the registers of the Maternity Hospitals. Of course, the higher classes did not go to the Maternity Hospitals, and it was therefore impossible to have a record of miscarriages in those families.

Dr. FISCHER, replying to questions, said that he had not any definite knowledge of the abortion-rate; his paper had only included live births. He had no data comparable to that of Dr. EDIN of the fertility-rates in towns of families of different incomes.

UNTERSUCHUNGEN ÜBER DIE DIFFERENZIERTE FORT-PFLANZUNG AM DEUTSCHEN VOLK NACH HERMANN MUCKERMANN

In den letzten drei Jahren hat das Kaiser Wilhelm-Institut für Anthropologie, Menschliche Erblehre und Eugenik die Aufgabe unternommen, die Unterschiede in der Fortpflanzung einiger wichtiger sozialer Gruppen des Deutschen Volkes zu untersuchen. Es bedarf kaum des Hinweises, dass die einzelnen sozialen Gruppen nicht nur nach wirtschaftlicher Lage nach Zahl und Bedeutung für das Gesamtvolk ausserordentlich ungleich sind, sondern auch nach Eigenschaft und biologischem Verhalten ihrer Menschen. Die eine Gruppe—etwa der Bauer—erhält auf natürlichem Wege ihren Bestand an Menschen, ja gibt dauernd deren Überschuss ab; die andere—der Arbeiter, die Industriebevölkerung—vermehrt sich stark an Zahl, neben eigener Fortpflanzung vor allem aber durch Aufnahme zahlloser neuer Mitglieder ohne Auswahl; und wieder eine andere—akademische Berufe, obere Kaufmannsschichten—knüpfen den Zutritt an Eignungsprüfung und Auslese, ihre natürliche Vermehrung steht heute in Frage. Vor allem wird auch nach den geistigen Eigenschaften, deren erbliche Unterlage grossenteils heute feststeht, ein starker Unterschied zwischen den sozialen Gruppen bestehen. Selbstverständlich wird man nichte die eine Gruppe ohne weiteres als biologisch wertvoller und besser denn die andere bezeichnen dürfen, jede ist absolut unentbehrlich, jede kann in sich absolut hochwertig sein, aber ebenso kann durch besondere kulturelle und biologische Umstände in einer Gruppe oder einer gewissen Schicht diese minderwertiger und dadurch für das Ganze schädlich werden. So wird die Frage, wie stark sich die einzelnen Gruppen und einzelne Schichten in den Gruppen an der Gesamtfortpflanzung ihres Volkes beteiligen, immer von besonderer Bedeutung sein. Diese Wichtigkeit aber wächst ins Ungeheure in einer Zeit, wo die Fortpflanzung der Gesamtheit sinkt. Bei einem Geburtensturz, wie wir ihn heute erleben, grösser und schneller als je in der Geschichte der Kulturvölker, wird die Zahl der Erblinien, die das Gesamtvolk in die Zukunft hinüberführt, im Verhältnis zu Zeiten der Vermehrung sehr klein. Die Qualität der Zukunft hängt also jetzt vielmehr von

der einzelnen Linien ab als in anderen Zeiten. Trifft der Geburtenrückgang alle sozialen Schichten gleich, dann ändert er nur die Kopfzahl des künftigen Volkes, berührt aber seine qualitative Zusam-
mensetzung nicht. So besteht also wohl das lebhafteste Interesse an
der Aufklärung der Frage nach den Unterschieden in der Fortpflanzung
jeder einzelnen sozialen Gruppe und Schicht. Muckermann nennt das
die Frage nach der differenzierten Fortpflanzung.

Die allgemeine Bevölkerungsstatistik pflegt Stadt und Land, Gross-
und Kleinstadt usw. zu trennen, eine Reihe von Schülerarbeiten
versuchten nach Einkommenhöhe oder Steuersatz differenzierte
Gruppen zu erfassen. Wir haben uns entschlossen die einzelnen
Individuen bestimmter ausgelesener sozialer Gruppen persönlich zu
untersuchen. So mussten wir Fragebogen verwenden. Sie gehen je
an das Familienoberhaupt aller eine Gruppe zusammensetzenden
Familien. Bei den Gruppen, deren allgemeine Bildung und Verständnis
für das Problem uns eine gute Gewähr für die Erlangung wahrheits-
gemässer Antworten bieten, wählten wir unmittelbare Frage und
Antworten, bei den anderen wurden die Erhebungen Familie nach
Familie durch Vertrauensleute (Ärzte, Doktoranden, Geistliche, Für-
sorgepersonal) durchgeführt.

Folgende Gruppen sind in Arbeit (in runden Zahlen): 4,500 Profes-
soren aller deutschen Universitäten und Hochschulen, 1,500 Privat-
dozenten ebendaher, 60,000 Mann der uniformierten Schutzpolizei
(aller Dienstgrade), 3,000 Reichswehroffiziere, 2,500 Arbeiter eines
industriellen Werkes in Westfalen, 1,240 Familien einer kleineren
westfälischen Stadt und 625 desselben Landbezirkes und endlich 328
Familien aus 3 kleineren Dörfern aus verschiedenen Landesteilen.
In Vorbereitung (aber nur durchführbar, wenn es gelingt, weitere
Geldmittel zu erhalten) die Erfassung der gesamten preussischen
Lehrerschaft (Volks- und höhere Schulen) und der evangelischen
Geistlichkeit. Noch einige andere sollen folgen.

Bisher ist ein erstes fertiges Ergebnis über die Gruppe der Hochschullehrer von Hermann Muckermann vorgelegt worden.*

Ihre Fortpflanzung wird mit der von 250 Bauernfamilien verglichen.
Ich hebe aus Muckermann's umfangreichen Darlegungen folgende
Hauptpunkte heraus.

* *Archiv für Rassen- und Gesellschaftsbiologie*, Band 24, 1930.

DIE DURCHSCHNITTLICHE KINDERZAHL BETRUG

	Kinder
Professoren der Universitäten	2,8
Professoren der Techn. usw. Hochschulen	2,4
Bauern	6,5

DURCHSCHNITTLICHE ZAHL DER KINDER, DIE SICH
SELBST WIEDER FORTPFLANZTEN

	Kinder
Professoren der Universitäten	1,8
Professoren der Techn. usw. Hochschulen	1,6
Bauern	4,2

Die soziale Gruppe der eigenartig ausgelesenen Hochschullehrer hält
also in zwei Generationen nicht einmal ihre Kopfzahl.

Ein helles Schlaglicht wirft auf die Art der Fortpflanzung das
Verhältnis der kinderarmen- und kinderreichen Ehen.

Es hatten durchschnittlich:

Kinder	Professoren	Bauern
	Per Cent.	Per Cent.
1–2	31	3,6
3–4	36	14
5–6	5,7	17
7–8	2,7	27
9	0,7	34

Jede Bermerkung zu dieser vollkommenen Umkehr ist überflüssig.
Auch die folgenden Ziffern zeigen dasselbe Bild. Die Kinderzahlen
waren durchschnittlich:

	Professoren	Bauern
Im ersten Jahrfünft der Ehe ..	1,65	2,3
Im zweiten Jahrfünft der Ehe..	0,65	2,0
Später	0,3	1,8

Mit dem ersten Jahrfünft ist also der Durchschnitt der Ehe praktisch
am Ende ihrer Fruchtbarkeit (für die Art der Berechnung, die Grenze
der vollendeten Ehe und andere Einzelheiten verweise ich auf die
Arbeit von Muckermann).

Endlich sei noch aus ihr die sehr interessante Übersicht über die zeitliche Entwicklung dieser Gebrutenarmut angeführt.

VOLLENDE EHEN DER PROFESSOREN HATTEN

		Kinder je Ehe
1879–1886 im Durchschnitt	..	3,37
1887–1890 ,,	..	2,9
1891–1894 ,,	..	2,96
1895–1898 ,,	..	2,65
1899–1902 ,,	..	2,62
1903–1906 ,,	..	2,70
1907–1910 ,,	..	2,65

Man sieht, dass der niedrige Stand der durchschnittlichen Kinderzahl schon 1895 vorhanden war und sich seitdem nicht nennenswert geändert hat, die kleinen Schwankungen dürften auch die kleineren Zahlen der einzelnen Ehen je Jahrfünft (1–11 bis 303) durchzuführen sein. Der Geburtenrückgang dieser Familien hängt offensichtlich mit wirtschaftlichen Notzuständen wie wir sie heute haben nicht zusammen. Dass er nicht biologisch ist, etwa in ursächlichen Zusammenhang mit geistiger Arbeit zeigt die Tatsache "dass in allen Zeiträumen kinderreiche Väter durchweg zu jenen Gelehrten gehören, die in der wissenschaftlichen Welt klangvollste Namen tragen," es sind deren immerhin 13–15 per cent. aus der Professorenschaft. Nach Fakultäten getrennt, ist die Kinderzahl der evangelisch-theologischen Fakultäten ebenso wie die Zahl der kinderreichen Familien am grössten.

Die wenigen Angaben sollen hier genügen, es soll nur gezeigt werden, wie die Einzeluntersuchungen und restlose Erfassung eines ganzes Standes den furchtbaren Zustand beleuchtet, in dem sich ein Volk befindet, dessen Fortpflanzung man als die eines sterbenden Volkes bezeichnen muss.

PAPER No. 8

THE OUTLOOK FOR THE AMERICAN BIRTH-RATE

By LOUIS I. DUBLIN, Ph.D.

(Third Vice-President and Statistician Metropolitan Life Insurance Company, New York)

THE OUTLOOK FOR THE AMERICAN BIRTH-RATE

THE birth-rate has declined sharply in nearly all civilized countries during the last half-century. In the years preceding 1880, the rate in many countries reached from 35 to 40 per thousand of population, which is not far from the limit of human reproductive capacity. To-day the figures are more like 15 to 20. With very few important exceptions, as in Russia, the average married couple of to-day is bringing into the world half as many children as did their grandparents, or less. In the United States, where accurate birth registration on a wide scale was begun in 1915, the rate has fallen from 25 per thousand to 19, or about a quarter in fifteen years. It is needless to say that so rapid a change in the fundamental habits of the whole civilized world is utterly unprecedented so far as history records, and carries with it serious economic, social, and political consequences. The situation has attracted the attention of careful scholars and statesmen everywhere, who see in it a possible threat to national survival, and in any case disturbing implications in the international distribution of the various races.

There is as yet no indication that this tendency has reached its culmination. The decline in the current birth-rate is continuing, and, in some countries, especially in the United States, it is faster than ever. In the last few years the birth-rate has been falling about one unit per thousand per year. This decline, moreover, is very widespread, and affects especially our cities and the industrial areas of the country. The City of New York, for example, which has always been characterized by its youth and high fecundity, last year had a birth-rate of 17·6 per thousand. Chicago, the second city of the country, showed a rate of 17·1 per thousand, and our large cities on the Pacific Coast show rates varying from 12 to 14. The phenomenon is country-wide, in spite of the fact that our people are favourably constituted to give high birth-rates. Our age distribution, owing to the heavy immigration of young adults and the high birth-rates of the past generation, is heavily loaded with persons at the reproductive ages which makes the present birth-rate considerably higher than the current fertility actually calls for. Recent studies which Dr. Lotka and I have made show, for example, that in 1928 the true birth-rate was 17·3, as contrasted with the observed rate of 19·4. By the "true birth-rate" we mean that which would ultimately become established by the existing fertility and mortality after the age distribution had had time to assume the corresponding stable form. We have also shown that the true rate of natural increase under current conditions is practically zero.

It is this situation which invites our speculation as to how far the decline may go. While the recent attitude of many writers and workers in this field has been altogether favourable to smaller families, it is doubtful whether many have realized how far this tendency has already gone, what the indications are for the near future, and what ultimate consequences are implied in the constantly diminishing number of births for the very organization of society in the next few generations.

In discussing the prospects of the future birth-rate it is necessary to bear in mind the several forces that have operated in the past, and that are now operating to depress the birth-rate. We may roughly classify these under two main heads, namely, biological on the one hand and social on the other.

How far a direct biological diminution of fertility may have been responsible for the recent decline in the birth-rate is at present an open question. Certain writers, including your own Drs. Yule and Snow, have pointed out that fertility always declines with advancing civilization, that there are cycles in fertility, with rise and fall succeeding each other over long periods of time. These writers further hold that the spread of education and other advantages of modern civilization which are favourable to the standard of living of the common people work in the direction of diminishing the capacity to breed. I am afraid that these authors have not sufficiently refined their research to differentiate between internal and external causes, between the loss of natural fertility and the conscious control of fertility from without. For, after all, it seems fairly certain that the main causes of the decline in birth-rate are not biological, but social and economic.

Among the forces so operating is the rise in the standard of living which has followed as a consequence of the modern industrial civilization. Side by side with the increase in population, there has occurred a great increase in man's control over nature, with the result that civilized peoples to-day are undoubtedly better housed, better clothed, and better fed than they were generations ago. The general standard of living is incomparably higher to-day than it was fifty or a hundred years ago; one glance at our streets, often more congested with automobiles than with human beings, gives evidence of this fact. The same machine civilization which has made it possible to feed, house, and clothe a greater population on the product of inhabitable and arable land has whetted our appetite for machine-made products of all kinds, apparently at the cost of men's natural desire for the old-fashioned type of home, with its family of many children. In competition with children, as an alternative, the automobile, the radio, and the innumerable accessories to modern life are at an immense advantage, if advertising is at all effective. Who ever saw, among the vari-coloured displays in our street-cars or elsewhere, any glowing advertisement praising in similar terms the virtues of a large family?

While some loss of natural capacity to bear children may be granted, the evidence, in my judgment, is altogether convincing that the major cause of the phenomenon we are discussing is the conscious control through the spread of the knowledge and use of contraceptive methods. This is the new force which has spread over the world in recent decades, and has been accepted with almost religious fervour especially among professional people and high-grade industrial workers in the city populations of the world. With ever-increasing discussion and controversy which this subject has brought about, more and more people of all classes have become aware of the power that is within their reach to determine the size of their families. To-day, virtually the entire civilized world is aware of the possibilities of birth control.

I am fortunately able to make available to you in advance of publication the results of a very interesting study of the habits of 10,000 women who in recent years have availed themselves of the services offered by the Birth Control Clinic of New York under the direction of Mrs. Sanger and her associates. This study shows that 93 per cent. of the women reported having used some birth-control method prior to consulting the clinic. Of these women all but 9 per cent. reported some success by one or other method they had employed. Nevertheless they came to the Birth Control Clinic for further advice and help. They are, in a sense, a selected group, but they also show how widespread the practice of various contraceptive methods is. The principal races and religions are represented. Jews, Catholics, and Protestants were all represented in large numbers. Reports of similar groups in England and in other countries of the world show very definitely that the knowledge of birth-control methods is fairly universal. That such knowledge is not always effective is also very clear, but there can be no doubt that the current low birth-rates can be traced in large measure to the success of the various methods employed.

It is, therefore, reasonable to assume that, as the methods of birth control become more widespread and more effective, the birth-rate will continue to decline not only in Europe, but in America also, and other continents as well. This result is all the more to be expected in view of the weakening of moral, legal, and religious restrictions on the practice of birth control. Your own bishops have spoken for the first time and clearly. In my country the Federal Council of the Churches of Christ has brought in a report favourable to the spread of birth-control information under guarded conditions. The subject is still very controversial, but more and more those who unqualifiedly condemn the practice are finding themselves reduced in number and with diminished public support. The outlook, therefore, is very clearly toward the wider application of birth-control methods to the whole people, and, consequently, toward lower birth-rates.

How far this phenomenon will go is an open question. I shall discuss this subject under two heads. The first is on the assumption that the future fall in the birth-rate is such as will ultimately give virtually a stabilized population under the conditions of the best mortality which we believe our people capable of. Studies we have made at other times indicate that the life expectation can be extended to about 70 years. This is on the assumption that the entire country will avail itself of all the advances of modern medicine and of public health work and will control the preventable diseases in accordance with our knowledge. The corresponding death-rate for this favourable expectation is 14·28 per thousand living. The equilibrium birth-rate corresponding to this death-rate will be the same figure. The indications are also that this condition of equilibrium will be reached in the decade distributed around 1970. We have further assumed that the birth-rate is maintained practically at this level for a relatively long period of years up to 2100.

Chart I shows the curve of population that will result under the conditions of optimum mortality coupled with a slightly diminishing birth-rate after the point of stabilization has been reached. The uppermost broken curve indicates that the population will reach its maximum between 1980 and 1990 with about 154 millions, and will slowly decline thereafter. At 2100 it will have fallen to 140 millions. These figures do not make any provision for additions through immigration.

The supposition on which this first estimate is based seems altogether too optimistic, however. Guided by the precipitate declines in the birth-rates that are now occurring, not only in America but all over the world, I expect the birth-rate to drop below the curve indicated by the broken line. This is all the more likely to occur because of the operation of two forces: (a) the Americanization of the foreign-born; (b) the movement

BIRTHRATE *and* POPULATION

U.S. 1915–1930 OBSERVED; 1930–2100 ESTIMATED

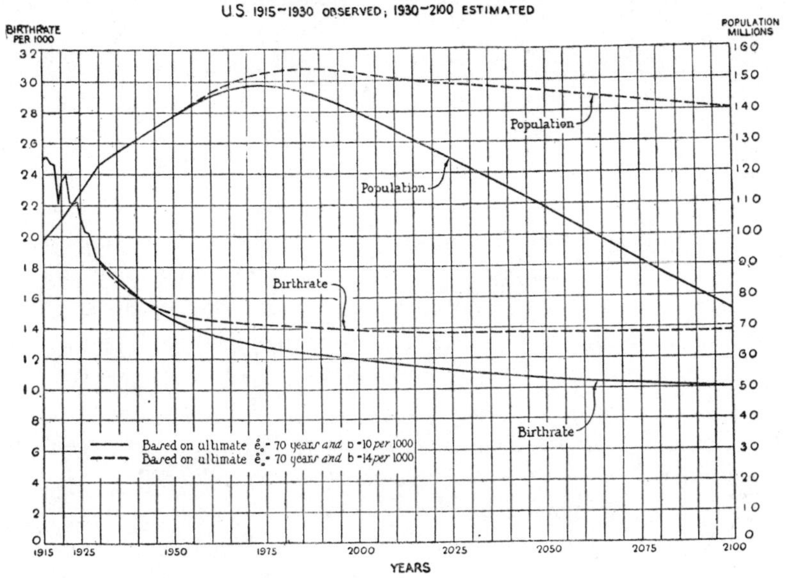

CHART I

of population from the country to the cities. Recent analyses have shown that an appreciable part of the current birth-rate in many of our States is traceable to our first generation foreign stock. We find also that in succeeding generations the fertility more and more approximates that of the native population. The next one or two generations will, therefore, see the dilution, if not the elimination, of the additions that have come from this source in the past. In like manner, the movement from the farms to the cities will expose large numbers of people to influences and a mode of life conducive to low birth-rates. What now keeps the natural birth-rate up to its present level is the fact that nearly half of the people still live on farms or in small towns. Contraceptive practices are not as yet countenanced in such locations. Moreover, there is an economic motive for large families on the old-fashioned farm. But the mechanization of the farm will modify all this. Dr. O. E. Baker, the senior Economist of the United States Department of Agriculture, estimates that, with the present drift, the proportion of our population living on farms will be reduced to one-sixth of the total, and that furthermore, if certain machine processes become successful for the harvesting of cotton and corn, the farm population will be reduced to an eighth. This is, of course, speculation. Nevertheless, it is fairly certain that in the near future the cities will continue to grow at the expense of the country, and that birth-rates will decline seriously on this account alone.

We have accordingly traced an alternative curve of the birth-rate which calls for 13 per thousand by 1970, for 12 by 2000, and 10·7 by 2050, and 10 in the year 2100. This may seem like a very low figure, but it has already been experienced in a number of large cities, as, for example, in Berlin after the War, and in a number of other large urban areas where exceptional social standards prevail. My extreme prediction for 2100 may turn out to be conservative after all. At this point we have assumed that the birth-rate becomes stabilized. Under this second condition, the total population will reach a lower maximum and will fall rather rapidly thereafter. The chart shows that the maximum at about 1970 will be about 148 millions. The population then will decline to 140 millions by the year 2000, to 109 millions by 2050, and to 76 millions by 2100. It is clearly understood that these figures and estimates are, like the previous ones, based on the assumption of no increase through immigration. If this rapid decline in population should materialize, it will surely be the first time in recorded history that, with a low population density and with rich natural resources, such as prevail in the United States, a nation will follow a downhill curve even to the point of reducing its total by half in the short period of a hundred years.

It will be of interest to analyse some of the changes in the structure of the population that will follow on each of the two assumptions. Under the first condition, that is, of a population approaching ultimately an expectation of life of 70 years, associated with a birth-rate giving a stationary condition, the age distribution will be materially changed from that at present. The number of young people in the population will be materially reduced. There will be approximately 29 per cent. of the population under 20 years of age in 1950, as contrasted with a percentage of 52·5 in 1850 and 40·7 per cent. in 1920. In the middle registers, that is, between ages 20 and 50 years, the population proportion will change only slightly and vary around 40 per cent. The changes in the proportion of the population at the older ages will, therefore, be as marked as in those at the younger ages, but in the opposite direction. In 1950, 25·3 per cent. will be over 50, as contrasted with 9 per cent. in 1850 and 15 per cent. in 1920. Ultimately, under the first and moderate supposition (of an ultimate birth-rate of 13·7 per thousand in the year 2100), the proportion of persons 50 years old and over will be 35·5 per cent.

Under the second assumption, that is, of a more marked decline in the birth-rate even down to 10 per thousand per annum, the changes in the age composition will be more marked. Again, we find that the proportion of persons in the middle years of life (between ages 20 and 50) remains fairly constant, constituting about 40 per cent. of the population. On the other hand, the proportion of the population under 20 declines very markedly. This is compensated for by a corresponding increase in the proportion of those 50 years of age and over. Under the conditions we are discussing, the percentage of those 20 years of age and under will be about 21 per cent. in the year 2100, while those 50 years of age and over will be somewhat more than 40 per cent.

I have in another place discussed the implications in these changes, and I shall not do that here again. But it will be sufficient to say that changes as fundamental as these in the organization of society are matters of the greatest importance, and should receive the careful attention of all students of population and of the intelligent public as well.

Chart II shows not only the ultimate situation for which figures have just been cited, but also exhibits the intervening stages from the age distribution in 1850 and carried forward through 250 years. The two curves divide the chart into three areas or bands. The central one of these is of practically uniform width, indicating that the population within the working ages of life forms a practically constant proportion of the whole. Very different is the aspect of the lower and the upper areas in the diagram. If what we have outlined actually occurs, America will become a population of old people instead of the youthful one it is now.

Chart III, furthermore, shows the ultimate age distribution that would be attained by the population of the United States under the conditions of an optimum death-rate and with birth-rates varying from the figure of 14·28 per thousand as the upper limit down to the minimum figure of 10 as the lower limit, with the three intermediate steps of 13, 12, and 10 per thousand. Each of the curves corresponds to the conditions of diminishing birth-rate indicated. It will be seen that all five curves have practically a common point at about age 40. The proportion of the

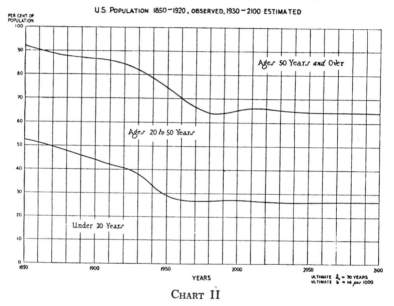

PROGRESSIVE CHANGES IN AGE DISTRIBUTION

U.S. POPULATION 1850−1920, OBSERVED, 1930−2100 ESTIMATED

CHART II

population at this age is apparently independent of the birth-rate, being 1·25 per cent. of the total. But at all the other ages the proportion of persons does vary with the birth-rate, directly for ages under 40 and inversely for ages over 40. The higher the birth-rate, the younger the population; the lower the birth-rate, the older the population. And under the conditions of a birth-rate of 10, we find the extraordinary situation that the largest single age group is that of persons between 55 and 60. Each year of age in this period corresponds to a little over 1·3 per cent. of the population.

One thing is certain. The changes that are now occurring in the birth-rate and those that are likely to occur are bringing in their train consequences of the first importance. These have not received the attention they deserve, for the conditions that will ultimately result will determine the kind of a world we shall live in. The psychological as well as the economic and social atmosphere will be largely determined by the demographic situation that I have described. These are primarily internal considerations confronting each country. There will also be

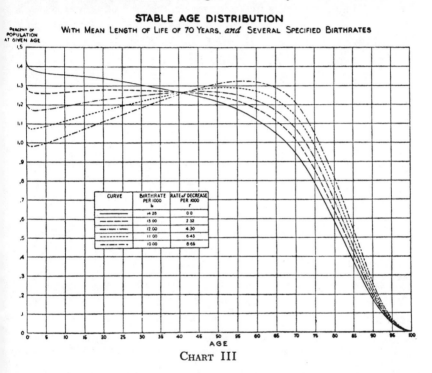

STABLE AGE DISTRIBUTION

WITH MEAN LENGTH OF LIFE OF 70 YEARS, *and* SEVERAL SPECIFIED BIRTHRATES

CURVE	BIRTHRATE PER 1000 b	RATE OF DECREASE PER 1000 r
	14 25	0 0
	13 00	2 32
	12 00	4 30
	11 00	6 43
	10 00	8 65

CHART III

need of external readjustments of equal importance. Changes such as we have considered for the United States will have their repercussions on the peoples of the whole world. Similar changes will undoubtedly occur in most other countries; but if certain of them, for example, Russia, and especially China and India, continue to increase their populations, or even maintain their present numbers, the question forces itself upon us what the international relations in the future will be like. In the last analysis, numbers must count, and in the future more than ever, when different political and economic ideals will strive for supremacy.

The changes that are coming through the differential decline in the birth-rate will make a totally different kind of a world for our grand-children and our great-grand-children to live in. Those groups that will maintain higher rates will dominate the scene. There are signs that the era of ruling and of subject peoples is rapidly coming to an end. At the same time, experiments are being made to demonstrate that the most effective society is that in which every man is a significant unit—an end in himself, irrespective of class, station, or tradition. If this aim is realized, the individual will come into his own. Under such conditions, if the people of Russia, of India and China, continue to people the earth, they will in all probability dominate it also.

DISCUSSION

Dr. DUNLOP referred to Dr. DUBLIN's statement that in the country districts and in the small towns of America contraception was not countenanced. If there were no contraception, however, he would have expected a much higher relative birth-rate.

Dr. DUBLIN said that the present expectation of life was nearer 60 than 70. If the expectation of life was 60, the reciprocal of that figure, about 16·7, would be necessary as a birth-rate to balance that figure.

Professor FAIRCHILD said the over-weighting in the middle-age groups due to immigration was largely responsible for the change of birth-rate. Immigration was about one-third female to two-thirds male. Had Dr. DUBLIN taken account of the effect of immigration?

Captain PITT-RIVERS asked if Dr. DUBLIN had made any attempt to correlate the fall in the birth-rate with the change in the adult sex-ratio?

Dr. DUBLIN said there had not been a marked change in the sex-ratio in his country; it was not anything like as marked as it was in Great Britain. There was an excess of males, due to their coming in from other countries.

Captain PITT-RIVERS said that his suggestion that a fall in birth-rate and a slowing up of population was likely to accompany a change in the adult sex-ratio was based particularly on his investigations of Pacific populations, which showed that there was actually some correlation between a decline in the birth and survival rates, and an apparent change which was less easy to detect in the differential sex survival-rate. A factor in the decline was the less usual phenomenon of a greater pre-ferential survival of males over females in the later age categories. Thus a decline was marked by increase in masculinity.

Dr. DUBLIN said that in America there was not that difference in the survival-rates of the sexes.

Professor FAIRCHILD disagreed that the difference in the sex distribu-tion was offset by marriages of immigrants. There were hundreds and thousands of men living in boarding-houses and such places in the United States in which there were no women.

Mrs. HOW-MARTYN doubted the value of Dr. DUBLIN's curves for future forecasting. Dr. DUBLIN thought the fall in birth-rate had been due to birth control and not to biological infertility. Was it not just as likely that conditions would arise that might make people want to change and have more children? Control was surely desirable; it was now being used to bring about a fall in birth-rate; at another time it might be used in another direction in response to different ideas.

Dr. DUBLIN agreed that there were some prospects of a reversal of habit. This was, of course, a possibility. His own feeling was that the indications were for an increase of the practice of birth control. At present a large part of the population of the United States living in small towns and country places was as yet little touched by the knowledge and practice of birth control, but that knowledge would become more and more available to those people and would be used. It was possible that in future when the man in the street realized what he, Dr. DUBLIN, had predicted, there might be an appreciation on the part of some people of their obligations as individuals to Society, but it would require nothing short of a religious revolution to bring about a change in attitude to undo what had already happened. Individuals did pretty much what suited them personally.

Dr. DUNLOP said that Dr. EDIN's experience pointed in the other direction.

Dr. DUBLIN replied that, although extremely interesting in itself, Dr. EDIN's experience could only be considered a drop in the bucket; it was the smallest fraction of population, and in the totals was washed out.

FIRST FINDINGS OF THE BELGIAN INVESTIGATION OF THE CONDITIONS OF LIFE IN LARGE FAMILIES

By M. EUGÈNE DUPRÉEL

(*University of Brussels*)

FIRST FINDINGS OF THE BELGIAN INVESTIGATION OF THE CONDITIONS OF LIFE IN LARGE FAMILIES

A DETAILED questionnaire was devised and 870 copies issued to investigators. About 130 replies have been received. A first analysis of the data received confirmed certain tendencies already noticeable by less searching methods.

The mother plays the dominant part in bringing up the family; where State or charitable aid encourages large families, this fact becomes more pronounced. Where small families predominate, the large families stand out as divisible into two distinct groups. The "accidental" or passive, and the deliberate and intentional.

The accidental or involuntary type may be regarded as a survival, they are clearly becoming less frequent. From the nature of the case, the parents being dull or irresponsible, the family sinks in standard.

The "voluntary" large family appears to be successful. Economic incentive is denied (except in one case), and the responsibility is undertaken as a moral and virtuous course.

All observers concur in assessing the restricted family as less socially valuable than the "voluntary" large family: the hard work and self-sacrifice of the parents, and the more rigorous upbringing of the children being cited as the cause.

The solidarity of the family as an institution is said to be growing.

The writer envisages the time when the large family, though rare, will be regarded as a superior social class. This may bring about a change in public opinion tending to a fashion for large families, reversing the present demographic trend.

PREMIERS RÉSULTATS DE L'ENQUÊTE BELGE SUR LES CONDITIONS DE VIE DES FAMILLES NOMBREUSES

Par le Professeur EUGÈNE DUPRÉEL

Peu de temps après sa fondation, l'Association belge pour l'Étude des Problèmes de la Population a décidé de procéder à une enquête sur les conditions de vie des familles nombreuses en Belgique. Un questionnaire très détaillé a été imprimé et 870 exemplaires ont été distribués à des enquêteurs de différentes catégories. Environ 130 réponses ont été obtenues jusqu'ici. La recherche ne s'en tiendra pas à ces premières démarches. Comme l'expérience a montré que les meilleures réponses proviennent des infirmières-visiteuses et en général des personnes préparées pour le service social, l'Association a l'intention de provoquer de nouvelles enquêtes émanant de cette catégorie de personnes, au moyen d'une rémunération appropriée.

D'une première étude des réponses obtenues, certaines indications se dégagent, qui ne sont pas nouvelles, et qu'une observation moins rigoureusement conduite a pu mainte fois procurer.

Par exemple, on est frappé du *rôle primordial de la mère* dans le statut et la destinée des familles nombreuses. Fréquents sont les cas où le père est manifestement insuffisant et où cependant les choses tournent à bien grâce aux aptitudes et à l'effort soutenu de la mère. Il semble même que les mesures législatives ou privées prises en faveur des familles nombreuses, tendent à accentuer cette inégalité de l'importance relative du père et de la mère dans la destinée du groupe familial: le rôle de la mère reste aussi fondamental que jamais, tandis qu'il n'en va pas ainsi pour le père. On pourrait dire que cette tendance rapproche le groupe familial humain des sociétés d'hyménoptères. . . .

Notre enquête vérifie aussi cette courbe d'évolution selon laquelle le moment critique dans une famille nombreuse est celui où les enfants sont en bas âge. A ce moment, la chute sociale est menaçante ou s'accomplit; mais un relèvement est régulier dès que les aînés deviennent adultes. Quand les enfants sont petits, ils empêchent les distractions, les relations, et la famille est isolée. Au contraire, lorsqu'ils grandissent, la grande famille devient un centre d'attraction et de divertissement.

Enfin, à la demande du questionnaire: la famille se comporte-t-elle comme un petit groupe social distinct? la réponse la plus fréquente est l'affirmative. Tantôt on juge que ce fait est un bien, tantôt que c'est un mal.

Mais je voudrais insister surtout sur un fait sociologique d'une importance méconnue, que notre enquête paraît révéler.

Dans un milieu où la majorité des familles sont de petites familles, les familles nombreuses tendent à se répartir en deux espèces profondément différentes. Cette différence s'accuse probablement beaucoup moins dans les milieux où la famille a comporté plus régulièrement un grand nombre d'enfants. Il y a d'une part les familles nombreuses *de fait*, ou *non voulues*, ou *passives*; la seconde espèce est la famille nombreuse délibérée où le grand nombre des enfants est soit voulu d'avance, soit justifié a posteriori.

La première espèce, la famille nombreuse involontaire, quelle qu'en soit la proportion dans l'ensemble de la population, apparaît comme *une survivance*, en voie de diminution évidente. Et l'on comprend aisément pourquoi les familles de ce type font si pauvre figure: les gens avisés, éclairés, réfléchis, ou bien n'ont pas beaucoup d'enfants, ou, s'ils en ont, les familles qu'ils fondent rentrent dans notre seconde espèce. La famille nombreuse involontaire paraît donc en voie de régression et de qualité déclinante.

Quant à la famille nombreuse volontaire ou délibérée, c'est le type de famille que notre enquête met le mieux en lumière et sur lequel elle nous donne des détails hautement suggestifs.

Les *avantages économiques* que pourrait présenter pour les parents une nombreuse postérité sont presque totalement inaperçus (un seul cas). Enquêteurs et intéressés considèrent comme un axiome que le grand nombre des enfants ne peut entraîner pour les parents que détriment et sacrifice.

Les raisons invoquées pour se justifier comme un bien, sont exclusivement d'ordre moral. Le plus fréquemment, les familles nombreuses délibérées et fières de leur statut professent des convictions religieuses ardentes, mais il en est aussi chez lesquelles le facteur religieux n'entre guère en ligne de compte.

Le point sur lequel tous les intéressés sont d'accord, au moins *implicitement*, le voici: tous sont convaincus de *valoir mieux* que les membres de familles restreintes. Ils se jugent supérieurs, comme parents, par l'abnégation, le sacrifice, le travail, la contribution finale au bien public, sans oublier la pureté ou la sévérité des mœurs; et de même, les enfants sont jugés devoir être meilleurs par une éducation plus rigoureuse leur inculquant la solidarité, le courage, et l'esprit d'entreprise.

A la question: la famille recensée a-t-elle reculé sur l'échelle sociale, beaucoup d'enquêtes répondent: Au contraire, la famille est en voie d'ascension. Il va sans dire que cet optimisme est sujet à critique, car ce sont les familles qui réussissent que des enquêtes du genre de celle-ci rencontrent le plus facilement. Celles où l'infortune a pris le dessus sont moins enclines à se déclarer enthousiastes de leur propre statut.

Malgré les réserves d'une critique prudente, il me paraît que l'on peut généraliser les constatations que nous venons de faire, et attirer l'attention sur un fait de portée sociologique universelle. Qu'on le déplore ou qu'on l'approuve, il semble bien qu'une très grande partie de la population du globe, enveloppant presque toute la race blanche, soit destinée, d'ici peu de temps, à apparaître comme *une espèce biologique à fécondité formellement limitée*. Dans un tel milieu, la famille nombreuse deviendra l'exception. La distinction entre deux espèces de familles nombreuses que notre enquête nous a suggérée, s'imposera dès lors. D'une part, la famille nombreuse involontaire deviendra de plus en plus rare et d'une qualité sociale de plus en plus basse; elle sera pratiquement en voie de disparition. D'autre part, la famille nombreuse voulue ou systématique, quelle qu'en soit l'abondance ou la rareté, apparaîtra comme *une variété de l'espèce humaine caractérisée par une grande fécondité*.

Sociologiquement, ces familles nombreuses s'accorderont entre elles pour se considérer comme *une classe sociale supérieure*, ou comme une minorité aristocratique caractérisée par ses qualités morales. Le grand nombre d'enfants sera comme une *vertu symbolique*, c.a.d. l'attestation matérielle d'une supériorité.

N'y a-t-il pas là une application aux conditions démographiques d'une loi sociologique beaucoup plus générale? Dès qu'une pratique quelconque ou une manière de penser devient universelle, elle devient aussi *vulgaire*, et n'entraîne plus avec elle aucune *distinction*. Dès lors il y a toute chance pour que la pratique ou la manière de penser diamétralement opposée retrouve au moins quelques partisans qui prennent ce que les autres appelleront *un paradoxe*, comme une source de distinction et un facteur de satisfaction intime.

Au XIXᵉ siècle, lorsque la restriction voulue de la natalité était encore un peu comme un secret, les petites familles ont plus ou moins fait figure de minorités supérieures ; la masse des familles nombreuses, d'ailleurs la plupart involontaires ou non délibérées, représentait alors la majorité vulgaire. Nous assistons au renversement de cet état de choses. Dans une humanité presque universellement constituée de petites familles, les familles systématiquement nombreuses apparaîtront à elles-mêmes comme une aristocratie morale ou une élite sociale fondée sur *des mérites*.

L'influence de cette minorité sera toujours sensible ; cependant, il y a peu de chance que son prestige suffise pour qu'elle soit imitée par le plus grand nombre, car à mesure qu'une grande progéniture deviendrait de plus en plus fréquente, dans cette même mesure elle deviendrait moins significative et moins révélatrice d'un niveau social ou moral avantageux.

Quoi qu'il en soit, et quelque opinion que l'on professe sur l'état démographique général le plus désirable, l'importance du phénomène sociologique entrevu ici ne saurait être contestée. Il pose d'innombrables problèmes sur le rôle des *réactions minoritaires* dans l'activité des hommes en général, et en particulier dans les conditions démographiques.

RESEARCH ON INCOME, NATALITY, AND INFANT MORTALITY IN HOLLAND

By Dr. H. W. METHORST

(Holland)

For the report of the Dutch National Committee in the field of Commission I see Report No. 3, p. 358

RESEARCH ON INCOME, NATALITY, AND INFANT MORTALITY IN HOLLAND

I

BEING A REPORT OF THE ACTIVITIES OF THE SECOND COMMISSION OF THE DUTCH NATIONAL COMMITTEE

THE Dutch Central Commission for Statistics once conducted an inquiry into the number of births and the number of deaths among children of all undissolved marriages contracted between 1877 and 1881 inclusive, for a period ending in 1897, in a few towns and forty country places. These families were divided into groups according to their degree of prosperity, based on the house-taxes paid.

The Dutch National Committee has now decided to study, after a lapse of thirty years, the births and infant mortality in all marriages contracted in the years 1907-11, i.e. the marriages which continued for fifteen to twenty years, for a period ending in 1927.

It is very satisfactory to note that 135 country places with populations varying from 4,000 to 10,000 inhabitants have consented to help us to carry out these investigations. Out of these 135 places, 27 requested us to let them have the questionnaires immediately, while the other communities wished to wait until the work in connection with the General Census of December 31, 1930, and the subsequent elections was over. A number of communities have already returned the questionnaires with the information we asked for, and it has been possible to prepare calculations for three groups, viz.:

1. Questionnaires, which are not going to be included in the investigations, because the marriage was dissolved before 1927 for any of the following reasons:

    (a) Death.
    (b) Divorce.
    (c) Separation.
    (d) Departure of either husband or wife, or of both, without there being any trace of their whereabouts.

2. Questionnaires, which are not excluded for any of the above reasons, and which deal with families, which have remained in

the community for the periods of 1907, 1908, 1909, 1910, and 1911 to 1927.

3. Questionnaires relating to families which moved, previously to 1927, to another place in Holland.

These questionnaires will later on be forwarded for completion to the communities where these families now live, if they have moved to communities with from 4,000 to 10,000 inhabitants. The information about income is entered in those questionnaires which are to be included in the investigations as they are received. This is done by means of the entries in the registers of the income-tax.

Two towns, viz. Utrecht and Dordrecht, have consented to collaborate also. Besides the contribution of $300 which the Union has granted for the years 1930 and 1931, and for which the Dutch National Committee is particularly indebted to Professor Pearl, a few other amounts have been received from interested Societies and Institutions in Holland. The towns and other communities give their help free of any charge. In the second half of 1931 and the first half of 1932 the work will be well on its way.

The method followed for these investigations is generally the same as the one applied thirty years ago. This is done on purpose, in order to be able to find out whether, and if so to what extent, matrimonial ideas have changed during this period of thirty years.

It is very probable that there will be changes in this respect, for whereas in 1877 the birth-rate was still over 36, and in 1897 still over 32, it had gone down to 23 per 1,000 inhabitants in 1927. The investigations of thirty years ago showed that in the two towns Rotterdam and Dordrecht almost half the number of families had six or more children, and in the forty country towns 46 per cent. of the families had six or more children. It is a well-known fact that since 1900 the birth-rate in the towns has gone down below that in the country, and has increasingly fallen, whereas, almost simultaneously with the birth-rate, the death-rate has rapidly gone down since 1900, and has dropped below the death-rate in rural districts, this being the case both with general and infant mortality.

The most striking result shown by these previous investigations is that when families were divided into three groups according to the rental value of houses, we find that in the two towns Rotterdam and

Dordrecht there were 5·6 births per family in the lowest prosperity class, 5·2 in the second, and 4·3 in the highest. So there was a regular drop from 5·6 to 4·3 in the birth-rate corresponding to classification by this standard of prosperity. In the forty country towns there was also a drop to 5·2 births per family in the lowest prosperity group to 5·1 in the second, and to 4·7 in the highest. It follows that in the rural districts the difference between the three prosperity groups was smaller than in the towns.

Infant mortality under one year of age per 100 live births was 16·6 in the lowest prosperity class in the two towns Rotterdam and Dordrecht, 15·7 in the second, and 12·3 in the highest. In the rural districts these proportional figures were: 11·2, 10½, and 9½.

When we bear in mind that for the larger towns in Holland the annual death-rate is now only 4 or 5 of the group of children under one year, we are justified in presuming that in this respect, too, there must have been great changes during the past thirty years. We are led to expect that in the towns the birth-rate and the death-rate under one year of age have fallen rapidly in the lowest prosperity group, not only absolutely but also relatively to the highest prosperity group.

In order to be able to adopt a purer standard for the present investigations, we have now chosen the income-tax paid by married couples, instead of their house-taxes. For the purpose of obtaining further indications of social status, questions are put with regard to the husband's position at the beginning of his married life, his present position, and the husband's and the wife's religious denominations.

The questionnaire states also the husband's age and the wife's age.

II

Notes on the Latest Dutch Census

With reference to this report, I may add that the latest Census taken in Holland also included questions with regard to matrimonial fertility.

The form used for women also contained a few questions with regard to married women concerning—

1. Date of marriage, and place where it was contracted.
2. Town or village where the married couple now lives.

3. Age of wife and her occupation.
4. Age of husband and his occupation.
5. Number of live births (boys and girls).
6. Number of children alive on December 31, 1930.

Thus it is possible not only to calculate matrimonial fertility for the groups of towns and the groups of rural districts, but also for each province and each town or village, with reference to marriages that had lasted one year, two years, three years, etc., at the moment of the Census, taken on December 31, 1930. It will be particularly interesting to study the degree of fertility in marriages which, as regards fertility, are terminated, as the wives have reached an age at which, humanly speaking, they can bear no more children.

As the husband's and the wife's occupations are known, and whether they are employers or employed, it is possible to find out, if among working people fertility is greater or smaller than among employers and among retired persons, and it will be possible to state whether there is a difference between groups of workers in factories and groups of workers in agriculture, and what is the degree of fertility among officials, teachers, etc.

It will be easier this time than it used to be to divide matrimonial fertility into as many groups as is thought fit, because this is the first time that Hollerith machines are being used by the Census. The Census was taken on December 31, 1930, and the municipalities forwarded the forms to the Central Bureau of Statistics, after comparing the information with the population registers which have existed in Holland since 1850, and which are kept up to date by means of the data concerning birth, death, arrival, and departure. These two institutions (Census and Registers of Population) complete each other. By means of the Census it is possible, every ten years, to find out whether too many or too few inhabitants have been registered, and which are the most recent data concerning occupation and religious denomination. The Registers of Population show whether any people were omitted by the Census.

The municipalities forwarded the forms to the Central Bureau of Statistics before July 1, 1931. On April 1st 220 persons began checking the forms. It is expected that on December 1st of the current year it will be possible to start sorting and adding by machines, and that this work will be ready in the course of 1932.

As regards the registers of population in the Netherlands, we may add that at present in my native country a trial is being given in forty communities to a new system, with a view to the introduction of uniform and personal bulletins into the population administration. If this trial proves successful, an entirely new system will be introduced in Holland, in accordance with which a bulletin will be devoted to each individual at his or her birth. This bulletin contains all particulars of a demographic nature, and it follows the individual from one place to another.

This leads to the following three great advantages:

1. There can be only one bulletin for each individual, thus preventing in future any overlapping, which in the present system may at any time occur.
2. It will no longer be necessary to copy particulars in case of removal (from registers of population on removal form, and from removal form in registers of population of new domicile). Thus numerous mistakes will be avoided. The identical bulletin follows the individual.
3. As the bulletin gives the pedigree, and in case of death also the cause of death, with which it is forwarded to the Central Bureau of Statistics, a collection of such bulletins is thus gradually made, which will be useful for genealogical, demographical, and heredity studies.

I hope to witness the introduction of this system during my official career; posterity will reap the fruit, which will need a lifetime to attain maturity.

These bulletins will give in the future the most interesting data on fertility.

Third Session

GENERAL POPULATION

Chairman: Dr. Louis I. Dublin

Papers read:

11. THE RELATION OF SOCIAL STATUS TO THE FERTILITY OF NATIVE-BORN MARRIED WOMEN IN THE UNITED STATES. By Dr. Frank W. Notestein.

12. NUPTIALITY, FERTILITY, AND REPRODUCTIVITY. By Dr. S. D. Wicksell.

THE RELATION OF SOCIAL STATUS TO THE FERTILITY OF NATIVE-BORN MARRIED WOMEN IN THE UNITED STATES

By Dr. FRANK W. NOTESTEIN

(*Department of Research, Milbank Memorial Fund*)

THE RELATION OF SOCIAL STATUS TO THE FERTILITY OF NATIVE-BORN MARRIED WOMEN IN THE UNITED STATES*

DIFFERENTIAL fertility according to social class is a fact thoroughly established by many studies in Europe and Great Britain. Only a few American inquiries have been made, and these either were confined to small samples, such as those by Baber and Ross,† and Sydenstricker,‡ or were indirect statistical approaches to the question, such as those by Ogburn and Tibbits,§ and Pearl.|| In 1910 data analogous to those employed in the English Census Report on the "Fertility of Marriage,"¶ were collected by the Federal Census, when each married woman in the United States was asked, among other things, the number of children she had borne, and the number of years she had been married. Unfortunately, the returns were never tabulated by the Bureau of the Census.

The importance of these unpublished Census data led the Milbank Memorial Fund to undertake the tabulation of a sample of them from

---

* From the Division of Research, Milbank Memorial Fund. This paper summarizes the material presented in the following studies:

   (a) "Differential Fertility According to Social Class," by Edgar Sydenstricker and Frank W. Notestein, *Journal of the American Statistical Association*, March 1930.

   (b) "Social Classes and the Birth-rate," by Frank W. Notestein, *Survey Graphic*, April 1931.

   (c) "Differential Age at Marriage According to Social Class," by Frank W. Notestein, *The American Journal of Sociology*, July 1931.

   (d) "Trends in the Size of Families Completed Prior to 1910 in Various Social Classes," by Xarifa Sallume and Frank W. Notestein, *Proceedings of the American Sociological Society*, 1931.

† R. E. Baber and E. A. Ross: "Changes in the Size of American Families in One Generation," *University of Wisconsin Studies in the Social Sciences and History*, No. 10.

‡ Edgar Sydenstricker: "Differential Fertility According to Economic Status," *Public Health Reports*, August 30, 1929, vol. xliv, No. 35, pp. 2101–2106.

§ W. F. Ogburn and Clark Tibbits: "Birth-rates and Social Classes," *Social Forces*, September 1929, pp. 1–10.

|| Raymond Pearl: "Differential Fertility," *The Quarterly Review of Biology*, vol. ii, No. 1, March 1927, pp. 102–118.

¶ *Census of England and Wales*, 1911, vol. xiii.

the original enumeration schedules. It is the purpose of this paper to summarize the results thus far obtained from an analysis of this tabulation.

The sample, which adequately represents each of the broad social classes, comprises data for 99,226 married women who were living with their husbands north of the Mason and Dixon Line in 1910. It is limited to women from families in which both husband and wife were of native–white parentage and had married only once. This group is divided into two parts: the urban sample, which was taken from the thirty-three northern cities with populations of between 100,000 and 500,000 in 1910; and the rural sample, which was taken from rural parts of seventy-four counties adjacent to those cities.* Altogether records were obtained for 56,687 city and 42,539 country women.

The women of the urban sample were separated, on the basis of the Census Returns of the husband's occupation, into four broad social classes: professional, business, skilled workers, and unskilled labourers; and those of the rural sample into: farm owners, farm renters, and farm labourers.† The rural classes are exactly what the names indicate, but the titles of the urban classes, which include a wide range of occu-pations, must be suggestive rather than precise. Nevertheless, the urban classes were dominated by the groups from which the titles are taken, and it is believed that each of them differed from the others with respect to its standards of living, education, and achievement, and in its general social environment.

Since changes in the birth-rates for these classes have a different significance before than after the end of the child-bearing period, we shall postpone our consideration of the data for women over 45 years of age, pending an examination of those for women still in the fertile period when the Census was taken.

The number of children ever born to a group of married women prior to the Census date is the resultant of many factors, among the more important of which are age of the wife, age of the wife at marriage, sterility, fecundity, and a host of factors relating to the economic and social environment of the class. Of these factors, the age of the wife is

---

* Appendix Tables I and II indicate the number of women for whom data were obtained in each city and county.

† The chief occupational groups included in each of these classes, and the number of women considered in each group, are shown in Appendix Table III.

unique in that it determines the length of time during which the other factors are operative, or in a sense the opportunity which any group of wives has for bearing children. To obtain a fair comparison of the net fertility of the social classes, these opportunities must be equal, that is, comparisons must be made between groups having the same age distributions. For example, the fact that the wives of farm labourers had borne on the average fewer children than the wives of farm owners does not indicate that the wives of farm labourers were less fertile. It only reflects the fact that they were younger and had had less opportunity to bear children prior to the date of enumeration. The true relation of the net fertility of these two classes can be shown only by comparing the average number of children born to the wives of farm owners and farm labourers who were of the same age.

This requirement, that age of the wife should be held constant in any expression of net fertility, is met by the cumulative birth-rates for specific age groups, that is, the number of children ever born per 100 wives in each quinquennial age group. These rates are presented in Table I and Fig. 1 for the total urban and rural samples, in Table II and Fig. 2 for the urban social classes, and in Table III and Fig. 3 for the rural social classes. Less accurate but useful summary ratios are given by the standardized cumulative birth-rates shown in Table IV and Fig. 4, which indicate the number of children that would have been born to the women of each social class had the age distribution of those women been the same as that of a standard population—the standard in this case being the combined urban and rural samples.

Before attention is turned to a detailed consideration of the cumulative birth-rates, a common and at first glance anomalous characteristic of all of them should be noted. As the age of the wives advances there is no tendency for the curves of the birth-rates to approach an asymptote toward the end of the child-bearing period. If this material represented one cohort observed at successive ages, such results would lead to the absurd conclusion that the average annual increment to the family did not decrease with advancing age of the wife. But instead of representing one cohort observed at successive dates, these data represent successive cohorts observed at one date, that is, women who entered their child-bearing period between 1880 and 1910 and who reported the number of children born prior to 1910 at ages ranging from 14 to 44. Since these years witnessed a sharp decline in the birth-rate, the families of

TABLE I

CHILDREN BORN, WIVES, AND TOTAL NUMBER OF CHILDREN
EVER BORN PER 100 WIVES IN EACH QUINQUENNIAL AGE
GROUP UNDER 45, FOR THE URBAN AND RURAL SAMPLES

Children Born, Wives, and Children Born per 100 Wives for Urban and Rural Areas	Age of Wife at the Census of 1910						
	Total under 45	Under 20	20–24	25–29	30–34	35–39	40–44
Children born							
Urban*	59,522	393	5,112	11,128	13,664	14,788	14,437
Rural	72,543	549	5,557	11,772	16,203	18,838	19,624
Wives							
Urban*	37,206	865	6,125	9,092	8,238	7,082	5,804
Rural	27,864	1,012	4,676	5,988	5,831	5,476	4,881
Children born per 100 wives							
Urban*	160	45	83	122	166	209	249
Rural	260	54	119	197	278	344	402

* In order to obtain an adequate sample of the professional class it was necessary
to search three times as many schedule pages as were used for the other urban
classes. For that reason the data for the professional class are given one-third their
actual weight.

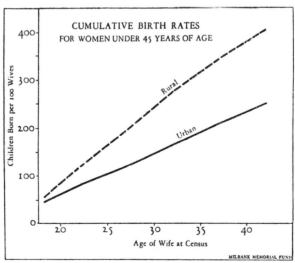

FIG. 1.—Total number of children ever born per 100 wives in
each quinquennial age group under 45, for the urban and
rural samples.

TABLE II

CHILDREN BORN, WIVES, AND TOTAL NUMBER OF CHILDREN
EVER BORN PER 100 WIVES IN EACH QUINQUENNIAL AGE
GROUP UNDER 45, FOR EACH URBAN SOCIAL CLASS

Children Born, Wives, and Children Born per 100 Wives for each Social Class	Age of Wife at the Census of 1910						
	Total under 45	Under 20	20–24	25–29	30–34	35–39	40–44
Children born							
Professional ..	9,661	9	349	1,364	2,352	2,856	2,731
Business ..	25,420	87	1,580	4,324	5,871	6,732	6,826
Skilled workers ..	24,463	201	2,657	5,065	5,666	5,585	5,289
Unskilled labourers..	6,419	102	759	1,284	1,343	1,519	1,412
Wives							
Professional ..	6,827	26	587	1,538	1,764	1,616	1,296
Business ..	17,475	235	2,401	4,146	3,997	3,653	3,043
Skilled workers ..	14,354	449	2,857	3,699	3,066	2,377	1,906
Unskilled labourers..	3,100	172	671	734	587	513	423
Children born per 100 wives							
Professional ..	142	35	59	89	133	177	211
Business ..	145	37	66	104	147	184	224
Skilled workers ..	170	45	93	137	185	235	277
Unskilled labourers..	207	59	113	175	229	296	334

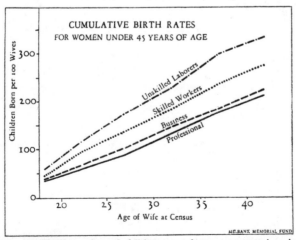

FIG. 2.—Total number of children ever born per 100 wives in
each quinquennial age group under 45, for each urban social
class.

TABLE III

CHILDREN BORN, WIVES, AND TOTAL NUMBER OF CHILDREN
EVER BORN PER 100 WIVES, IN EACH QUINQUENNIAL AGE
GROUP UNDER 45, FOR EACH RURAL SOCIAL CLASS

Children Born, Wives, and Children Born per 100 Wives for Each Social Class	Age of Wife at the Census of 1910						
	Total under 45	Under 20	20–24	25–29	30–34	35–39	40–44
Children born							
Farm owners ..	38,470	78	1,515	4,432	8,225	11,112	13,108
Farm renters ..	24,372	226	2,440	5,102	5,781	5,773	5,050
Farm labourers ..	9,701	245	1,602	2,238	2,197	1,953	1,466
Wives							
Farm owners ..	13,770	156	1,238	2,356	3,109	3,423	3,488
Farm renters ..	9,912	438	2,164	2,621	2,036	1,571	1,082
Farm labourers ..	4,182	418	1,274	1,011	686	482	311
Children born per 100 wives							
Farm owners ..	279	50	122	188	265	325	376
Farm renters ..	246	52	113	195	284	367	467
Farm labourers ..	232	59	126	221	320	405	471

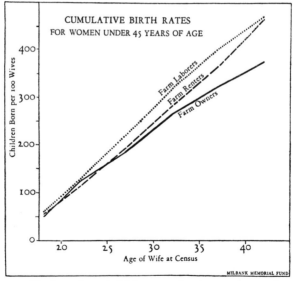

FIG. 3.—Total number of children ever born per 100 wives in each
quinquennial age group under 45, for each rural social class.

TABLE IV

STANDARDIZED CUMULATIVE BIRTH-RATES FOR THE URBAN
AND RURAL SAMPLES AND FOR EACH URBAN AND RURAL
SOCIAL CLASS FOR WOMEN UNDER 45 YEARS OF AGE *

Urban Sample	160
Professional	129
Business	140
Skilled workers	179
Unskilled labourers	223
Rural Sample	260
Farm owners	247
Farm renters	275
Farm labourers	299

* Obtained by applying the rate for each quinquennial age group under 45 to
the age distribution of the combined urban and rural samples.

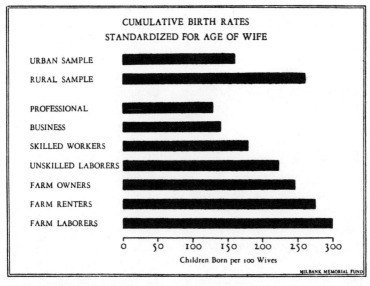

FIG. 4.—Standardized cumulative birth-rates for the urban and rural
samples and for each urban and rural social class.

(Obtained by applying the rates for each quinquennial age group under 45 to the age distribution
of the combined urban and rural samples.)

the younger wives of this study were not only less nearly complete, but never did become so large as those of the older groups. No attempt is made to determine the respective influence of these two factors in shaping the curves. It is sufficient to note that the influence of the falling birth-rate was probably least in the younger groups and became of increasing importance as the age of the wife advanced.

It is apparent from Fig. 1 that the rural wives were more fertile than those living in cities. The specific rural rates were from 20 to 67 per cent. higher than the corresponding urban rates, and the standardized rural rate was 63 per cent. higher. When the Census was taken the average country wife had borne one more child than her urban neighbour.

The ranking of the urban social classes by fertility was exactly opposite that conventionally given to their social status. The specific rates for the most fertile class, the unskilled labourers, were from 58 to 97 per cent. higher than those for the least fertile, the professional class, and the standardized rate was 73 per cent. higher. The differences between the rates of the business and professional classes were less than half as large as those between the other classes, and probably reflect the relatively similar social status of the two classes.

The rural rates, though less divergent than those of the urban sample, also indicate a definite inverse relation between fertility and social status. The specific rates for the most fertile class, the farm labourers, were from 3 to 25 per cent. higher than those for the least fertile class, the farm owners, and the standardized rate was 21 per cent. higher. But even the least fertile women of the rural sample had larger families than the wives of the urban unskilled labourers.

Only two of the many factors associated with the differential net fertility of the social classes may be examined here. They are age of the wife at marriage and the no-child family.

Marriage age is an important factor in determining the net fertility of any population group, since it limits the length of exposure to the risk of childbirth, and determines the ages during which that exposure takes place. The marriage ages considered here have been limited to those for women whose marriages were contracted between 1900 and 1905, in order to avoid various selections inherent in our data.* For present purposes the modal ages presented in Table V and Fig. 5

* "Differential Age at Marriage," op. cit.

TABLE V

MODAL AGE AT MARRIAGE OF WOMEN IN THE URBAN ANI
RURAL SAMPLES, AND IN EACH URBAN AND RURAL SOCIA
CLASS*

Social Class of Husband	Modal Age of Women at Marriage
Total Urban	20·5
Professional	23·5
Business	21·4
Skilled workers	19·6
Unskilled labourers	18·5
Total Rural	19·2
Farm owners	20·0
Farm renters	19·0
Farm labourers	18·1

* Based on data for women who were under 40 years of age at their marriage,
married between 1900 and 1905, and living with their husbands at the Census
of 1910.

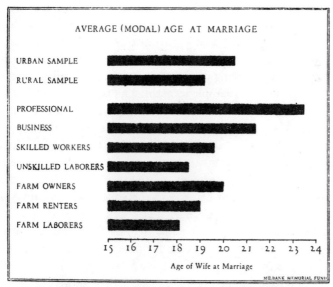

Fig. 5.—Modal age at marriage of women in the urban and rural samples
and in each urban and rural social class.

(Based on data for women who were under 40 years of age at their marriage, married between 1900
and 1905, and living with their husbands at the Census of 1910.)

adequately describe the distributions obtained from this group. The typical woman in the professional class married five years later than her counterpart in the farm-labourer class. It is rather surprising in view of this wide maximum difference to find that the most popular age for marriage in the urban sample was only 1·3 years higher than that in the rural sample. This relatively small difference is due to the fact that wives of farm owners who dominate the rural sample married later than the women in the two "lowest" urban classes. However, within both the urban and rural samples the modal ages at marriage rose with the rising social status of the classes.

The bearing of this direct relation between social status and age at marriage on the inverse relation between social status and fertility may be seen from the birth-rates for specific marriage-age groups presented in Table VI and Fig. 6. The rates for each of these groups have been adjusted to a standard duration-of-marriage distribution, so that within any one marriage-age group all classes have the same exposure to the risk of childbirth. In every class these birth-rates fall with advancing age at marriage. The relatively low fertility of the urban and upper classes appears therefore to be due in part to delayed marriage.

A closer examination of these rates brings out the fact that their decline with advancing age at marriage was more rapid in the lower than the upper classes. Of course, this is to be expected. The birth-rates of the most fertile classes must decline rapidly as marriage approaches the end of the child-bearing period when only small families are possible. But at least in the urban sample something more was involved. The rates for the professional class were actually higher than those for corresponding marriage-age groups of the business class from 20 on, and than those of the skilled-worker class from 25 on. When marriage took place before the wife's twentieth birthday, the rate for the professional class was only 63 per cent. of that for the unskilled labourers, but when it occurred between the twenty-fifth and thirtieth year, the rates for the two classes were virtually equal. The inverse relation between fertility and social status, so definite for women who married before 20, was no longer present for marriages contracted between 25 and 30 years of age. In fact, the rates for this and the next higher marriage-age group indicate a direct rather than an inverse association between fertility and social status. Therefore, in the urban classes, the inverse relation between net fertility and social status found in

TABLE VI

TOTAL NUMBER OF CHILDREN EVER BORN PER 100 WIVES UNDER 45 YEARS OF AGE, ACCORDING TO THE WIFE'S AGE AT MARRIAGE, FOR EACH URBAN AND RURAL SOCIAL CLASS*

Age at Marriage	Social Class of Husband						
	Professional	Business	Skilled	Unskilled	Farm Owners	Farm Renters	Farm Labourers
14–19	171	184	226	270	288	318	353
20–24	148	146	170	206	221	248	253
25–29	127	115	119	128	173	186	211
30–34	95	81	72	—†	127	122	—†
35–44	—†	43	43	—†	48	—†	—†

* The rates have been calculated on the assumption of a standard duration-of-marriage distribution for each age-at-marriage group.

† Less than 100 married women.

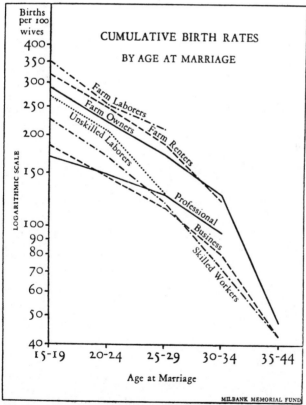

FIG. 6.—Total number of children ever born per 100 wives under 45 years of age, according to the wife's age at marriage, for each urban and rural social class.

(The rates have been calculated on the assumption of a standard duration-of-marriage distribution for each age-at-marriage group.)

each age-at-Census group was due entirely to the women who married under 25 years of age, and to the greater frequency of early marriage in the lower than upper social classes.

The cause of this shift from an inverse to a direct association between fertility and social status as marriage age advances cannot be determined from our data. Probably a number of factors were involved. As pointed out in the English Census Report, "Fertility of Marriage,"* the fact that the upper-class birth-rates were relatively high for women whose late marriages offered slight inducement to family limitation, and relatively low for those whose early and perhaps impecunious marriages made family limitation most desirable, suggests that for early marriages birth is increasingly subject to voluntary control as social status rises.

Less voluntary control of birth may account for the relatively high birth-rates of late upper-class marriages, but it cannot account for the fact that certain of these upper-class rates were absolutely higher than those of the lower classes. This greater fertility suggests that upper-class couples had greater reproductive potentialities than those of the lower classes when marriage was postponed. Such greater fecundity of the upper classes would not necessarily be inconsistent with a general opposition of individuation and genesis. Perhaps marriage is a selective process which operates differently in the different social classes. It is possible that in all classes there is a tendency for the most fecund women to marry earliest, but that this tendency is more inhibited in the upper than lower classes by intellectual interests or the maintenance of a higher standard of living. Quite apart from such a selection, it is possible that the reproductive ability of lower-class women was lessened by prolonged industrial employment before marriage. At present we cannot demonstrate that any of these factors were actually involved in the change from an inverse to a direct association of fertility and social status as marriage age advanced. We can only put them forward as suggestions consistent with our present knowledge, which more than anything else illustrate our ignorance of the fundamental causes of variation in human fertility.

The extent to which differences in the net fertility of the social classes may be due to differences in the proportion of married couples who are either unable or unwilling to have any children is a problem

* Op. cit., p. lxxxvi.

of the greatest biological and sociological significance, and one upon which it has been virtually impossible to obtain trustworthy information in the United States. Table VII and Fig. 7 show for each class the proportion of married women 40 to 49 years of age who had borne no children. Since only a negligible number of these women would have borne their first child after that age, the ratios give an adequate picture of the situation. There is a striking difference in the proportion of childless marriages found in the urban and rural populations. In the country, no-child families constituted only about 9 per cent. of the total, but in the city they comprised nearly 16 per cent. As we proceed down the social scale, the proportion of childless marriages falls in the urban sample from about 18 per cent. for the professional class to 14 per cent. for the unskilled-labourer class, and in the rural sample from 11 per cent. for the farm-owner class to 7 per cent. for the wives of farm renters and farm labourers. There can be no doubt that such differences in the proportion of childless marriages, like those found in age at marriage, played an important part in bringing about the relatively low net fertility of the urban population, and the particularly low birth-rates of the upper urban classes.

The birth-rates for women over 45 years of age at the Census, unlike those for women under 45, to which we have thus far confined our attention, do not reflect the growth of individual families as the age of the wife advances. They indicate rather the size of families which were completed between 1870 and 1910 as returned by women 84 to 45 years of age, and should therefore throw a unique light on the incidence of the declining birth-rate during a period which antedates the establishment of the birth registration area.

The actual decline in the size of completed families was probably somewhat more rapid than that shown by the rates, because of the fact that women in certain low birth-rate areas were relatively old, and constituted a larger proportion of the total sample in the most advanced than in the younger age groups. To avoid this difficulty the rates for each age group presented in Table VIII and Fig. 8 have been calculated on the assumption of a standard geographic distribution of the women.

It is conceivable that there is a direct association between fertility and longevity which influenced the trends by preventing women who reached an advanced age with their marriages unbroken from reporting a size of

TABLE VII

TOTAL NUMBER OF MARRIED WOMEN 40–49 YEARS OF AGE, AND THE NUMBER AND PER CENT. OF THEM WHO HAD BORNE NO CHILDREN, FOR THE URBAN AND RURAL SAMPLES AND FOR EACH URBAN AND RURAL SOCIAL CLASS

Social Class of Husband	Married Women 40–49 Years of Age		
	Total Number of Married Women	Number of Married Women who had Borne no Children	Per Cent. of Total Married Women Childless
Total Urban (adjusted)	10,215	1,604	15·7
Professional	2,368	420	17·7
Business	5,302	850	16·0
Skilled workers	3,305	499	15·1
Unskilled labourers	819	115	14·0
Total Rural	9,107	841	9·2
Farm owners	6,690	676	10·1
Farm renters	1,859	126	6·8
Farm labourers	558	39	7·0

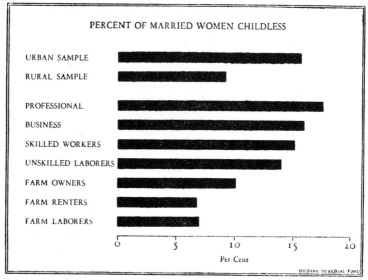

FIG. 7.—Per cent. of married women 40 to 49 years of age who were childless, for the urban and rural samples, and for each urban and rural social class.

TABLE VIII

TOTAL NUMBER OF CHILDREN EVER BORN PER 100 WIVES IN
EACH AGE GROUP OVER 45, FOR CERTAIN URBAN AND
RURAL SOCIAL CLASSES, STANDARDIZED FOR GEOGRAPHIC
DISTRIBUTION OF WIVES*

	Age of Wife at Census of 1910					
	45–49	50–54	55–59	60–64	65–69	70–84
Professional	250	264	300	301	369	392
Business	254	278	314	326	358	370
Skilled workers	312	353	377	392	397	—†
Farm owners	403	425	447	463	484	498

* From "Trends in the Size of Families Completed Prior to 1910 in Various
Social Classes," op. cit.
† Data inadequate.

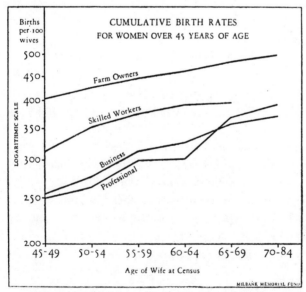

FIG. 8.—Total number of children ever born per 100 wives in
each age group over 45, for certain urban and rural social
classes.

(The rates have been calculated on the assumption of a standard geographic distribution of the women.)

family typical of their generation as of the end of the child-bearing period. However, the existence of such a direct association between fertility and longevity after the end of the child-bearing period has never been demonstrated.* In view of the known decline in the American birth-rate, it seems unlikely that the trends observed are attributable to such an association, and probable that they reflect the decreasing size of families during the period studied.

The fertility of married women appears to have declined in rural as well as in urban areas, and in the lower as well as in the upper classes. In each class for which we have adequate data, the birth-rates were highest in the oldest age groups, which include women whose families were completed as early as 1870, and declined consistently as the end of the child-bearing period approached the Census date. The curves for these rates suggest that this decline was more rapid for the urban than for the rural areas, and for the upper than the lower classes. But none of the curves, except possibly that for the skilled-worker class, show any signs of approaching an asymptote in the earliest period covered by these data. It seems likely, therefore, that the size of completed families had been declining in both urban and rural social classes for some years before 1870.

The results of this study of the fertility of 99,226 native-white married women enumerated in the Federal Census of 1910 may be summarized as follows:

1. Women of the rural population were more fertile than those of the urban.
2. In both the urban and rural populations there was a definite inverse relation between the net fertility of the classes and their social status as conventionally ranked.
3. This inverse association between fertility and social status is in part accounted for by a direct relation between marriage age and social status.

* An opinion that there is a direct association between fertility and the length of life after the end of the child-bearing period was expressed by Beeton, Yule, and Pearson in their paper, "On the Correlation Between Duration of Life and the Number of Offspring," *Proceedings of the Royal Society*, 1900, vol. lxvii, pp. 159–179. However, the evidence adduced does not seem conclusive, since it rests on the assumption that there was no secular trend in the size of the families whose genealogical records furnish the data for the study.

4. A classification of the urban women by marriage age indicates that the inverse association of fertility and social status was characteristic only of early marriages, and that among women who married after age 25 fertility and social status were directly related.

5. The proportion of childless marriages varied directly with social status in both the country and city, but was distinctly higher in the urban than the rural classes.

6. The trends in the birth-rates for women over 45 years of age in 1910 seem to indicate that in all classes for which the data are adequate, the size of completed families had been declining at least since 1870, but that this decline was less rapid in rural than in urban areas, and probably somewhat less rapid in the "lower" than in the "upper" urban classes.

APPENDIX TABLE I

GEOGRAPHIC DISTRIBUTION OF 59,149 MARRIED WOMEN, OF NATIVE-WHITE PARENTAGE, FOR WHOM CERTAIN FERTILITY DATA WERE EXTRACTED FROM THE 1910 CENSUS RECORDS OF 33 CITIES

Area and Locality	Number of Women Considered*	Percentage Distribution of	
		Total Women Considered	Total Women of Similar Colour, Marital Status, Nativity, and Parentage in the Population
Total from cities	59,149	99·9	100·0
New England	4,838	8·2	8·9
Massachusetts	2,541	4·3	3·9
Cambridge	683	1·2	0·9
Fall River	230	0·4	0·5
Lowell	359	0·6	0·8
Worcester	1,269	2·1	1·7
Rhode Island	938	1·6	2·4
Providence	938	1·6	2·4

Area and Locality	Number of Women Considered*	Percentage Distribution of	
		Total Women Considered	Total Women of Similar Colour, Marital Status, Nativity, and Parentage in the Population
Dayton	2,684	4·5	3·3
Toledo	1,967	3·3	3·3
Indiana	5,878	9·9	7·4
Indianapolis	5,878	9·9	7·4
Michigan	2,733	4·6	6·2
Detroit	1,712	2·9	4·4
Grand Rapids	1,021	1·7	1·8
Wisconsin	608	1·0	2·0
Milwaukee	608	1·0	2·0

	Number		
Connecticut	1,359	2·3	2·6
Bridgeport	423	0·7	1·1
New Haven	936	1·6	1·5
Middle Atlantic	11,650	19·7	19·3
New York	7,869	13·3	11·0
Albany	1,386	2·3	1·6
Buffalo	2,869	4·9	4·1
Rochester	1,707	2·9	2·8
Syracuse	1,907	3·2	2·5
New Jersey	3,230	5·5	7·0
Jersey City	997	1·7	2·4
Newark	2,056	3·5	3·5
Paterson	177	0·3	1·1
Pennsylvania	551	0·9	1·3
Scranton	551	0·9	1·3
East North Central	18,918	31·9	32·8
Ohio	9,699	16·4	17·2
Cincinnati	1,695	2·9	5·3
Columbus	3,353	5·7	5·3
West North Central	4,817	8·2	7·7
Minnesota	2,831	4·8	5·5
Minneapolis	1,591	2·7	3·6
St. Paul	1,240	2·1	1·9
Nebraska	1,986	3·4	2·2
Omaha	1,986	3·4	2·2
Mountain (Colorado)	3,439	5·8	5·0
Denver	3,439	5·8	5·0
Pacific	15,487	26·1	26·3
Washington	4,234	7·1	7·1
Seattle	2,729	4·6	4·6
Spokane	1,505	2·5	2·5
Oregon	2,694	4·6	4·5
Portland	2,694	4·6	4·5
California	8,559	14·4	14·7
Los Angeles	6,232	10·5	8·4
Oakland	1,787	3·0	2·4
San Francisco	540	0·9	3·9

* Preliminary hand count. Includes 2,462 wives for whom data are excluded from the remaining tables. Of this number 2,240 were wives of persons not gainfully employed whose previous occupation was not stated, and twenty-two were wives for whom the data were inaccurate.

Appendix Table II

GEOGRAPHIC DISTRIBUTION OF 43,352 MARRIED WOMEN, OF NATIVE-WHITE PARENTAGE, FOR WHOM CERTAIN FERTILITY DATA WERE EXTRACTED FROM THE 1910 CENSUS RECORDS OF THE RURAL PARTS OF 74 COUNTIES

Area and Locality	Number of Women Considered*	Percentage Distribution of	
		Total Women Considered	Total Women Considered in Urban Sample (Appendix Table I)
Total from rural districts	43,352	100·1	99·9
New England	3,114	7·2	8·2
Massachusetts	1,690	3·9	4·3
Berkshire	190		
Hampshire	574		
Middlesex	353		
Worcester	573		
Rhode Island	601	1·4	1·6
Kent	174		
Washington	427		
Connecticut	823	1·9	2·3
Litchfield	823		
Middle Atlantic	7,878	18·2	19·7
New York	5,368	12·4	13·3
Albany	778		
Cattaraugus	1,538		
Cortland	694		
Delaware	1,317		
Wayne	1,041		

Area and Locality	Number of Women Considered*	Percentage Distribution of	
		Total Women Considered	Total Women Considered in Urban Sample (Appendix Table I)
West North Central	3,056	7·1	8·2
Minnesota	1,643	3·8	4·8
Dakota	101		
Dodge	182		
Faribault	186		
Fillmore	220		
Goodhue	57		
Le Sueur	84		
Mower	208		
Olmstead	275		
Ottertail	260		
Scott	18		
Wabasha	52		
Nebraska	1,413	3·3	3·4
Custer	352		
Gage	818		
Washington	243		
Mountain	2,086	4·8	5·8
Colorado	2,086	4·8	5·8
Delta	362		

	Number		
New Jersey	2,092	4·8	5·5
Monmouth	1,584		
Morris	508		
Pennsylvania	418	1·0	0·9
Bradford	277		
Columbia	141		
East North Central	16,717	38·6	31·9
Ohio	10,336	23·8	16·4
Fayette	1,469		
Highland	2,248		
Madison	1,018		
Medina	1,360		
Tuscarawas	1,164		
Wayne	1,889		
Wood	1,188		
Indiana	4,058	9·4	9·9
Orange	1,049		
Randolph	1,379		
Steuben	818		
White	812		
Michigan	1,909	4·4	4·6
Allegan	600		
Gratiot	469		
Huron	61		
Lenawee	779		
Wisconsin	414	1·0	1·0
Grant	142		
Jefferson	100		
Sheboygan	99		
Trempealeau	73		

	Number		
Larimer	501	24·2	26·1
Mesa	794		
Washington	429	6·4	7·1
Pacific	10,501		
Washington	2,766		
Chelan	165		
Columbia	234		
Skagit	246		
Whitman	1,067		
Yakima	1,054		
Oregon	1,791	4·1	4·6
Linn	918		
Morrow	205		
Yamhill	668		
California	5,944	13·7	14·4
Butte	385		
Colusa	189		
Eldorado	68		
Glenn	159		
Imperial	404		
Kings	397		
Modoc	273		
Orange	482		
Riverside	538		
San Bernardino	615		
Solano	174		
Sonoma	799		
Tulare	1,461		

* Preliminary hand count. Includes 813 wives for whom data were excluded from the remaining tables. Of this number 126 were wives of farmers whose tenure was unknown, 102 wives of farm overseers, 309 of farm managers, and 276 wives for whom the data were inaccurate.

APPENDIX TABLE III

DISTRIBUTION OF 99,226 MARRIED WOMEN, OF NATIVE-WHITE PARENTAGE, FOR WHOM FERTILITY DATA WERE EXTRACTED FROM THE 1910 CENSUS RECORDS, ACCORDING TO OCCUPATIONAL GROUP AND SOCIAL CLASS OF THE HUSBANDS

Social Class and Occupational Group	Number of Women		
Total			**99,226**
Total from cities			56,687
Professional		9,910	
Lawyers, judges, and justices	2,433		
Physicians and surgeons*	1,957		
Technical engineers	1,329		
Teachers in college and school†	983		
Clergymen	827		
Dentists	635		
Accountants and auditors	410		
Authors, editors, and reporters	367		
Architects	323		
Other professional persons‡	646		
Business		23,992	
Salesmen and clerks in stores..	3,514		
Retail dealers	3,216		
Other clerks	2,630		
Commercial travellers	1,730		
Real estate agents and officials	1,498		
Book-keepers and cashiers	1,487		
Builders and building contractors	1,147		
Manufacturers and officials of manufacturing ..	1,268		
Managers and superintendents of manufacturing ..	774		
Insurance agents and officials of insurance companies	830		
Brokers, commission men, and promoters	597		
Wholesale dealers, importers, and exporters ..	430		
Agents, canvassers, and collectors	741		
Draftsmen	411		
Conductors (steam railroad)	399		
Bankers and bank officials	322		
Other owners, proprietors, and managers§	1,259		
Other clerical and kindred workers‖	1,739		

* Includes osteopaths.   † Includes teachers of athletics and dancing.
‡ Includes: artists, sculptors, and teachers of art; chemists, assayers, and metallurgists; designers and inventors; veterinary surgeons; librarians; selected public officials; and other professional persons.
§ Includes: managers and operators engaged in transportation and extraction of minerals; proprietors of employment offices, elevators, and warehouses; undertakers; owners, managers, and officials of places of amusement; hotel-keepers and managers; owners and managers of laundries; restaurant-keepers; and saloon-keepers.
‖ Includes: baggagemen and freight agents; ticket, station, and express agents; express messengers and railway mail clerks; mail carriers; telegraph and telephone operators; floorwalkers, decorators, inspectors, gaugers, and samplers; musicians and teachers of music; semi-professional pursuits; actors and showmen; housekeepers and stewards; and stenographers and typists.

APPENDIX TABLE III—*continued*

Social Class and Occupational Group	Number of Women	
Skilled workers		18,454
Carpenters	2,641	
Semi-skilled operatives* in manufacturing industries	2,060	
Machinists, millwrights, and tool-makers	1,846	
Conductors and motormen (street railroad)	1,094	
Painters, glaziers, and varnishers	1,026	
Foremen and overseers	763	
Other skilled workers in building trades	748	
Locomotive engineers and firemen (steam railroad)	713	
Engineers (stationary), cranemen, hoistmen, etc.	683	
Brakemen, switchmen, flagmen, and yardmen	586	
Electricians	581	
Compositors, linotypers, and typesetters	521	
Barbers and hairdressers	454	
Plumbers and gas and steam fitters	413	
Blacksmiths, forgemen, and hammermen	324	
Other skilled workers†	2,770	
Other semi-skilled workers‡	1,231	
Unskilled labourers		4,331
Draymen, teamsters, expressmen, and carriage and hack drivers	1,043	
Labourers (building, general, and not specified)	827	
Deliverymen	536	
Labourers in manufacturing industries	598	
Other labourers engaged in transportation	341	
Janitors and sextons	210	
Other labourers§	776	
Total from rural districts		42,539
Farm owners	25,697	
Farm renters	11,886	
Farm labourers	4,956	

* Not otherwise specified.
† Includes: bakers; boilermakers; electrotypers, stereotypers, and lithographers; engravers; jewellers, watchmakers, goldsmiths, and silversmiths; mechanics; moulders, founders, and casters (of metal); pattern- and model-makers; pressmen and plate printers (printing); tailors; tinsmiths and coppersmiths; other skilled workers in non-precious metal; proprietors and managers of garages, transfer companies, and livery stables; inspectors (transportation); firemen (fire department); policemen; photographers; detectives, sheriffs, and keepers of institutions; and cooks.
‡ Includes: mine, quarry, and oil and gas well operatives; filers, grinders, buffers, and polishers (metal); chauffeurs; telegraph and telephone linemen; other semi-skilled operatives engaged in transportation industries; boarding and lodging-house keepers; launderers, and laundry operatives; waiters; and bartenders.
§ Includes: firemen (except locomotive and fire department); labourers in coal and lumber yards, warehouses and stores; labourers in public service; bootblacks, charmen, elevator tenders; other labourers in domestic and personal service: guards, watchmen, doorkeepers, and guides (public service).

NUPTIALITY, FERTILITY, AND REPRODUCTIVITY

By DR. S. D. WICKSELL

(*Sweden*)

NUPTIALITY, FERTILITY, AND REPRODUCTIVITY*

DURING the last few years quite a number of investigations—private as well as official—have been devoted to the study, by numerical methods, of the effect of a given mortality, and fertility (or nativity) on population growth. Considerable progress has also been made— above all by the researches of A. J. LOTKA—with the abstract mathematical treatment of this problem which leads to certain integral equations with interesting asymptotic properties. Until quite recently, however, no account has been taken of the effect of different marriage-rates, or rates of nuptiality. For the sake of simplicity the fertility has, in fact, been assumed to have a certain value for each age group of women as a whole, without any distinction whatever between married and unmarried women. This is of course only a first approach to the more general and more important problem of studying the combined effect of a given mortality, a given nuptiality, and a given fertility of married as well as of unmarried women.

In a paper published last year in the Swedish Journal, *Ekonomisk Tidskrift*, I sketched a simple method of taking into account also different sets of nuptiality-rates, and I also gave some numerical results of their influence on reproductivity. Only a few months later the German Federal Statistical Office published some detailed computations on the probable future of the German population (*Statistik des Deutschen Reichs*, Bd. 401, II. Anhang), where also some changes in the marriage-rates and civil status distribution of the women are foreseen and, to a certain extent, taken account of.

On studying this German work it occurred to me how well the method worked out by me will serve to simplify and also to amplify investigation as regards the part played by the changes in the marriage-rates. I also have reason to think that my theoretical results might be of use in extending and generalizing the mathematical treatment of the problem. The introduction of nuptiality as one of the arbitrary factors in the problem of population growth proves, as a matter of fact, to be surprisingly simple. It is in consideration hereof that I have undertaken to give, in the *Skandinavisk Aktuarietidskrift*, a fuller account in

* A full account of the investigation is given in the *Skandinavisk Aktuarietidskrift*, Stockholm, 1931.

English of the investigation of which only the broad outlines were presented in the Swedish paper referred to above.

The method of computing the age distribution of the women in a population having a given function of nuptiality, $n(x)$, into spinsters and married women centres in the formula

$$\log s(x) = - \log e \int_0^x d\xi n(\xi) \quad \cdots \quad (1)$$

Here 100 $s(x)$ is the percentage of spinsters at age x, and the formula is easily applied numerically by summation for one-year intervals, or, where $n(x)$ is given only for quinquennial age intervals, by a method of graduation or by mechanical quadrature. The formula only assumes that the mortality of spinsters is practically the same as the mortality of married women, an assumption which is shown to be sufficiently valid for the Swedish women in the ages of any relevance for the investigation of fertility and reproductivity.

The formula is, under the assumption mentioned, very easy to prove. It also follows very simply from some formulæ given by WESTERGAARD in the paper "On the Study of Displacement within a Population" (*Journal of the American Statistical Association*, 1920).

After a mathematical discussion of the upper limit of the crude marriage-rate in a stationary population, formula (1) and some differential formulæ derived from it are used to decompose the stationary population, corresponding to the Swedish female mortality table of 1921–25, and for constructing the curves of $s(x)$ and of the age distribution at first marriage. Extensive tables are also given.

Using the simple formula

$$s_a(x) = s_1^a(x) \quad \cdots \quad \cdots \quad (2)$$

which immediately follows from (1) for the case that the nuptiality is in all ages multiplied by the factor a, the tables and diagrams are carried out under the assumption that the nuptiality is equal to a times the Swedish nuptiality function for the decennium 1901–10, a being put equal to 1/2, 1, 3/2, 2, and 3. Thus the effect of any reasonable proportional stimulation of the nuptiality is easily studied.

By using a set of factors of correction derived from current Swedish vital statistics, the classification into spinsters and married women is changed to one of single women and wives. This classification is applied to the stationary population already mentioned, and by the aid of it for the cases $a = 1$, and $a = 2$, the net reproductivity rates (KUCZYNSKI) are computed, using the fertility tables of single women and of wives, respectively, as observed in Sweden in the year 1926. Thus the general net reproductivity-rate R is resolved into two additive components, viz. the illegitimate net reproductivity-rate R_2 and the legitimate net reproductivity-rate R_1.

The following figures were found:

Case a = 1: $R_1 = 0 \cdot 782$ *Case a = 2:* $R_1 = 1 \cdot 132$
                $R_2 = 0 \cdot 133$ $R_2 = 0 \cdot 096$

                $R = 0 \cdot 915$ $R = 1 \cdot 228$

The results show that whereas the general net reproductivity rate corresponding to the fertility of 1926, the mortality of 1921–25, and the pre-War nuptiality is below unity (i.e. insufficient to maintain a stationary population), the same net reproductivity-rate will be 23 per cent. above unity if the nuptiality is doubled. Such a rise in the nuptiality is by no means an exceedingly high one, the result being still behind the nuptiality-rate of, for instance, the Frenchwomen of corresponding ages. The effect on the crude marriage-rate is only to increase the figure (for first marriages) from $5 \cdot 4$ pro mille to $6 \cdot 6$ pro mille.

The investigation finally concludes with some mathematical developments and numerical examples giving and illustrating a new simple method of computing the "true rate of natural increase" (LOTKA), and also of the theoretically and so practically important complex roots of the fundamental equation of the mathematical theory of population, $R(t) = 1$.

Fourth Session

GENERAL POPULATION

Chairmen: (*a*) PROFESSOR DR. EUGEN FISCHER
(*b*) DR. H. W. METHORST

Papers read:

13. HAS THE REPRODUCTIVE POWER OF WESTERN PEOPLES DECLINED? By Professor FRANK H. HANKINS.

14. SOME FACTORS IN POPULATION DENSITY. By Professor C. B. FAWCETT.

15. SOME EFFECTS OF CURRENT MIGRATION RESTRICTIONS. By Professor J. W. GREGORY.

16. THE RESPONSIBILITIES OF THE OBSTETRICIAN IN THE PROBLEM OF POPULATION. By Dr. G. W. KOSMAK.

17. ANIMAL POPULATION AND MIGRATION. By Mr. CHARLES ELTON.

18. SOME EXPERIMENTS ON POPULATIONS OF MICE. By Professor F. A. E. CREW.

19. THE FUTURE OF THE POPULATION OF BELGIUM. By FERNAND BAUDHUIN.
L'AVENIR DE LA POPULATION BELGE. Par Professeur FERNAND BAUDHUIN

PAPER No. 13

HAS THE REPRODUCTIVE POWER OF WESTERN PEOPLES DECLINED?

By Professor FRANK H. HANKINS

(*United States of America*)

HAS THE REPRODUCTIVE POWER OF WESTERN
PEOPLES DECLINED?

IT would seem clear that every explanation of the decline in the birth-rate must relate directly or indirectly either to innate fecundity, or to the processes of fertilization or gestation. They, therefore, reduce in final analysis to three types. In the first and most obvious category are the direct artificial interferences with the processes either of fertilization or gestation. These interferences are respectively contraception and abortion. In the second category are the biological factors, or changes in inherited racial constitution. In the third category are the physiological factors—that is, changes in bodily metabolism or in the distribution of bodily energies tending to reduce reproductive vigour.

We may pass over the first category, admitting them to be very probably the principal factors, though the weight to be attached to either of them is far from clear. Much uncertainty exists also as to the efficiency of Neo-Malthusian practices among the different social classes. Nor do we know either the present extent of abortion or its increase or decrease during recent decades.

In the category of biological factors may be noted first Professor Gini's theory of the cyclical rise and fall of racial reproductive vigour.*

Gini speaks of the youth, maturity, and old age of a race or people in terms strictly analogous to the youth, maturity, and old age of an individual. He implies† that the low fertility of the upper classes is due to their being farther along on "the parabola of their evolution"; they are viewed as old and biologically incapable of an adequate fertility. He traces the evolution of nations through four stages marked by a progressive weakening of the reproductive instinct. He holds that not only nations and races, but individual family strains pass through this evolutionary parabola, with a period of rapid rise in fertility, a period of moderate fertility, and then a rapid plunge into the oblivion of sterility. This parabola is conceived as a predestined course, like the maturity and senescence of the individual. A population is thus conceived to become biologically senescent. He speaks of "The slow exhaustion

* Gini, Professor Corrado, *Population—Lectures on the Harris Foundation, 1929*. Chicago, 1929.
† Ibid., p. 25.

of the reproductive powers of human populations and of animal species, that is to say, of their germinal cells."*

This theory leads Gini to mention the Eskimos as a senile race and the Italians as a young one. Now it may be doubted whether such phraseology has any factual basis. The germ cells are renewed each generation; they are just as young in one generation as in another. If they had a tendency to senescence, it would seem that the whole human race must have perished long ago. Moreover, there are both mystical and fatalistic qualities about such a theory that render it unpalatable. If we designate as fecundity the capacity to produce mature gametes, this is an inherited trait, and can change in numerical value in a population only in consequence of mutations or of those selective processes which favour the more or the less fertile strains to the detriment of their opposites. Homogeneity of stock, to which Gini also attributes a detrimental effect, is not necessarily injurious to fecundity; in fact, this is one of the conditions emphasized in breeding domestic strains of plants and animals. At the same time, homogeneity plus selection in favour of strains of low fertility would tend to spread through a population a low degree of inherent fecundity. This presumably might happen, or may have happened, in such a population as parts of the old American stock where inherited wealth has favoured the preservation of low fertility strains; that is, upper-class infertility may in part be accounted for by the more facile rise of less fertile strains, and by the preservation and spread of their low fertility through class or caste mating and inherited wealth. In general, however, reproductive selection throws the balance in racial evolution in favour of the more rather than the less fertile strains. I do not see, therefore, how Gini reaches his conclusion that there are old races, that these old races exhibit a certain exhaustion of the germinal cells, and that nations of European culture are now exhibiting this senescence.

We come then to the third category of factors, namely, the physiological. Here are included all influences affecting either the total sum of bodily energy or the division of such energy between reproduction and all other demands upon it. Organic energy is made available through food assimilated. The relations of food and fertility are too complex to be treated here, but one seems warranted in saying in general that a

* Gini, Professor Corrado, *Population—Lectures on the Harris Foundation, 1929*, p. 9. Chicago, 1929.

generous diet is associated with high fertility, and a meagre diet and famine conditions with low fertility. Energy assimilated is expended in a variety of ways, and over a period of time a balance must be struck between energy income and expenditure. There are four principal ways in which the adult expends energy: maintenance of bodily heat and vital processes; increase in size; physical and mental activity in adjustment to environment; and reproduction.*

Other things being equal, an increase in expenditure in one or more directions must involve reduction in one or more others. The whole level of the equation may be elevated or depressed by the quantity and quality of food assimilated, and this in turn may be greatly affected by mode of life. It would seem that civilization greatly increases the available energy in a population by improvements in food and manner of living and by reduction of energy expended in maintaining bodily heat. Both activity and reproduction can thus be maintained at a higher level than is possible for populations at lower stages of culture. With every increase in the dynamic quality of culture, however, there must be established a new physiological balance between that proportion of the total energy devoted to external adjustments and that devoted to reproduction.

Some such reasoning seems very plausibly to account for the apparent increase in the fertility of civilized man in spite of his more active social life. It does not follow, however, that continued advance in civilization will continue to increase the energies displayed in both directions. The total of energy available is always limited. It seems reasonable to suppose that, when the individual is put under ever-increasing pressure to advance or maintain his social position, his sex activity and fertility will begin to decline after a certain equilibrium point is passed. To be sure, there are many such equilibrium points depending on the manner in which all the factors in the equation are adjusted; but, however high the food intake, and however careful the conservation of health and energy, the general proposition that excess of social activity leads to a decrease of fertility should logically hold true. It would seem that just some such readjustment of the budget in physiological expenditures has been and is taking place among Western nations.

The progress of our civilization has been attended by an unprecedented stimulus to individual activity. The growth of population and

* Compare Pearl, Professor Raymond, *The Rate of Living*, pp. 100 and 148.

the marvellous increase in agencies of communication have placed every individual within numerous currents of social suggestion. It is not the mere increase of density of population that appears significant, but the rapid rise of the tide of social stimulation. Personal ambition, ego drives, and self-consciousness have been awakened and maximized. Life is more complex, and the problems of adjustment which daily require individual decision and initiative have multiplied apace. Along with increased complexity, the tempo of life has been accelerated. Competition has been enormously intensified; and it is competition, not merely for the food, clothing, and shelter necessary for bodily security, but it is competition for that social approval which alone can give a sense of ego satisfaction and security. This competition is not limited to the adult years, but through mass education has been extended far below the adolescent period, only to be intensified at the ages immediately before and after puberty. Such intensification of demands upon the resources of the central nervous system as our culture is now making is wholly unprecedented in the life-history of the races involved. That it has set up important selective processes can hardly be doubted. The question is whether this intensity of living has been a factor in the decline of fertility during the past two generations. Phrased somewhat differently, our query is whether, quite apart from any undemonstrated change in hereditary capacities, the mode of life is not undercutting sexual vigour.

We may briefly suggest some of the evidence that this is true. Most of this evidence is equivocal, and all of it needs amplification and verification. In the first place, there is evidence that sex intercourse is more frequent among farmers and labourers than among business and professional classes. The significance of this would seem to be twofold. Fertility is correlated positively with frequency of coition, and sterility in marriage is correlated negatively therewith. Secondly, sex vigour is associated with an active physical life rather than with sedentary occupations and intellectual pursuits.

In this connection it might be argued that a considerable decline in the frequency of coitions would have little effect on fertility; it might seem that one coition annually would be sufficient to maintain families at or near the normal number. Such argument neglects the law of chances, as well as the correlation that seems to exist between the intensity of the sex drive and the vigour of the gametes. The male gametes are known to range from a state bordering on non-viability and immobility to that of great viability and vigorous motility. The sex vigour of the female is likewise variable. It seems probable, therefore, that low sex vigour and inferior gametes would go together. Hence a mode of life reducing sex vigour would reduce the probability that intercourse would be synonymous with impregnation. Those most active sexually are, as shown by the studies of Miss Davis and Mr. Hamilton,* less prone to sterile unions, and have the largest families; and this is true of persons of like social class. In this connection one may observe that the relatively infertile unions find control of births comparatively easy as compared with the relatively fertile ones.

One may cite here, for whatever significance attaches to it, Professor Gini's finding that there has been an increase in the lapse of time between marriage and fecundation. Of like import is the increase in the lapse of time between births. Gini shows that there has been a considerable decrease in the proportion of unprejudiced marriages giving rise to offspring ten to twelve months later. While this would be expected in view of the fact that an increasing number of couples marry with the intention of postponing the commencement of a family, Gini gives reasons which have a degree of plausibility for supposing that some part of the phenomenon may be due to reduced fertility.

We find a progressive increase in the percentage of childless unions in all social classes, especially since 1850, with larger proportions in city than in country, among upper than lower classes, and among native whites of native parents in the United States as compared with other nativity classes. If one may rely on genealogical studies, the percentage of childless unions is now fully six times as high in the United States as in the eighteenth century. I need not recall in detail those numerous investigations which have shown high percentages of childless unions among the graduates of both men's and women's colleges, the intellectual classes, American men of science, women who attain *Who's Who*, British men of genius, and so on. Infertility and small families are extraordinarily frequent in these classes even when, according to their own testimony, no effort at family limitation has been made. Ellis found that very superior men come from families distinctly larger

* Davis, Katherine B., *Factors in the Sex Life of Twenty-Two Hundred Women.* New York, 1929. Hamilton, Dr. G. V., *A Research in Marriage.* New York, 1929.

than the normal. Genius thus seems to be an offshoot of vigorous stock, men of genius should inherit high fertility, whereas in fact they show a marked percentage of childlessness. Women geniuses have shown a much higher percentage of infertility than gifted men. Cope found more than half of 531 women in *Who's Who* who had married were without offspring.* These classes also show a pronounced tendency toward celibacy, a fact that would be of significance, if it were certain that in general celibacy is associated with low sex potential. Here may be mentioned also the general failure of upper classes to maintain themselves, not only now, but in times past. The disappearance of knightly and aristocratic houses in England and Germany is a striking illustration of the constant flux of population composition. There are several causes for such a phenomenon: later age of marriage; greater celibacy; perhaps a desire for small families; knowledge of family limitation; perhaps also a low natural fertility owing to the fact that small families ascend the social scale more easily than large ones. One can only conjecture, therefore, that mode of life may also have been a factor affecting the reproductive resources of such classes.

Turning now to considerations of a somewhat different sort, we may note that diseases of pregnancy and confinement have not been reduced in recent decades, but may have actually increased. They are thus assimilated to the organic diseases of heart and kidneys. Maternal mortality seems almost certainly to have increased in the United States during the first quarter of this century; it increased during the first two decades in Germany, Scotland, and Sweden, and remained about the same in some fifteen other countries.† This is remarkable in view of the attention given the matter, increased prenatal care, hospitalization and medical attendance. In the United States the rate has been higher for native-born mothers than for foreign-born, except English and Irish. The rate is higher in the better economic classes and in urban centres, among both of which improvements in environmental and medical conditions have been greatest. Associated with these increased difficulties of childbirth are the increased infertility of all classes, and especially of the upper, the increased inability of mothers to nurse their offspring, the

* Cope, Persis M., "The Women of Who's Who—A Statistical Study," *Journal of Social Forces*, VII, 1928, 212–223.
† Woodbury, R. M., "Maternal Mortality," United States Department of Labour, *Children's Bureau Bulletin*, No. 158, 1926.

very probable increase in the proportion of still-births and the probable increase in the frequency of sex perversions. All of these phenomena appear to be associated positively with income and urbanism.

These facts suggest that cultural evolution is interfering with normal racial reproduction. They suggest that the improved social status of woman has not been all clear gain to her, and may be entailing some loss to the race. From the standpoint of the thesis we are here considering, these facts, if we find them fully substantiated, lead to the query whether the emphasis placed upon education, personality development, social ambition, and vocational success may not entail some loss of fertility and perhaps some tendency to underdevelopment of reproductive structures and capacities.

It is a well-known fact that worry, nervous strain, and neurasthenia reduce sex activity; and ours seems to be becoming a neurasthenic age. About thirty-five years ago Miss Brownell showed that there was an association by geographical areas between decline in the birth-rate and increase in the rate of deaths from nervous diseases.* This latter she took to be an index of the level of civilization, a mark of the intensity of social life. The correlation seems perfectly logical. Speaking broadly, there is associated with the decline of the birth-rate an increase of neurasthenia, nervous breakdowns, insanity, suicide, and like evidences of mental strain. It may seem somewhat far-fetched, but it is nevertheless possible, to discover common ground for the rise of the suicide-rate, the increase of nervous diseases, the rise of psychiatry, and decline in the natural fertility of the population.

The case for the physiological factor is, obviously, far from convincing. The arguments for it are necessarily inferential, rather than direct in nature. Moreover, there are strong countervailing arguments. Modern man lives so much longer, knows so much better how to maintain his health and vigour, is so much more free from various debilitating diseases, that it would seem as though there should have been no reduction in his reproductive capacities. One seems to have a choice between placing the whole responsibility for the decline in births on birth control and abortion, and dividing it between them and some physiological factor. The view that birth control is the sole factor seems to me as much of an error in one direction as the view that it is of no particular significance

* Brownell, J. L., "The Significance of the Decreasing Birth-rate," *Annals*, Amer. Acad. Pol. and Soc. Sc., v, 1894, pp. 48–65.

is in the other. Birth control may well be the primary cause of the general decline in the birth-rate, but it is of less significance as the cause of the infertility of marriage. It certainly does not account for the high proportion of infertile unions among British and American intellectual and scientific men and college women who disavow attempts at family limitation. It may well be doubted whether more than half the population even now has command of anything like effective contraceptive knowledge, and likewise whether the number of married couples desiring no children, and who also succeed in circumventing nature in this regard, has increased as fast as the number of infertile unions.

In conclusion, then, it seems plausible to hold that, although biological inheritance may be much the same, the physiological balance has been altered in necessary adjustment to the rising tempo of social life. Men living under sedentary conditions lose stamina; they become incapable of activities requiring physical strength and endurance, unless they place themselves in training under conditions which will develop their latent resources in these respects. So also a part of their potential reproductive powers may remain undeveloped or incapable of effective expression for like reasons. The civilized mode of life is not only inimical to the full development of fertility, but the latter is, in fact, also inimical to the former. Intensity of social life carried beyond a certain point not only requires, but may even compel, a reduction in the birth-rate. One can see a certain validity in Gini's figure of the "parabola of evolution," but its basic cause is not some more or less mysterious racial senescence, but the parabola of civilization itself.

It is conceivable, and Gini asserts it as a foregone conclusion, that Western Europe is doomed. If so, it is not because its potential powers of renewing its populations have disappeared from the inherited racial factors, but because the strenuosities of life and the ambitious strivings of a highly competitive social order have compelled birth restriction and have apparently also reduced effective reproductive capacities. This does not necessarily spell doom. It means only that the Western World is more full of people than is desirable in view of the state of culture. There seems no reason to doubt the possibility of a restoration of the birth-rate when and if the cultural opportunity develops.

PAPER No. 14

SOME FACTORS IN POPULATION DENSITY

By Professor C. B. FAWCETT

(*University of London*)

SOME FACTORS IN POPULATION DENSITY

DENSITY of population is a measure of its geographical distribution, which is a principal fact to be considered in any complete study of population. It is second in importance only to its magnitude, and of the same order as the main facts of its composition. In this paper I propose to consider some of the more important of the many factors which influence this density.

Population density is the numerical relation between the numbers of a population and the extent of the land which they inhabit. It is usually expressed by stating number of persons per unit area: $D = P/A$. It is a term whose precision is apparently limited only by the accuracy of the data, of numbers and area, on which it is based. But in fact it is by no means easy to agree upon a completely satisfactory definition of the word "inhabit" in this relation; e.g., Where a man sleeps in one area and works in another, in which of the two is he an inhabitant? This difficulty has been met in every Census. It is the cause of the distinction between *de facto* and *de jure* populations in Census returns.

The total land area of the world is about 56 million square miles. And if we exclude the uninhabitable ice-covered lands of the Polar Regions, we may estimate the area available for human habitation at about 50 million square miles, or nearly 130 million square kilometres. This is an approximate figure for the land area; but our knowledge of the total numbers of the human race is probably even less precise. We may for our present purpose take it at the round number of 2,000 millions. Thence it is a simple calculation that the mean density of population over all the inhabited land of the world is about 40 persons per square mile, or 15 per square kilometre, or one person to 16 acres. This refers the population to the whole of the accessible land. But it is also fair to regard the world's population as essentially dependent for its food on the products of the cultivable land only. The extent of land to be taken into account in this case is only one-third of the total;* and the world density is about 120 persons per square mile of cultivable land. These world densities of 40 and 120 are chiefly of value as standards of comparison to be

* See paper, "The Extent of the Cultivable Land," in *The Geographical Journal*, December 1930.

borne in mind when we speak of any particular area as densely or sparsely peopled. In a modern civilized community it is not possible to define any area to the resources of which any individual, or group of individuals, is limited. Ultimately every such group is dependent on world-wide resources. And hence the only density figures of ultimate value are the world densities. No smaller area can be self-contained.

The most obvious fact of the actual distribution of population over the land is its extreme unevenness. Local densities vary very widely. The following table shows some mean densities for a few countries for which reliable statistics are available:

	Country	Year of Census (c) or Estimate (e)	Density—Persons per Square Mile
I	England ..	1931 (c)	742
	(Great Britain	1931 (c)	520)
	Belgium ..	1930 (e)	712
	Japan	1930 (c)	450
II	Germany	1930 (c)	369
	Italy	1931 (c)	362
	Switzerland	1930 (e)	262
	India	1931 (c)	200
	France	1931 (e)	200
	Spain	1930 (e)	120
	Irish Free State ..	1926 (c)	111
III	United States of America	1930 (c)	42
IV	New Zealand	1930 (e)	14
	Newfoundland ..	1929 (e)	6
	Canada ..	1931 (c)	3
	Australia ..	1930 (e)	2·2

Most of the lands listed in this table may be readily classed in four divisions in respect to population density.

First there is a small number of very densely peopled countries such as England, Belgium, and Japan, with which may be classed the industrialized regions of the Rheinland and Southern New England and some parts of India and China. These have densities more than ten times as great as the world average, i.e. more than 400 persons per square mile.

Next is a larger number of countries of a high density, ranging from two to ten times the world's average, or 80 to 400 persons per square mile. These include nearly all the long-settled lands of the fertile regions of the Old World, i.e. nearly all Europe and most of Monsoon Asia, but no large countries outside these regions.

The third division, countries whose density is near to the world average, is represented here by only one large country, the United States of America. It is also of interest to note that the world average density of 40 per square mile is near to the actual local densities of some agricultural areas in Western countries. In the United States the agricultural state of Iowa, which contains only one large town, had in 1920 a mean density of 43. And some local studies in England have shown the rural densities to range from 25 to 100 per square mile.

At the lower end of the scale (IV) are the lands whose mean density is less than half the world average. This is a very large group; it includes the majority of the "new" countries, with all the overseas Dominions of the British Empire, South America, and Africa. It also includes the greater part of the lands between Europe and South-Eastern Asia, e.g. Arabia, Persia, and Siberia. For many of the countries in this group we have not sufficiently reliable statistics to justify us in stating a precise figure for their density.

Within any of these areas, which are in general purely political, there are similarly wide differences in local densities; e.g. in England the county of Lancashire has 2,600, and its neighbour, Westmorland, only 83; but even this, the most thinly peopled county of England, has twice the mean world density. In the United States of America, Rhode Island has 680 and Nevada less than one. In nearly all countries there are considerable areas which have no permanent inhabitants, though they are more or less frequently visited. These form an extreme contrast with the parts of our large cities where the urban population is crowded at the rate of some hundreds to the acre, or more than 10,000 per square mile.

What are the chief factors which have produced the wide variations in local densities which are so prominent in all the inhabited lands? It is difficult, perhaps impossible, to give a quite satisfactory answer to this question; but it is possible, and it may well be useful, to indicate some of the chief of these factors.

First I would place the natural resources of the land. Among these resources the one which has been of prime importance in the past is that of natural fertility, a resultant of favourable climates and good soils. A glance at climatic and population maps of the Old World is sufficient to show that it contains two great marginal regions of oustanding fertility —the Monsoon Lands of South-East Asia and the well-watered temperate lands of Europe. All the rest suffers from lack of either warmth or moisture, or both. These fertile regions are also by far the most populous: so much so that these two great regions together contain two-thirds of the world's population on not more than one-seventh of its habitable land area; while the vast regions between them are all relatively thinly peopled, with less than a sixth as many people on four times the area. Here the correlation between natural fertility and density of population seems very obvious; but we have only to note that other regions of apparently equal natural fertility, in Africa and in the Americas, are thinly peopled, or even, as in the Amazon Valley, almost uninhabited to realize that natural fertility, however important, is not the only factor involved. There are also some regions, e.g. New England, in which a high density of population is associated with a low natural fertility.

Next to fertility among the natural resources we may place mineral wealth and power resources. The influence of the exploitation of mineral wealth on the concentration of population has often been noted. Usually its direct influence has been limited to small areas and to comparatively short periods of time, though its indirect effects have been of very great importance in the attraction of immigrants to some "new" countries. But at the beginning of the modern industrial age the exploitation of the coal and iron resources of Great Britain led to the growth of dense populations on our coalfields, where we now have a group of industrial areas in which the total population is more than twenty-five millions, with a mean density of over a thousand per square mile and local densities of over four thousand, or from twenty-five to one hundred times the mean world density. Nowhere else has the modern exploitation of coal led to so marked a concentration actually on the coalfields, though there are other comparable industrial concentrations; so that here again it is evident that other factors are also involved. One of the chief of these is, I believe, the particular stage of the development of transport at the time when the coalfields were first exploited on a large scale.

The third main factor of the natural resources in this relation is that of geographical location. Every large city in the world owes a very large part of its population and importance to its advantageous location. And the particular distribution—but not the growth—of the vast urban agglomerations which have now gathered more than a tenth of the world's population into less than a hundred great cities* is in large part due to the geographical factors of location, factors which are of prime importance to every city.

Before the development of modern mechanical transport food resources were essentially local, and therefore no large region could be densely peopled unless it was fertile, and any fertile region which was inhabited by agricultural peoples who could make use of its fertility tended to accumulate a dense population. Similarly the coalfields which were exploited before the middle of the nineteenth century accumulated a dense industrial population. But to-day the products of local resources, of fertility and its food supplies, of mineral wealth and of power, need not necessarily be used locally. The mechanization of transport and of agriculture has made it possible to increase the food-production of a fertile land without a proportional increase in its population, and to use the food there produced to maintain the populations of distant lands. Thus the age-long tendency of local populations to increase in density on fertile lands has lost much of its strength. And in some countries, e.g. U.S.A., we have the phenomenon of an increase in food-production being accompanied by a decrease in the agricultural and rural population. There is no indication that the fertile regions of the New World are likely to become the homes of densely crowded peasant populations comparable to those of India and China.

Similarly the local density of population due to the exploitation of mineral resources varies very widely, according to the methods and intensity of that exploitation. It is at a minimum where this is limited to the extraction of the mineral and its dispatch to other areas, as in the case of the coal of Spitsbergen and the nitrates of Chile. It is at a maximum where the mineral is used locally as a base for large manufacturing industries, as in Lancashire. In general the location of the mineral deposits is becoming of relatively less importance in the determination of the location of the industries and populations engaged in the exploitation of those resources.

But population density is also influenced very strongly by non-

* Omitting China, for which there are no adequate statistics.

geographical and non-economic factors. In India and China the social traditions which make the family the principal unit of society, and for the maintenance of the family insist on early marriage and the essential need of children, have played a large part in the accumulation of their dense populations. The same solidarity of the family tends to keep all its members near their ancestral home, and so to check outward migration and a free spreading of the population. Such traditions have influenced the distribution of population in many lands, particularly among agricultural peoples. And they have been a very important factor in the growth and continued concentration of many Old-World populations. In the United States of America, on the other hand, we see the influence of a recent tradition of free migration within the country in the ease with which population is drawn to any local area of favourable economic opportunity, and the readiness of a large proportion of the people to change their place of abode within their country. Attachment to locality seems to be much weaker there than in Europe.

Some of the ways in which political forces, acting through Government policies, may affect the distribution and density of populations will be dealt with in Professor Gregory's paper,* since restriction on free movement across political boundaries is one of the most prominent of these. In this country the Poor Law of one hundred years ago, and the Unemployment Insurance of to-day, are both examples of Government action which has had the unforeseen, and undesired, result of restricting freedom of internal movement among the sections of the people to whom they are applied.

But the growth of the town-planning movement, and of the consciousness of the need of a considered policy of country-planning in many lands, indicates the likelihood of a far greater Governmental interference in this matter in the near future; for any control of the exploitation and use of a country involves some control of the distribution of the population within it, and so a general control of local densities. For this control to be effective and useful it should be based on much more knowledge of the factors influencing density, and of the relation of density of population to economic efficiency and to social well-being, than we possess at the present time.

Last among the few factors I have been able to refer to in this brief paper I have placed the time-lag. It is an obvious fact that the accumula-

* See p. 201.

tion of dense agricultural populations on the wide fertile lands of the Old World is the result of many centuries of growth. And it is probably true that the great difference in the length of time during which the Old and the New Worlds have been accessible to civilized men is the principal reason why the Old World still contains more than three-fourths of the human race on less than half of the total land area. All the lands which we commonly term "young" or "new" countries are areas of low density of population. The greatest and oldest of them, the United States of America, has only just reached the mean world density.

It does not follow, however, that the fertile regions of such "new" countries as the Americas and Australia will become as densely peopled as the corresponding regions of Asia and Europe are to-day. Many of the conditions of population growth have changed within the last two or three generations; in particular there is no longer the former close localization of the relation of a people to the natural resources on which they are dependent. And the movements, or migrations, necessary to adjust population to changing conditions can now be carried out more rapidly. In this sense the time-lag is less to-day than in any period of the recorded past.

Some of these factors which influence the distribution and density of population are, in part at least, susceptible to control by organized human effort. Deliberate transfers of population on a large scale have taken place in South-East Europe since the War, and may be copied elsewhere. And attempts to control the growth and distribution of population are likely to become more frequent and more effective as human societies become more fully organized. It is largely because of this tendency that there is need for a fuller study of the facts of population density. Such a paper as this can only be an introductory statement. What is wanted is a considerable number of intensive studies over limited areas of different kinds, from the combined results of which we may expect to be able to obtain some useful knowledge as to the past and present distribution of population density and the relation it bears to many other aspects of the study of population.

PAPER No. 15

SOME EFFECTS OF
CURRENT MIGRATION RESTRICTIONS

By Professor J. W. GREGORY, LL.D., D.Sc., F.R.S.
(*University of Glasgow*)

SOME EFFECTS OF CURRENT MIGRATION RESTRICTIONS

THE World Population Conference at Geneva (August 29—September 3, 1927) held an illuminating discussion on the control of International Migration, to which I was invited to contribute a paper on "The Principles of Migration Restriction." The restriction of European emigration has since gone to lengths which were not then contemplated.

The speakers at the discussion in 1927 were unanimous as to the profound importance of the problem and the need for international agreement on the regulation of migration. M. Albert Thomas, Director of the International Labour Office of the League of Nations, warned the Conference of the probability of a war if no agreement be reached on the main principles of international migration. The Conference itself, however, failed to agree as to either the effects or ethics of migration. Professor E. M. East* defended the hypothesis that migration has no permanent effect on population, as the numbers removed are soon made up by an increased birth-rate. This view was in accordance with the theory expounded by Lothrop Stoddard (1920), that if there had been no immigration into the United States since 1800 "the population to-day would be larger and better than it is." But the view that the greatest long-distance mass transfer of population that the world has seen added nothing to the population of the country that received, was tacitly rejected. Dr. Cederblad† held that the experience of Sweden proves that emigration has a direct important influence on unemployment. That immigration is beneficial to the immigrant country by raising wages in it was upheld by Professor L. Hersch of Geneva.‡

At the Conference no agreement was reached on the then fundamental issue whether an emigrant country should be allowed to maintain its hold over its emigrants as Italy urged, or whether, as Brazil insisted, emigration should be so disciplined in the interest of the world that an emigrant would be assimilated into the people among whom he settled —a view admitted by Dr. K. S. Iniu of Japan.§

The Conference also failed to remove the deadlock upon the right of an over-populated country to send emigrants, under reasonable

* *World Population Conference*, 1927, p. 295.
† *Proceedings World Population Conference*, pp. 276–277.
‡ Ibid., p. 284.   § Ibid., p. 271.

conditions, to an under-populated country. The claim was mentioned and was not formally contradicted; but the feelings between the emigrant and immigrant countries on this issue were so deep that the question was left without serious discussion. M. Thomas* uttered an emphatic warning that unless this issue can be settled it may lead to a war even worse than that of 1914–18.

The one proposal that was generally accepted was the advisability of an international organization for the solution of migration problems. M. Thomas† advocated the foundation of such an institution to organize the control of migration; and its establishment as a branch of the International Labour Organization was recommended by Dr. W. Keilhau of Norway.‡ Senhor Pedro Paulet of Peru.§ A German representative, Professor H. Grothe,‖ approved the scheme, and described what was wanted as an Emigration Court. M. Thomas, in his opening speech, suggested "a sort of supreme institution to settle the different migration problems between nations," and to establish principles which it could put into force "by means of suggestions, or advice, or even executive machinery."¶ At the close of the discussion he, however, agreed to more limited functions for the proposed institution, and that it should be "wholly free and scientific," and should not be given executive powers.**

During the Conference, especially in conversations at the social functions, strong feelings were expressed in favour of the establishment of an International Institution or Court, which should either be given executive powers at once or after its establishment should agitate to obtain them. After the Conference I was moved to prepare a work— *Human Migration and the Future*††—to state at greater length than in my paper the principles of migration restriction,§§ while directing attention to the absolute need for continued emigration from the British Isles and some other European countries.

Since the Conference the whole position of migration has been radically changed, for the failure of some part of the international commercial organization has led to the almost complete suppression of

* *Proceedings World Population Conference*, p. 264.
† Ibid., pp. 269–271, 300–301.   ‡ Ibid., pp. 273–274.
§ Ibid., p. 292.   ‖ Ibid., p. 297.   ¶ Ibid., pp. 270–271.
** Ibid., pp. 300–301.   †† Seeley, Service & Co., 1928.
§§ *Proceedings World Population Conference*, pp. 302–305.

immigration by the countries that formerly received the bulk of European emigrants. The reasons for the suppression are so obvious that the emigrant countries have acquiesced. The effect on the emigration countries has, however, been serious. Thus in Great Britain industrial employment has increased unexpectedly since the War, for despite the displacement of many men by mechanization, the British factories in 1928 employed 165,000 more workpeople than in the factories of Britain and Ireland combined in 1914. Unemployment has, however, greatly increased owing in part to the reduction in emigration.

In 1927 I hoped that the United States, Australia, and Canada would together receive 197,000 British emigrants a year,[*] as without such an outlet the facts would justify such pessimistic views as those of Sir Charles Close,[†] that the British Isles have a population of several millions too many, and that the country would be afflicted with chronic unemployment and poverty until birth control or disease had reduced our numbers. It is true that Dr. R. R. Kuczinski, in *The Balance of Births and Deaths*, vol. i, "Western and Northern Europe" (1928, holds that the British population is already decreasing in number; but that conclusion rests on calculations based on abnormal conditions due to the War,[‡] and we must await the results of the recent Census, and especially the proposed Census of 1936, for a final test of his theory.

The desirability of emigration from this country is not due simply to the removal of surplus population. The rights of any country to refuse to be the dumping-ground for another country's unemployed and to restrict immigration to the number that it can accommodate and assimilate without disturbance of its economic system are universally admitted. The main advantage to a nation of emigration is that by increasing the population and thereby the output of materials of some under-populated land, the market for the products of the emigrant country is enlarged. The ultimate effects of the suppression of migration are, however, likely to be more unfavourable to the immigrant than to the emigrant country.

The United States has received from Europe one and a quarter million immigrants in a single year. It is generally agreed, as established by Professor Carr-Saunders, that emigration does not remove the

[*] *Migration and the Future*, p. 192.
[†] *Population and Migration Geography*, XIV, 1927, p. 23.
[‡] Cf. *Nineteenth Century*, November 1929, p. 679.

difficulties of a country that has the maximum possible population, for every emigrant is there replaced by a survivor from those who would otherwise have added to the infant mortality. But the view that immigrants into a sparsely peopled land do not add to its population is generally set aside as fantastic.

The reduction of the annual immigration into the United States from over a million to 357,803 by the 1921 Act has had already profound and generally unexpected effects. The influence was increased by the further restrictions of the 1924 Act, which was designed to reduce the number to about 150,000 per annum, and will doubtless be strengthened by the practical suppression of immigration by recent action. Thus, in addition to fresh legislation, restriction has been rendered more complete by administrative regulations. Thus it is reported that the United States consuls in Europe are refusing visas to applicants who have secured work on their arrival on the ground that this arrangement is an enfringement of the laws against the entry of labour under contract; and visas are being refused to those who have not secured work on the ground that they might fail to secure employment and so become a public burden.

One early effect of the immigration restriction was a dearth of labour in the eastern and northern industrial cities and on the railways. The employers had resisted immigration restriction on the ground that it would cause a labour shortage. As they were deprived of cheap European labour they turned to the South to engage negroes and Mexicans. The wage of negroes was raised, and the more favourable and safer conditions in the Northern States led to an extensive northward migration. Wages were thereby raised in the Southern States to the embarrassment of some of the agricultural industries. The improvement in the hygienic, educational, and social conditions of the negroes has accelerated that lengthening of life and reduction of infant mortality which have already been remarked. Hence the better survival rate of the negroes and the absence of the inflow of a million or more European immigrants a year must raise the negro proportion in the population.

Moreover, as the negroes are being spread through the Northern States, the opportunities of miscegenation with the white population are inevitably increased; and though American opinion was indignant at any suggestion that the negroes are being absorbed in the general population, some American authorities are emphatic that such must be the result of present conditions.* The increase in the negro population and its ultimate absorption must have an important influence on the American race.

A second effect of the immigration restriction is financial. American industries have been founded on a scale adequate for a much larger population. According to some popularly accepted estimates, the existing 120 millions will have grown to 180 or 200 millions by the end of the present century. The present railways and factories would serve the needs of an increased population, and to repay their cost expanding markets are necessary. If the population increases at a much slower rate than has been expected, or begins to decline in a few decades' time, the American industries will be less profitable. The market in the European countries will probably be restricted as their impoverishment will lead, in order to provide employment at home, to the protection of their own industries by higher tariffs; when tariffs prove inadequate they are supplemented by ingenious devices such as milling regulations for wheat, quarantine regulations for live stock, and precautions against infection.

Canada has recently reduced immigration in order to cope with the unemployment due to the depressed markets for its wheat. Its wheat production has multiplied thirty-fourfold between 1871 and 1928, and more than tenfold between 1901 and 1928, thanks to improved cultivation and machinery and the conversion of once profitable cattle ranches into wheat farms. This conversion had the recommendation that the area would support a denser population; and the financial success of the 55,000 miles of Canadian railways requires a much larger population. At present they are a heavy burden. Their deficit, which was 80½ million dollars in 1920, has been reduced by severe economies to less than 30 million dollars in 1928; but it is still a serious annual charge on the Dominion. At the beginning of last year the railways were estimated to have cost 4,000 million dollars; their excess of income over expenditure in 1929 was only about 100 million dollars, which is inadequate for interest and depreciation.

The greatest immigration into Canada—402,432—was in the year 1912–13. After 1923 propaganda in favour of immigration was actively renewed; but the number of immigrants has fallen to 90,000 in 1930, and they are expected to be many fewer this year. The condition of the

* E.g., E. B. Reuter, *American Race Problems*, 1927, pp. 427, 434.

wheat trade has resulted in conditions in Canada which may render impracticable at present the continuation of immigration to the previous extent; but it nevertheless appears obvious that the financial position in Canada will be harassing until the population has been considerably increased.

Australia is also in serious trouble owing to its generous expenditure on development having exceeded the needs of the existing population. Australia has a Federal and State debt of £1,250 million, or over £170 per head of population. The railways in the year 1928 had cost £311,000,000, and in 1928 their receipts were £9,827,918 more than the working expenses, and they earned 3·18 per cent. on their capital, so that they are not quite remunerative. A large part of the capital spent in their construction was expended in accordance with a far-seeing land settlement policy, and with full knowledge that the back-block development railways could only pay when the country had a larger population.

Victoria has spent more than £10,000,000, on irrigation works; but the enterprise has proved so far not fully profitable, as the farmers are too few and the farms too large to make full use of the water supply provided. Australia has developed her manufactures so successfully that their annual addition of wealth is greater than that of the pastoral and agricultural industries. But manufacturing in Australia is so costly, owing to the high wages, that the extensive export of manufactures in competition with those of Europe and Asia can hardly be hoped for. The continued success of the Australian factories is dependent on the growth of the home market, and that growth requires a larger population.

The question of how many people Australia can support at a reasonable standard of comfort is one that vitally concerns its future. I made an estimate, based on extensive calculations, that the continent and Tasmania could ultimately support a population of 100 million. The late Admiral Sir Edmond Slade, after a tour of inquiry upon the resources and possibilities, told me that mine was an extreme under-estimate, as Australia could easily support a population of 200 million.

On the other hand, the bulk of Australian opinion in recent years has been in favour of much smaller figures, ranging from 10 to 30 million. Thus F. C. Benham, of Sydney University, in his contribution to the *Peopling of Australia* (1928), puts forward the estimate of 10 million; Griffith Taylor of 20 million (or 80 million at the European state of saturation); H. Barkley of 30 million; and H. L. Wilkinson of 23 million, in his *The World's Population Problems* (1920, p. 143). Professor Ellsworth Huntington has added to the low estimates one of 15,100,000. According to Benham's view, Australia can only carry a population of half the density of that existing in Arabia! Such estimates seem to me unnecessarily pessimistic and injurious to the credit of Australia. The conclusion that Australia can never support a population of more than from $1\frac{1}{2}$ times to 2 or 3 times as large as the present, seems to me highly improbable in view of the large tracts in the coastal districts near convenient harbours, that have a rich soil, an ample rainfall, and a climate favourable to luxuriant vegetation, and yet are practically unoccupied. Some of these tracts have a delightful climate, such as Croajingolong, the eastern province of Victoria, and the area around Twofold Bay in New South Wales.

There is no need to rediscuss these estimates here, as I stated some objections to them in the *Contemporary Review* (October 1929, pp. 476-782); but if they are true, the outlook for Australia is gloomy, as it would have greatly overspent on development. Many of the railways and irrigation and other public works will not repay their working expenses, apart from interest on their cost of construction, until the continent has a much larger population.

In view of the natural resources of many parts of Australia, the estimate that it could support as many inhabitants as France and Germany still seems to me reasonable; but any such population is only possible by continued immigration. Without it, Australia will be embarrassed by the cost of over-development, and by its products being undersold by countries that have a larger labour supply and are nearer the great northern markets.

The current breakdown in the migration from Europe to North America and Australia is inconvenient to Europe; but if it be long maintained, it will ultimately be far more costly to the countries who have been suddenly thereby cut off from this contribution to the growth of their populations.

DISCUSSION

Professor JENS WARMING showed by diagram how wages depended upon the number of workers. It would be seen that the total wealth of the world would increase if people migrated from one country to another. His diagram showed how migration from Europe to America would be an advantage to all. The workers in America were interested in opposing emigration, whereas the landowners took the opposite view. The amount of money invested in railroads in Australia would repay better when there was a larger population. The total wealth of the world would be greater the more evenly the population was distributed among the different countries.

Dr. DUNLOP asked Professor GREGORY if production would not become dearer in Australia as the population became denser through the action of the law of diminishing returns. At present wool was obtained from Australia very cheaply because they were working on a very sparse population with large tracts of land, enabling them to produce cheaply. As the country filled up the production would become dearer, and the goods would become more costly, or else the standard of living would have to be reduced.

Professor GREGORY agreed that in certain industries that was undoubtedly the case, and if the population filled up the cost of production increased; but in large parts of Australia the cost of production would fall with a larger population. There would be a better service on the railways, better roadways would be maintained at a reasonable cost, and for a long time in Australia the increased population would have the effect of reducing the cost of production.

Professor BLACK did not feel as certain as did Professor WARMING that increase in the population of the United States by migration or otherwise would reduce the cost of production. The question was not one that migration produced a lower *per capita* return, but a lower *per capita* return than would be the case at some time in the future. The prospects for population increase presented here were steadily increasing *per capita* returns. The rate at which this had occurred in the United States since 1920 had given a *per capita* return, which was such that they were on an appreciably higher plane than they were before. He did not think the analysis Professor WARMING had presented was complete, as it seemed that this migration was likely to be accompanied by decreasing *per capita* returns.

Professor FAIRCHILD agreed with Professor BLACK that the productivity and *per capita* returns of a nation were largely dependent upon its development. Over-population was always a relative matter.

He disagreed with him, however, as to the possibilities of the future as a result of the technical improvements going on in America and other parts of the world. The general principle was that the very nature of these technicological improvements was to get the same product, and often a very much larger product, from the same amount of land, and the developments on that line in the United States in the last few years had been very striking. He believed he was correct in saying that in the five years between 1923 and 1928 the industries of the United States actually employed about 800,000 fewer labourers. The railroads were employing 150,000 fewer labourers than they did sixty-five years ago. The same principle was running through all industries at an enormous rate. This was the peculiar paradox and the menacing feature of modern civilization. As population was increased, a lesser demand for population was created. This was one thing that had to be faced seriously in the future.

Professor FAIRCHILD said that to him it always seemed somewhat superfluous to speak about the need for more population in the United States when they recalled that they had some nine million people unemployed. These unemployed were not unfit, incompetent, or unemployable; they were a normal group of working people who could work and had worked.

Professor BLACK said there was no inconsistency between Professor FAIRCHILD and himself, excepting that Professor FAIRCHILD added the further fact that the unemployed were involved in the matter. The situation in the United States at the present time of unemployment was not due to the fact that there was not work to do, but that the work was not properly distributed between different people. Some people had all the work, and some had none. In a time of rapid evolution and technicological improvements there was always a period of unemployment while the work was getting passed round and distributed. The matter called for readjustment, and it was a painful readjustment.

Dr. DUBLIN said that there were similar international relationships calling for readjustment. The reserves of the world had not yet been tapped.

Professor BLACK thought the time was drawing nearer when a rational programme would be able to be made out under control, and the distress would be relieved.

Professor WHELPTON said Professor GREGORY had referred to the increase in the mortality-rates among the negroes. A study recently made on that point indicated that the rather rapid movement of negroes to urban centres tended to lower the birth-rates much more rapidly than the death-rates, and, as a matter of fact, the negro population was likely to continue increasing at a lower rate, tending to become less and less. This study showed that the growth of the negro population would stop before that of the white population.

Professor GREGORY said he could quite anticipate that fact as a first consequence of the movement of negroes to the towns, but he thought that in time, when things had readjusted themselves, the fertility would tend to increase. Two or three years ago he had gone into all the figures he could get from America, and there seemed to be evidence that there was a greater increase in the life of the negro than of the white population of the States, that there was a considerable fall in negro infant mortality, and that when the negroes spread through the northern towns they would probably be followed by their women, or be led to intermarriage with whites, which would lead to the danger of increase of the negro-rate.

Professor FAIRCHILD thought it might be of interest to some present to know that there had recently been established in New York City a negro birth-control clinic, which was being largely patronized by the negro population and also to a certain extent by the white population. The birth-control factor was now coming into this question of the negro population.

PAPER No. 16

THE RESPONSIBILITIES OF THE OBSTETRICIAN IN THE PROBLEM OF POPULATION

By GEORGE W. KOSMAK, M.D.

(United States of America)

(Editor, American Journal of Obsetrics and Gynaecology)

THE RESPONSIBILITIES OF THE OBSTETRICIAN IN THE PROBLEM OF POPULATION

It may appear unusual for a physician to participate in the discussion of a problem which would seem to come more properly into the domain of the economist, the sociologist, the clergyman, the eugenist, the biologist, or even the much maligned statistician. For, judging from the literature on the much-debated subject of a lowering birth-rate among certain groups of nations, it might appear that the medical profession had little or no interest in this matter. Yet there are many angles to the problem of population increase or decrease in which the physician should not only interest himself, but in which, in my opinion at least, he must assume a direct responsibility. The phases of the problem which concern the sociologist, the economist, and others, must naturally concern the physician, but there are certain pacific aspects of the matter which I will venture to discuss that enter directly into medical practice, and in my belief have an important, if possibly a minor, bearing on the question of diminishing birth-rate.

The physician is interested quite naturally in the death-rate of the community in which he practises, not only in the course of his attendance upon the sick, but in the larger and more socially significant problems of Public Health administration, industrial hygiene, and the education of the public toward better co-operation with him in these activities. But infinitely more important than its duty to the present generation is the responsibility of the medical profession towards generations to come. The birth-rate, the real crux of the problem of population, depends, in its fluctuations, on the maintenance of fertility, on proper care during pregnancy and labour, on contraceptive measures, and on the incidence of abortion, premature labour, and still-birth. Definitely, this is the domain of the obstetrician; the other groups who have taken up the study of population problems must bear in mind these factors and accord to them proper importance in the general scheme.

It is an accepted fact that nations are subject to alterations in their degree of fertility; this seems to decline in more or less direct ratio to their condition of opulence and prosperity. As the economic need for large numbers of children diminishes in an advancing civilization, the desire for family limitation brings in its wake contraceptive devices and induced abortions. Moreover, present economic conditions make it increasingly difficult for parents to have many children; homes are smaller, the cost of medical care is higher, and fashion no longer seems to approve of large families, which are now regarded as a liability rather than an asset. (The effects of contraception on fertility is a subject to which I shall refer again.)

With the development of a higher civilization there must also be admitted a corresponding degree of biologic infertility which should constitute a topic for further investigation by the medically trained biologist. With this is likewise associated a variety of local and general diseased processes, the precise effect of which on fertility demands further study by the clinician and the pathologist.

With the tendency towards smaller families has grown, perhaps, a laudable desire to make child-bearing as easy and painless as possible. In this connection one need only refer to the growth of "twilight sleep," and other analgesic methods in labour, to the more frequent hospitalization of normal obstetric cases, and to operative methods of delivery in cases where the indications for interference are insufficient and based on convenience rather than necessity. All of these, as well as certain other factors about to be mentioned, have, apparently, contributed to, rather than reduced, the high maternal and infant death-rates in those countries which perhaps have shown the greatest interest in population problems.

It is, therefore, essential that every item in the declining birth-rate be thoroughly investigated from the medical point of view; there are, in other words, certain specific factors in the general problem of population maintenance for which the physician must, I believe, be held directly responsible. The prevention of a certain proportion of needless deaths among mothers and infants must contribute definitely towards the stabilizing of birth-rates, and it is essential therefore to preserve lives that are now sacrificed as well as to institute measures that will increase the numbers of those yet unborn.

Admitting the facts just stated, it is evident that the medical profession can no longer speak in generalities or avoid the issue of the obstetric aspects of a lowering birth-rate. Statistical information of a fairly reliable kind is gradually accumulating with respect to the number of abortions both spontaneous and induced, the incidence of operative deliveries with a fatal outcome for either mother or child, the frequency of puerperal infections, premature labour, and other so-called accidents of pregnancy, in all of which the question of preventability must be given due consideration.

In this connection I would like to refer more specifically to certain statistics based on conditions in the United States, a country which has also been so widely accused of furnishing one of the highest puerperal death-rates among civilized nations. Statistical methods and standards of accuracy vary so greatly among different countries, that until they are more firmly fixed on a common basis, international comparisons of this kind will be unsuited for practical purposes. I believe, however, that statistical comparisons between periods of time in the same country are of more value, and these show in a general way that in the United States, for the past twenty years, the maternal mortality-rate has varied little, the average figure being about five deaths of mothers per 1,000 live births.

On the other hand, by way of comparison, we find in the United States marked reductions in the death-rates of other illnesses. For example, early infant mortality has declined in a marked degree, due no doubt to an improved milk-supply and the more intelligent care of babies. In New York City, for example, a generation ago, one out of every five babies died during the first year; now only about one in every seventeen succumbs.

Many American communities disclose similar conditions. Diseases and complications of pregnancy and labour constitute a very large item in the general death-rate. For example, in the State of New York, during the decade ending with 1925, these were second in importance among the causes of death of women between the ages of 15 and 44, first place being held by tuberculosis, third by heart disease, and fourth by cancer.

If we accept pregnancy and labour as normal and physiologic processes, the above can only be regarded as very startling facts, and would label child-bearing as a decimating factor in the growth of any nation, unless checked by proper measures. Although it may be difficult to draw satisfactory or final conclusions from these statements, there are certain underlying medical facts that seem to point the way.

Progress in the obstetric art has brought about in its train certain developments that must be taken into consideration. For example, a recent and very valuable study made by Professor Plass, of the University of Iowa, for the White House Conference, held recently in Washington, contains the startling information that in about 4,800 scattered cases of puerperal deaths collected for this study, 48 per cent. died after operative deliveries, 16 per cent. of these following forceps operations, and 11 per cent. Caesarean section. The incidence of forceps deliveries which occurred in 217 general hospitals of the United States to which his questionnaire was addressed was 17·9 per cent. The Caesarean incidence in 119 hospitals was 2·9 per cent., varying from 1 per cent. to over 14 per cent.

Another investigation reported upon by Drs. Holmes, Adair, and Mussey at the 1929 meeting of the American Medical Association, was based on 2,500 puerperal deaths which occurred during 1927 in twelve scattered States of the United States Registration Area. In this series septic infection accounted for 41 per cent., toxaemia 23 per cent., haemorrhage 11 per cent., accidents of pregnancy 18 per cent. of the total. It is of interest to note that operations to complete delivery were done on almost 1,700 patients in this series.

Dr. De Porte, of the Department of Health of the State of New York, found a maternal death-rate of 58·5 per 10,000 total live births in the decade between 1915 and 1925, or approximately one in every 171 births resulted in the death of the mother.

A very thorough investigation of the maternal deaths in a three-year period in New York City is now under way by a special committee of obstetricians, and sponsored by the Academy of Medicine, each death being studied within a short time after its occurrence while the attendant facts are fresh in mind. During 1930, the first year of the study, 672 deaths took place of women pregnant twenty-eight weeks or over, out of approximately 122,000 births in the Greater City, or a rate of about 5·5 per cent. A decision as to how many of these deaths could have been prevented must wait the committee's further deliberations.

Reports for certain European countries, including among others England, Scotland, and Germany, disclose a similar tendency towards approximately equal mortality-rates from child-bearing, with a noticeable increase in the incidence of operative deliveries. When we add to the figures from these countries, those dealing with deaths in early pregnancy from abortions, induced or improperly handled, we meet with similarly startling results, for even where the mother survives an operation or other complications, there exists the probability of subsequent invalidism and sterility from infection and complication illness.

The bearing of children should be a moderately normal function, and in the majority of instances it proves to be such if the natural forces concerned with the process are allowed full play. Undoubtedly a great many things interfere with this, some of which have resulted from the changed, some say more civilized, existence which women lead, others from economic sources, and finally those due to a lack of proper care and treatment during pregnancy and labour.

Admitting the fairly well-established facts just noted, it is incumbent upon the medical and allied professions to preserve the health and life of a woman, who, by proving her fertility, is one of the most essential factors in population growth or maintenance. In order to accomplish an improvement in this situation, further studies must be carried out by individual countries and communities to demonstrate the effects of improper obstetric practice on fertility and on the birth-rate. A practical suggestion that might well go out from this Conference is to apprise the medical profession as well as the public of the effect which interference, especially unskilled, with the normal function of child-bearing has on the welfare of the nation in general and on the decline of population in particular. On the physician rests in great part this important duty.

The ready acquiescence toward the voluble propaganda of birth control has done much to instil into the mind of the public that actual and growing fear of pregnancy which it may take many years to overcome. There are certain phases of this problem in which the physician must come to a decision independent of economic aspects or religious influences. He is well aware of the uncertainties, failures, and dangers attached to the widely heralded contraceptive devices of the present day, and he should know that slight degrees of fertility may be destroyed or actual infertility obscured by these indiscriminate practices, until it is too late for effective remedial action. As a group, physicians have listened too much to the clamour of birth control rather than to the less popular appeal of "birth release." There are well-marked indications for the employment of contraceptive measures, but at the present moment there would appear to be a pressing need of better knowledge of increasing or retaining fertility and of relieving infertility. Moreover, the physician must study more effectively the disease factors underlying sterility and develop methods for their eradication. And to these must be added a practical knowledge of those more subtle and less physically evident disturbances of internal gland secretion which possibly underlie a condition of actual or relative sterility in many instances.

In addition to his salutary influence in overcoming the fear of pregnancy, the physician must endeavour to alleviate the fear of the actual labour which exists among so many expectant young mothers. I feel that he has been too receptive towards the propaganda of painless labours by resort to narcotic and analgesic measures, that are not only unsafe or unreliable in themselves, but their indiscriminate and routine employment leads to a feeling on the part of the patient that, by not resorting to them, the attending physician is not doing his full duty. Without denying the value of such analgesic measures when properly employed, I consider that their general adoption would lead to the belief that they are essential, and that without them child-bearing is dangerous. This, of course, is untrue.

Of the economic phases connected with child-bearing the physician also has some concern, for undoubtedly he has participated in the increased expenditures which have made pregnancy an economic burden to many young people. The quite unfounded supposition that hospitalization, special nursing, and surely other luxuries are necessary in normal obstetric cases has been a stumbling-block to many young couples who are perhaps most fit for the task of keeping up our birth-rates, and to the economist also the physician must answer for having his interests concentrated less on the birth-rate than on death-rates and the extension of the life cycle. In the course of time the postponement of adult deaths and the saving of lives of young children has resulted in retaining more of the age groups beyond the reproductive and active periods, with a corresponding increase in the factor of dependence. This has developed a situation which it may be difficult to deal with, combined as it is with the postponement of marriage for economic and other reasons.

In concluding, may I once more call attention to the important mission of the medical profession not only in maintaining but in improving the diminishing fertility-rate of civilized nations. It must do this not only in a material and physical sense by making child-bearing a safe, natural, and sane procedure, but by lending its weight and influence to develop a better and sounder knowledge of maternity among people at large, by educating more thoroughly its own ranks in obstetric knowledge, and by combining more intimately with other interested groups in endeavouring to overcome the baneful influences which are tending eventually to depopulate certain nations that must carry the burden of civilization in the very near future.

DISCUSSION

Dr. FRETS asked whether Dr. KOSMAK had taken the incidence of thrombosis and embolism into his death-rates?

Dr. KOSMAK believed personally that the incidence of thrombosis and embolism causing maternal deaths was largely over-estimated. The diagnosis of embolism as a cause of death was very often employed to cover the real cause which might not reflect credit on the attending physician. A great many errors in death certificates, intentional or otherwise, had been found. The diagnosis of embolism was a very frequent one, and in diagnosing deaths haemorrhage would probably have been better.

Dr. H. D. BRACKENBURY said that there had recently been two Departmental Committees inquiring into this question of maternal mortality, and while many biological observations had been made, he wanted to draw attention to two factors which had some definite bearing upon the problem. In the first place, out of all these cases of death, it was concluded that 48 per cent. at least were due to preventable causes, and it might be taken that that was approximately correct. If the existing maternal mortality-rate could be halved, all that was humanly possible in that direction would have been done. The various preventable causes were analysed, and some were found to be due to the action of the patient herself, some to the action of the patient's friends, and some to imperfect judgment on the part of either the midwife or the doctor concerned. The one fact he wished to inform the Conference of was this: that the preventable causes occurred in approximately 48 per cent. of the cases investigated, and that the rest were due to causes which could not have been prevented.

The other fact which was of great importance and was not commonly recognized was that childbirth could be made at least as safe in poor home surroundings as it could be made in good home surroundings or in institutional surroundings. If there were sufficient institutions to take the cases of major operations which were required, and with proper ante-natal supervision, it was shown by statistics that the external birth-rate, i.e. the births occurring in the poor homes of London and other large towns, had reduced its maternal mortality-rate by one-half. Poor home surroundings, provided there was proper attention, did not in themselves add the least bit to the dangers of childbirth.

Those two factors, preventable causes, and the fact that childbirth could be made as safe a thing in poor homes as anywhere, ought to be taken into consideration by all those considering the medical and social aspects of this subject.

Dr. WICKSELL asked if Dr. KOSMAK had observed in the United States any tendency for abortions and miscarriages to be proportionately more common in the early stage of marriage? Such observations had been made in Vienna. If this were so it had great bearing on the question of birth control.

Professor F. A. E. CREW said that they had been told both by the reader of the paper and in the discussion that child-bearing was a dangerous business, and that at least 48 per cent. of the maternal mortality was referable to what were allowed to be called "preventable causes." The assumption, therefore, was that 52 per cent. were unpreventable. Professor CREW suggested that they, as a group, could not accept that definition. Certainly many things were inefficient; the medical profession might even be allowed to be somewhat inefficient in this respect; but many mothers apparently were inefficient through lack of education. But might it not be that the human female—or a portion of the human female—was definitely inefficient in this matter of having and raising babies, and if that were so, was it not necessary to seek for a reason? The reader of the paper put his finger very nearly on this point. He referred, quite necessarily and naturally vaguely in a paper of this kind, to the consequence of the action of internal secretions. It seemed to him, Professor CREW, that the medical profession should have its focus drawn not only to the facts presented in this paper, but also to the ever-amassing facts of recent research in sex physiology. A great deal was known about these physiological factors that were responsible for normality, and therefore for abnormality, in the reproductive phenomena of the male and female, but only of that kind of female that could be kept and studied. It seemed to him that if what was known about the rat and rabbit were analogous in the case of human beings, one could no longer say that 48 per cent. of maternal mortality was preventable and 52 per cent. unpreventable, because it would *not* be so.

It was known that the pituitary and other internal secretions were definitely involved in the normal processes of pregnancy and parturition. There might be a biological type of woman in whom the quota of responsible hormones was imperfect. It was reasonable to assume that it was just as natural for people not to want to be born as for people not to want to die. He interpreted birth control as another example of all those attempts at immortality. He would only allow the type to develop that would benefit mankind.

Dr. DUBLIN said he would like to tell the Assembly of some work going on in New York to which Dr. KOSMAK had referred. In that city there had been for ten years a rather concentrated effort on the part of physicians and a great number of the public to reduce maternity mortality, and the results of that experiment were worthy of attention. He had recently studied the experience of those so-called maternal centres, and in a group of some 5,000 confinements it was possible to reduce the mortality of the mothers concerned to about one-third of the normal rate. Those women lived in one of the poorer sections of the city, and for the purpose of the experiment it was possible to follow the mortality of the whole community and the women under the care of the Maternity Centre nurses; those who received pre-natal care, whose confinements were supervised and who received after-care. The mortality instead of being 6·4, was actually 2·2 per thousand confinements.

To refer to the point made by Professor CREW, even without this knowledge, so much desired, of the action of the hormones and the application of the knowledge of general biology to man, it was entirely possible, without too extensive an effort, to reduce the mortality of women to one-third of what normally prevailed. What the ultimate reduction would be he had no doubt, but it was perfectly obvious that the current mortality was to a very large degree unnecessary.

Dr. KOSMAK had raised a number of very controversial subjects, but on the other hand he had raised one question which by no stretch of imagination was controversial. The mortality of women who had made up their mind to be mothers seemed a preposterous thing, a situation which called for every effort of the community to control. There should be no question as to that, for at present the world was concerned with a period of low birth-rates and a mortality of the birth agents—the mothers. But what seemed to be an even more important aspect was the repercussion of that mortality upon women who, fearful of the outcome, did not become mothers. Dr. DUBLIN said he did not know what the effect of that fear was, but it was a definite thing, and the direct effect was not only the curtailment of future births, but, what was more important, the increase in abortions by women who feared to go through pregnancy, and, in a very large number of cases, sterility, or lack of fertility, in women who feared to go through the ordeal, perhaps from the memory of a sister or friend who had died.

This resulted in social loss of the greatest consequence, and one which the medical profession could help to stop. The speaker had referred to the important place played by the physician in the population of to-day. For the most part that had been overlooked, and it seemed to Dr. DUBLIN that if there were another meeting of the Assembly, it would be very profitable to bring in a resolution suggesting to the members of the Assembly that they should go back to their respective countries determined more and more to bring into the picture of the population question the power, intelligence, and interest of the medical profession, and induce them not only to play their part in developing a proper attitude towards child-bearing, but to correct the present practices. It was unthinkable that the physician should be divorced from the economist and others who were interested in the population question.

Dr. DUNLOP said he would like the consideration of quality to be kept in mind. The latter speakers in the discussion had been emphasizing the idea of quantity. To quote one example, it was on record that the more Caesarean sections that were done to produce live children, the more Caesarean sections needed to be done; in other words, a population was being produced that would always require to be in the hands of the medical profession.

Dr. KOSMAK said he had been interested in the discussion and thanked Dr. DUBLIN for his remarks; it was Dr. DUBLIN who had interested him in this particular Conference and prevailed upon him to write this brief paper.

It was incumbent upon the medical profession to take a very definite interest in the population problem. They had listened to various records of the population increase, and the necessity for population maintenance, and it had seemed to him that most of these had looked to the future. But here was a cause operating at the present time—the maintenance of the lives of all women now engaged in this process. This was one of the small things in this large problem that must be taken care of.

With regard to preventable mortality, only the causes operating through the physician had been considered, i.e. neglect, fear of labour, and other factors of that kind.

As to the proportion of abortions in young women, Dr. KOSMAK said he could only speak for New York City, and he knew from the records of the Department of Health that the abortions were very much on the increase, not only among young women, but among all women.

Referring to Professor CREW's remarks, there was no doubt that the female of to-day was less efficient to bear children than the female of the past, or that the female of certain races was more inefficient than the female of other races. That was a problem that must be carefully considered, but it had not entered into any of the calculations he brought forward.

As civilization went on, the tendency to interfere with labour was increasing. If that interference was skilfully conducted by the highest and best-trained obstetricians, the results might not be so bad; unfortunately most of the obstetrics in the United States was in the hands of the general practitioner, who was led by the articles published in journals to believe in the ease of these various procedures that in the hands of the unskilled led to the deaths of mothers and of children.

PAPER No. 17

ANIMAL POPULATION AND MIGRATION

By CHARLES ELTON

(Department of Zoology and Comparative Anatomy, University Museum, Oxford)

ANIMAL POPULATION AND MIGRATION

AT a time when the importance of emigration and of a fluid labour population is admitted to be very great in human economic affairs, it is of some interest to consider the place which migration occupies in the "economic affairs" of animals.

Recent ecological investigations have proved that most animals migrate, either at regular or irregular intervals, whenever their surroundings become unsuitable for their life or breeding. In particular the supply of food, which varies from year to year and place to place, exercises a very important control over their movements. By such migratory movements the density of numbers of any species of animal becomes adjusted to the resources of its environment; and when, as frequently happens, such final adjustment is impossible, the migration may take place on a very large scale, leading to the death from starvation, disease, or other causes of the majority of the migrants.

Three illustrations may be given of this phenomenon. The first is the arctic fox, which inhabits the Polar regions of the globe. The records of the Hudson's Bay Company have provided an important index of the annual fluctuations in numbers of the arctic fox population of Northern Canada. There is a very marked fluctuation in their numbers with a periodicity of about four years, caused probably by a corresponding fluctuation in the population of lemmings upon which the fox depends for food. When food supply becomes scarce, the arctic foxes migrate for enormous distances; many of them invade the forest regions to the south of their normal arctic home; at the same time disease frequently breaks out among them, and probably gives rise to similar epidemics among the sledge-dogs of the north. It can be seen in this instance how the migratory activity of one animal may bring about a situation in which human beings of a primitive stage of economic life are themselves prevented from migrating in search of food supply, by the destruction of their main means of winter transport.

The second example is the Canada lynx, which fluctuates in numbers with its food supply, in this case the snowshoe rabbit of the Canadian forests, the periodicity being about ten years. At times of scarcity the lynx performs wide migrations, and when the supply of rabbits becomes exhausted, is frequently found in a state of starvation. Just as the arctic fox moves southwards, so it is found that the lynx at the northern edge of its range will move into the arctic tundras.

A third example is the field-mouse, grass-mouse, or vole, *Microtus*, which shows very marked local migratory activity in search of food. Under cage conditions, as soon as food becomes scarce, this mouse becomes feverishly active, completely changing its type of behaviour. It is possible by studying the reactions of the voles to show that migration occurs in response to a number of different conditions of its environment, varying from lack of food to the conditions of its cages, suitable cover, etc.

These are three examples of a type of behaviour which is found amongst a very large number of animals; in fact, it appears to be a general rule that animals that have any power of migration at all move about in response to the changes that take place in their surroundings. Furthermore, it is probable that this reaction occurs in response to conditions of discomfort, and not only to those of grave danger.

Among primitive human societies we find similar nomadic behaviour, later becoming suppressed to a very great extent by economic factors which tie men to one locality, and then to an increasing extent by cultural factors creating ties of sentiment which become equally strong.

In modern times it has become increasingly evident that the suppression of this deep-rooted migratory impulse may be harmful in two ways at least. First, it renders the supply of labour in a country like England less fluid than it might otherwise be. Professor Fawcett pointed out in his paper that in the United States (where traditional customs and habits are less fixed than in Europe, and where, moreover, the nation is recently derived from a migrant population) labour movements are much more extensive. Secondly, the suppression or repression of a strong impulse to move away from unpleasant or economically undesirable surroundings may be one cause of the strong tensions and emotional frictions which exist in highly civilized communities at the present day. The invention of motor transport has given effect to this fund of migratory impulse, as may be seen by watching any of the arterial roads leading from London on a Sunday. Thousands of people leave the unpleasant surroundings of the city at the highest attainable speed, only to return in the evening, drawn by the equally strong instinct of self-preservation.

The proper understanding of the relation of migration to ecological conditions among animal communities has therefore a definite bearing upon the population problem in man, since it will help to complete our knowledge of the manner in which our own communities have grown up.

SOME EXPERIMENTS ON POPULATIONS OF MICE

By F. A. E. CREW

SOME EXPERIMENTS ON POPULATIONS OF MICE*

PEARL and Surface (1909), Pearl and Parker (1922), and Pearl, Miner, and Parker (1927) have demonstrated that in the case of the experimental material used; the domestic fowl and *Drosophila melanogaster*, the death-rate varied directly with density of population, and that fecundity and the rate of reproduction varied inversely but according to the same law.

In an attempt to extend these studies to include a mammal the investigation now described was planned. Boxes of wood, each 21 in. × 9½ in. × 7 in., with a movable wire top and divided by two partitions, each 2 in. high, into three compartments, were used. The end compartments were prepared as sleeping-places, whilst in the larger central division the feeding-dishes were placed.

One hundred and seventy-six female mice, line-bred albinos, eight weeks old and virginal, were chosen as the experimental material, for the reason that mice breed freely throughout the year, and that their sexual activity and reproductive activity can readily be recognized and measured.

These females were placed in the boxes together with males from the same stock. In some of the boxes there was 1 male and 1 female; in others 2 males and 2 females, 4 males and 4 females, 8 males and 8 females, or 12 males and 12 females. Each day the females were examined for vaginal plugs (evidence of oestrus and mating), and all who were pregnant (recognized from the recorded account of their oestrous cycles and mating) were removed to single-unit mouse-boxes on the nineteenth day from the date when the plug was first recorded. Litters were destroyed as soon as they were found on the day of their birth, and the mother returned to the box to which she belonged. Any mouse that was removed or that died was immediately replaced from a reservoir of related mice of the same age by an individual with a similar reproductive history. The investigation continued from late July to early May.

Soon after its beginning it became clear that serious difficulties were to be expected. The death-rate amongst the males was remarkably

* A more complete account of this study appeared in *Biologia Generalis*, vii 2, pp. 239–250, 1931.

high; in the 4 × 4, 8 × 8, and 12 × 12 boxes the males fought perpetually unless some were dead or exiled. Certain boxes had to be withdrawn from the experiment, since all replacements and most of the originals were killed. This applies especially to the 4 × 4 boxes. In others, instead of males, ovariectomized females were introduced to take the place of the males that were killed, and in this way the correct number was maintained.

As time passed it became easily possible to tell to which density an individual belonged by manifest differences in general condition. Those from the 4 × 4, 8 × 8, and 12 × 12 boxes were thinner, duller, and rougher coated and more nervous.

Density	1 × 1	2 × 2	4 × 4	8 × 8	12 × 12
Total number of animals (females only) plus replacements after certain boxes had been withdrawn	8	12+6	12+12	32+27	24+18
Plug : Pregnancy ratio = $\dfrac{\text{Total number of vaginal plugs}}{\text{Total number of pregnancies}}$	1·25	1·35	1·73	2·10	2·17
Intensity of sexual life = $\dfrac{\text{Total plugs}}{\text{Total animals} \times \text{Total months}}$	1·39	1·34	1·35	1·56	1·33
Average individual contribution to population increase = $\dfrac{\text{Total offspring}}{\text{Total animals}}$	72·0	58·9	41·0	40·4	32·3
Reproductive rate = $\dfrac{\text{Total offspring}}{\text{Total animals} \times \text{Total months}}$	8·05	6·54	4·55	4·49	3·59
Average litter size	7·25	6·6	5·85	6·08	5·82
Death-rate (percentage)	—	33·3	50·0	45·7	42·8
Fertility-rate	80·0	73·7	57·5	47·4	46·0

The table summarizes the results obtained. The figures support the conclusion that the death-rate, the reproductive-rate, and the fecundity of a population are affected by population density. But since the life-history of each and every individual female during the course of the experiment was recorded in detail in respect of sexual activity, reproduction, and mortality, it was possible to recognize clearly that in this population there were individuals which endured with ease the conditions (of density) to which they were exposed, whilst there were others which could not adapt themselves to these conditions. There were many, for example, whose sexual activity was very high, yet who had no or few litters in the crowded boxes; but when removed therefrom and placed in the ordinary mouse-box ($10\frac{1}{2}$ in. $\times$ $9\frac{1}{2}$ in. $\times$ $4\frac{1}{2}$ in.) with three other females and one male soon exhibited an unremarkable plug-pregnancy ratio. This phenomenon was much more common among the individuals of the higher densities. For example,

> In the 4 $\times$ 4 one individual had 8 plugs and 0 litters in 4 months.
> In the 4 $\times$ 4 one individual had 13 plugs and 2 litters in 5 months.
> In the 12 $\times$ 12 one individual had 11 plugs and 0 litters in 4 months.

Certain females lived throughout the period of the experiment. There were 9 such in the 8 $\times$ 8 and 11 in the 12 $\times$ 12, and of these several produced abundant offspring, e.g. one in the 12 $\times$ 12 gave 76, whilst of the 8 $\times$ 8 one gave as many as 86.

There was no steady increase in mortality with increasing density, and the reason for this may be that in this experiment only adult individuals were employed.

SUMMARY.

The results obtained support the conclusions of Pearl and his colleagues that the death-rate, reproductive-rate, and the fecundity of a population are affected by population density, but they suggest that the cause for this is to be sought in the history of certain individuals in that population who are unable to adapt themselves to the existing conditions. The results show that in a population, the death-rate, reproductive-rate, and fecundity of which are deleteriously influenced by density, there are many individuals which, under the conditions existing, exhibit normality in respect of these phenomena.

BIBLIOGRAPHY

PEARL, R., MINER, J. R., and PARKER, SYLVIA L. 1927. Experimental Studies on the Duration of Life. XI. Density of Population and Life Duration in *Drosophila*. Amer. Nat., XLI, 1.

PEARL, R., and PARKER, SYLVIA L. 1922. On the Influence of Density of Population upon the Rate of Reproduction in *Drosophila*. Proc. Nat. Acad. Sci., 8, 7.

PEARL, R., and SURFACE, F. M. 1909. A Biometrical Study of Egg-production in the Domestic Fowl. I. Variation in Annual Egg-production. U.S.A. Dept. Agric. Bur. of Animal Ind. Bull. 110, Pt. 1

PAPER No. 19

THE FUTURE OF THE POPULATION OF BELGIUM

By Professor FERNAND BAUDHUIN

(University of Louvain)

THE FUTURE OF THE POPULATION OF BELGIUM

(ABSTRACT)

CALCULATIONS are made on the Census of 1921, taking age and sex distribution, marital status, etc., by which to forecast future numbers. Various methods are proposed for arriving at the number of children per family required to maintain the population at its present level. It is assumed that the present trends will be continued (if not accelerated) with the exception of the increased expectation of life. A considerable fall in population should appear in 1970.

Parallel figures are worked out for France.

Numbers of immigrants in recent years (largely from Poland) are shown to mask the true figures for both France and Belgium, this strong current of migration being compared with the East to West flow of peoples early in our era. A possible population surplus in Russia might, it is suggested, be attracted by under-population in France and Belgium to these countries and overrun the western edge of Europe.

A final table sets out the recent population figures for Italy, France, Germany, and Belgium, followed by a table calculating the Belgian vital statistic of future decennia to 1970.

L'AVENIR DE LA POPULATION BELGE*

Par FERNAND BAUDHUIN

(Professeur à l'Université de Louvain)

Read by M. EUGÈNE DUPRÉEL

I. Un des phénomènes les plus importants à prévoir dans les pays industriels et à civilisation matérielle avancée, est la régression de la population autochtone. Jusqu'à présent, l'Allemagne, la Belgique et même la France ont encore des excédents de naissances sur les décès. Mais, dès aujourd'hui, il faut s'attendre à la disparition de ces excédents, puis à leur remplacement par un déficit de naissances; sauf immigration, la population de l'Europe Occidentale et même Centrale va cesser de croître, et ensuite elle commencera à diminuer.

Les chiffres relatifs à l'année 1930 semblent devoir démentir cette tendance. En France, on enregistre, par exemple, un excédent de 100,000 naissances, contre un excédent de 13,000 décès en 1929. Les statistiques belges et allemandes, actuellement incomplètes, donneront des résultats du même genre. Mais il ne s'agit là que d'un accident. D'une part, en France et en Belgique, le léger relèvement de la natalité est en rapport avec la grande prospérité des années 1928 et 1929. D'autre part, dans tous les pays, la mortalité de 1929 avait été anormalement élevée, par suite de l'hiver très rigoureux.

Nous avons tenté d'établir, en ce qui concerne l'avenir de notre population, des calculs dont les résultats demeurent largement sujets à réserve, mais sont moins hypothétiques qu'on ne pourrait le croire. Ils font toucher du doigt la situation où nous sommes aujourd'hui et celle où nous allons nous trouver un jour. Malheureusement, nous n'avons en Belgique comme point de départ que les statistiques du recensement de 1920, dont nous sommes déjà fort éloignés, et qui surtout datent d'une époque très proche de la guerre, où beaucoup de facteurs importants étaient encore en mouvement.

D'autre part, ce calcul exigerait que l'on dispose de tables de mortalité correspondant réellement aux conditions existantes dans notre pays.

---

* Also published in *Bulletin d'Information et de Documentation*, of the Banque Nationale de Belgique, Sixth Year, Vol. I, No. 11, June 10, 1931.

Or, nous ne possédons pour la Belgique que de vieilles tables, périmées de toute évidence. Faute de mieux, nous avons utilisé les tables françaises dressées d'après les décès de 1920 à 1923.* Pour tenir compte des progrès récents de la médecine et de l'hygiène, nous avons pris pour base la mortalité féminine, plus réduite que la mortalité masculine. La vie moyenne accordée aux femmes par cette table est de 56 ans, au lieu de 54 aux deux sexes réunis, et 52 aux hommes. La confrontation de nos résultats avec le chiffre de la population calculée pour 1929 a semblé montrer qu'en estimant la vie moyenne à 56 ans, nous étions encore un peu au-dessous de la réalité.

Quoi qu'il en soit, c'est donc sous réserves, et en gardant la possibilité de modifier nos chiffres après la publication du recensement de 1930, que nous donnerons les indications contenues dans cet article.

Un raisonnement fort simple, appelant des retouches mais cependant exact dans ses grandes lignes, montrera que la diminution de la population est bien l'aboutissement inévitable des conditions démographiques actuelles. Pour qu'une population se maintienne stable, il faut qu'elle donne une moyenne de trois enfants par mariage. Deux enfants remplacent les parents, et le troisième compense la disparition de ceux qui meurent sans arriver à l'âge du mariage, ou qui demeurent célibataires. Les naissances doivent être plus nombreuses encore dans les pays où l'on se marie plus tard, et où la mortalité infantile est plus élevée. Voici, en effet, le pourcentage de célibataires parmi les morts:

PROPORTION DES CÉLIBATAIRES PARMI LES MORTS

				%
Belgique (1920)..	..	..	..	.. 43
France (1926) ..	..	..	..	.. 31
Allemagne (1927)	..	..	..	.. 32
Italie (1928) ..	..	..	..	.. 52

Le chiffre relatif à la Belgique se rapportant à 1920, date du dernier calcul établi, il est anormalement élevé par suite des plus nombreuses naissances consécutives à la guerre. Par ailleurs, on n'ignore pas qu'une forte natalité est, toutes choses égales d'ailleurs, une cause de forte mortalité de célibataires; c'est ainsi que l'Italie arrive à 52 pour cent, ce qui exigerait quatre naissances pour maintenir la population stationnaire.

Ajoutons qu'une certaine correction est nécessaire pour tenir compte

* *Annuaire Statistique*, Vol. XLIV, Paris, 1928, pp. 12-13.

des remariages de veufs ou de divorcés; on peut admettre de ce fait que pour maintenir une population stable, le nombre des enfants nécessaires est en réalité de 2·7 par mariage au lieu de 3. Or, voici comment se présente ce rapport pour les pays de civilisation matérielle très avancée:

NAISSANCES PAR MARIAGE (1928)

Allemagne	..	..	..	..	..	2·0
Belgique	..	..	..	..	..	2·2
France	..	..	..	..	..	2·2
Angleterre	..	..	..	..	..	2·2

Le cas de l'Italie est assez complexe, étant donné l'importance de l'émigration. D'après le pourcentage des célibataires parmi les morts, elle devrait avoir 4 naissances par mariage pour se maintenir, et elle n'en a que 3·8. Mais des corrections sont nécessaires, et au surplus elle pourra encore réduire sa mortalité infantile, actuellement assez élevée. Quoi qu'il en soit, il n'est pas douteux qu'elle ne disposera plus, dans un avenir plus ou moins lointain, d'excédents de population à exporter.

La menace dont nous parlons est actuellement masquée par le fait que l'âge moyen des habitants est relativement bas. Cette situation se présente dans les pays à population croissante, du moins lorsque cette croissance est due à l'afflux des enfants; elle persiste pendant un certain temps après que la natalité a fléchi, parce qu'il faut à la nation le temps de vieillir. C'est à ce stade que nous sommes. Il en résulte que la mortalité est anormalement réduite, et le nombre de femmes en âge d'avoir des enfants anormalement élevé. Mais au fur et à mesure que le nombre des vieillards augmentera, la mortalité s'élèvera; à l'excédent de naissances succédera un excédent de décès.

Le moment où le déficit apparaîtra variera d'après les pays. Ceux qui ont depuis longtemps une natalité très basse y parviendront les premiers. C'est le cas de la France, qui semble y arriver déjà; la Belgique suivra au bout d'un certain nombre d'années. L'Allemagne, qui a gardé plus tard une forte natalité, résistera plus longtemps, mais cédera finalement. Le Bureau Statistique du Reich vient, en effet, de faire des calculs minutieux en vue de déterminer quelle serait la population de ce pays à l'avenir. En possession de tables de mortalité toutes récentes, et de la répartition de la population par âge, cette administration pouvait établir avec un minimum de risques d'erreur, la population probable au cours des cinquante années qui vont venir.

L'Allemagne, qui comptait au début de 1931 près de 65 millions d'habitants, et en gagne 400,000 chaque année jusqu'à présent, atteindrait son maximum, quelque peu inférieur à 70 millions, en 1960. A partir de ce moment, la régression commencerait, assez lente cependant au début; en 1980, il resterait 68½ millions d'habitants en Allemagne.

En réalité, la régression sera plus prompte et plus vive. Cette estimation suppose que la natalité, c'est-à-dire le nombre de naissances par rapport à la population totale, ne fléchira pas. Mais elle fléchira, par suite de la diminution du pourcentage de femmes en âge d'avoir des enfants. En raison de la forte natalité qui prévalait encore il y a 20 ou 30 ans, la proportion d'adultes jeunes est aujourd'hui anormalement élevée.

En Belgique et surtout en France, le plafond de la population sera atteint beaucoup plus vite. La France y est déjà pratiquement, nous le montrerons plus loin; ses excédents actuels sont dûs à peu près entièrement à l'afflux d'étrangers jeunes, qui lui donnent des naissances en plus grand nombre, et abaissent l'âge moyen de la population. En Belgique, l'excédent des naissances est encore relativement considérable (40,000 par an). Mais cependant le plafond sera atteint assez vite.

Il faut prévoir en effet, en Belgique comme en Allemagne, un nouveau fléchissement du nombre des naissances. Dès à présent, il est déjà en cours. Les enfants viennent naturellement surtout chez les jeunes ménages; or, le grand nombre des mariages qui ont suivi la guerre a quelque peu forcé le nombre des naissances depuis dix ans, et ce stimulant tend aujourd'hui à disparaître.

Il y a plus grave. Le nombre des naissances dépend, cela va de soi, de celui des mariages récents; or, le fléchissement de la nuptialité s'annonce de façon permanente et irrémédiable. Les 71,000 mariages et remariages que nous avons actuellement sont le fait de personnes âgées en moyenne de 23 ou de 25 ans, c'est-à-dire nées vers 1905. Il y avait alors 190,000 naissances environ; il a donc fallu 2·7 naissances à cette date pour donner un mariage ou remariage aujourd'hui.

En 1935, se marieront des gens nés en moyenne en 1910; comme il n'y avait plus alors que 176,000 naissances, il n'y aura plus, toutes choses égales d'ailleurs, que 66,000 mariages, et sans doute 132,000 naissances, d'après la cadence actuelle de 2 naissances pour un mariage. En 1950, quand se marieront les gens nés en 1925, il n'y aura plus, d'après le calcul précédent, que 58,000 mariages et 116,000 naissances.

Il y aura une période plus déficitaire encore, celle qui correspond aux naissances de guerre, de 1940 à 1945. Les naissances tomberont alors au-dessous de 100,000, toujours conformément au même calcul.

Le caractère irrémédiable de cette régression est indiqué par le tableau que voici, et qui donne, calculé d'après la méthode utilisée dans toute cette étude, le nombre de personnes âgées de 20 à 30 ans, susceptibles donc d'avoir des enfants. On y voit que nous sommes en ce moment au point le plus favorable, et que nous allons l'abandonner bientôt.

POPULATION DE 20 À MOINS DE 30 ANS

1910	1,238,000
1920	1,287,000
1930	1,370,000
1940	1,070,000
1950	1,240,000
1960	1,100,000

La réduction de la mortalité infantile, revenue de 14 à 9 pour cent depuis vingt ans, apporte un certain correctif aux résultats de ces calculs. Un même nombre de naissances donnera lieu plus tard à un plus grand nombre de mariages, et partant, de naissances après vingt-cinq ans. Mais, par contre, la proportion adoptée comme base est forcée par l'existence d'un trop grand nombre de jeunes ménages, ce qui constitue une compensation au moins partielle. Une autre compensation doit être observée dans le fait que le nombre des mariages est actuellement trop élevé, semble-t-il, vu les naissances d'il y a vingt-cinq ans. Il est probable qu'il est enflé artificiellement parce que l'on se marie de plus en plus tôt; mais, bien entendu, ce facteur n'agira pas indéfiniment, il y a une limite.

On peut d'ailleurs présenter la situation actuelle de la Belgique sous un aspect plus saisissant. La classe née en 1905 comptait environ 190,000 naissances; elle ne donne que 146,000 enfants quand vient son tour de procréer. Elle ne comblera donc le vide qu'elle causera en disparaissant, qu'à concurrence des trois-quarts, mettons de 80 pour cent en tenant compte de la réduction de la mortalité infantile.

Sur ces bases, voici donc comment nous avons estimé le chiffre des naissances probables d'ici quarante ans. Mais il ne s'agit que des naissances de parents belges, à l'exclusion des immigrés, qui, comme nous le dirons plus loin, deviendront de plus en plus nombreux.

Le tableau qui suit suppose naturellement que la politique et les habitudes ne se modifient pas en ce qui concerne le nombre des enfants. Il tient compte de la réduction de la mortalité infantile, mais non des compensations signalées plus haut; il donne donc des estimations maxima.

NAISSANCES PROBABLES (MOYENNES DÉCENNALES)

1931–1940	..	..	..	.. 136,000
1940–1950	..	..	..	.. 110,000
1950–1960	..	..	..	.. 112,000
1961–1970	..	..	..	.. 98,000

Le relèvement de la période 1950 à 1960 surprend à première vue. Mais c'est qu'au cours de la période précédente la natalité s'était trouvée anormalement abaissée par suite de la guerre de 1914–18. Se marieront alors, en effet, notamment les personnes nées de 1915 à 1920—où, comme nous l'avons dit, les naissances furent largement déficitaires.

Les chiffres que nous venons de donner indiquent naturellement une natalité insuffisante pour compenser la mortalité. Au fait, quelle natalité faut-il pour y parvenir?

Tout dépend de la mortalité, cela va sans dire, et la proportion de naissances nécessaires à la stabilité d'une population varie selon les époques et les pays. Au temps où la vie moyenne était de 40 ans, il fallait chaque année un apport égal au quarantième du nombre des habitants, soit 25 pour mille. Actuellement, la vie moyenne est de quelque 56 ans; les naissances doivent donc représenter le cinquante-sixième de la population, soit 18 pour mille, sensiblement la proportion de l'Allemagne, de la France et de la Belgique. A première vue, la natalité de ces pays paraît encore suffisante.

Mais nous venons de montrer qu'elle devait baisser, à moins d'un changement dans la mentalité. Le coefficient de natalité par rapport à la population est actuellement faussé par le nombre anormal de femmes en âge d'avoir des enfants, la seule chose à considérer en cette matière. Ces pays ont peu d'enfants, et peu de vieillards encore; la proportion d'adultes est donc exceptionnellement élevée. Au cours des prochaines années, elle va décroître, et avec elle forcément la natalité.

Quoi qu'il en soit, il faut donc prévoir en Belgique la continuation du fléchissement du nombre des naissances. La tendance sera faible au début, puis elle s'accélérera, à partir surtout de 1940. Sauf apport étranger, nous descendrons de 18 à moins de 15 naissances ou peut-être même de 13 naissances pour mille.

II. Pendant que le nombre des naissances fléchira, comme nous venons de le dire, celui des morts augmentera. De nouveaux progrès de la médecine et de l'hygiène pourraient retarder le moment où cette tendance triomphera, mais ils ne pourront nous y faire échapper.

L'âge moyen de la population augmente, nous vieillissons. Précédemment, le grand nombre des naissances et l'accroissement de la population faisaient que le pays était peuplé d'hommes jeunes. Actuellement tel n'est plus le cas. On a calculé qu'en Allemagne, on devait prévoir un nombre de vieillards deux fois plus élevé dans trente ans, pour une population presque identique. Il en sera de même chez nous, même plus vite qu'en Allemagne.

La mortalité est conditionnée par des facteurs démographiques assez complexes. La Belgique compte actuellement chaque année quelque 105,000 morts, ce qui semble constituer un progrès par rapport à l'avant-guerre, où avec une population moindre, on enregistrait ordinairement plus de 110,000 morts. Mais ce fait est dû principalement à la diminution de la mortalité infantile. Toutes choses égales d'ailleurs, une forte natalité s'accompagne toujours d'une forte mortalité, étant donné les nombreux décès de la première année.

Par ailleurs, nous avons dit plus haut qu'une faible natalité élève l'âge moyen de la population, ce qui, après un certain temps, augmente la mortalité. En ce moment, la Belgique a encore une mortalité anormalement basse ; au lieu des 18 pour mille qui seraient indiqués pour une population stationnaire, nous n'avons que 13 ou 14 pour mille. Mais ce taux va augmenter, et faire face à un coefficient supérieur à la normale. Voici, en effet, comment se présentent les résultats d'un calcul que nous avons fait en nous basant sur la mortalité actuelle, mais en tenant compte de l'âge de la population. Ceci, sans les réserves faites au début de cet article, vu l'insuffisance des données statistiques indispensables.

NOMBRE MOYEN DE MORTS À PRÉVOIR

1931–1940	..	..	..	116,000 soit 14·5 pour mille
1941–1950	..	..	..	130,000 soit 16·2 pour mille
1951–1960	..	..	..	135,000 soit 17·3 pour mille
1961–1970	..	..	..	140,000 soit 18·8 pour mille

Il s'agit là, notons-le, de moyennes décennales approximatives. Pas plus que le calcul des naissances, celui-ci ne tient compte des immigrés ;

pour la commodité des calculs, nous avons écarté Eupen-Malmédy, la décomposition par âge de sa population de figurant pas au recensement de 1920.

Il résulte donc de tout cela que la Belgique connaîtra à bref délai l'équlibre des naissances et des décès, puis le déficit des naissances. La population belge arrive à un maximum. Elle y sera peut-être vers 1940. Après cette époque commencera une lente régression, qui ensuite s'accélérera. Le calcul très approximatif que voici donnera une idée de ce que pourra être la Belgique d'ici 70 ans, abstraction faite de l'apport des immigrés.

POPULATION BELGE PROBABLE, D'APRÈS LES NAISSANCES ET LES DÉCÈS*

1930	7,910,000
1940	8,110,000
1950	7,910,000
1960	7,680,000
1970	7,255,000
1980	6,725,000
1990	6,240,000
2000	5,760,000

La France, pays de basse natalité depuis longtemps, est déjà arrivée au point où pratiquement sa population autochtone cesse de progresser. En dépit de l'assimilation et de la naturalisation rapides, des grandes facilités d'option ou d'acquisition de la nationalité, le nombre des Français diminue, ainsi qu'il appert au tableau que voici. Afin de rendre les chiffres comparables, nous avons, d'une part, ajouté 1,700,000 habitants aux chiffres d'avant la guerre, pour tenir compte de la réintégration de l'Alsace-Lorraine; nous avons ajouté, d'autre part, aux chiffres d'après-guerre, 1,400,000 habitants pour compenser les pertes subies de 1914 à 1918. Il résulte de cela que le nombre des Français, après avoir atteint 40,171,000 en 1911, était revenu en 1926 à 39,646,000, dont il fallait déduire 1,400,000 morts de la guerre.

Ce résultat est dû, naturellement, à l'insuffisance de la natalité pendant la guerre; actuellement, la France a de nouveau des excédents. Mais ils sont imputables pour la plus grande partie à l'apport des étrangers immigrés.

* Non compris Eupen-Malmédy (62,000 habitants) et les immigrés de la période postérieure à 1920. La répartition par âge de la population d'Eupen-Malmédy n'est pas connue.

On a essayé récemment en France d'établir quel était le nombre des naissances dûes aux étrangers, et leur intervention dans les décès. Les chiffres, qui ne sont pas absolument complets, concernent l'année 1927 et viennent d'être publiés.*

Le nombre de naissances d'étrangers serait de 62,000, sur 744,000. Mais ce chiffre ne contient pas les enfants nés de mère française et de père étranger, parce qu'ils sont Français depuis la loi du 10 août 1927. Comme il semble en exister 15,000, le total serait de 77,000. Quant au nombre des décès d'étrangers, il serait compris entre 30 et 35,000. On peut donc estimer l'excédent des naissances étrangères à 40,000 sur les 68,300 enregistrés pour 1927.

MOUVEMENT DE LA POPULATION DE LA FRANCE

Années	Population légale totale (y compris à toutes les dates l'Alsace-Lorraine)	Étrangers	Français	Français (y compris les 1,400,000 morts de la guerre)
1901	40,661,000	1,038,000	39,623,000	39,623,000
1906	40,952,000	1,009,000	39,943,000	39,943,000
1911	41,304,000	1,133,000	40,171,000	40,171,000
1921	39,210,000	1,550,000	37,660,000	39,060,000
1926	40,744,000	2,498,000	38,246,000	39,646,000

Nous ignorons comment les choses se présentent depuis lors. L'année 1929 vit, par suite de l'hiver rigoureux, un excédent de 13,000 morts, alors que 1930 donna un excédent de 100,000 naissances. Si nous prenons une moyenne, il reste peu de chose pour un excédent proprement français, surtout étant donné que le nombre des étrangers n'a pas cessé d'augmenter jusqu'en 1930.

Les calculs esquissés plus haut ne nous permettent cependant pas de dire ce qu'en fait sera la population de la Belgique. La population d'un pays ne dépend qu'assez peu de sa natalité, et de ses excédents de naissances. Elle est conditionnée par les possibilités d'emploi que l'on trouve dans le pays en question. Lorsque la main-d'œuvre manque, elle vient de l'étranger; quand elle est en excès, elle émigre. Livrée à ses seules forces, la France verrait sans doute sa population reculer; mais le nombre des étrangers qui s'y rendent fait augmenter malgré tout le nombre des habitants.

* *Statistique du Mouvement de la Population,* Tome VII, 1re partie, Paris, 1930.

La population de la Belgique dépendra de l'activité industrielle du pays. Si nous supposons que non seulement cette activité se maintiendra, mais qu'elle progressera encore, nous devons admettre que l'immigration étrangère va s'intensifier. L'afflux de ces dernières années n'est donc pas un mouvement temporaire; c'est, au contraire, l'amorce d'une vaste transformation ethnique, qui affectera tout l'ouest de l'Europe, et en particulier la France et la Belgique.

On sait que la France, consciente du danger qu'elle court, s'efforce de hâter l'assimilation des étrangers. La loi du 10 août 1927, citée plus haut, poursuit ouvertement ce but. Aussi, le nombre des acquisitions de nationalité a été de 72,000 en 1928 et de 71,000 en 1929; celui des naturalisations, respectivement de 16,500 et de 14,000. Dans ces conditions, les statistiques divisant la population en Français et en étrangers n'auront bientôt plus de signification.

D'où viendrait l'afflux des immigrants? L'Italie pourrait en fournir pendant plusieurs dizaines d'années encore, mais guère au delà. Elle suit, en effet, le même chemin que les autres nations; sa natalité recule progressivement, et dès aujourd'hui elle ne permet plus d'entrevoir qu'un statu quo, pour un avenir assez éloigné. L'immigration italienne s'étendra probablement dans le Midi de la France, comme elle le fit déjà une première fois au début de l'ère chrétienne. C'est peut-être la Pologne qui fournira le contingent d'émigrants que le vide de nos pays appellera.

Nos pays seraient ainsi destinés à devenir progressivement slaves; la France a déjà commencé. Cette immigration atténuerait naturellement les dommages signalés plus haut, mais elle ne les ferait pas entièrement disparaître.

L'immigration à prévoir aura comme conséquence de modifier fortement les chiffres donnés plus haut, en ce qui concerne la natalité, la mortalité et la population. Les étrangers apporteront avec eux leur mentalité, et leur natalité plus élevée qui relèvera celle de la Belgique. D'autre part, cet afflux d'hommes jeunes maintiendra la mortalité plus bas qu'elle ne le serait sans cela. Nos chiffres ne doivent donc être retenus que comme des tendances.

Il reste cependant qu'en toute hypothèse la natalité des autochtones baissera, et que l'augmentation de la population sera plus de celle du passé. Ceci aura une influence sur beaucoup de choses et notamment sur les finances publiques.

Jusqu'ici, l'augmentation ininterrompue des dépenses et des dettes publiques a été rachetée par l'augmentation du nombre des contribuables. Ainsi furent effacées bien des fautes financières qu'on devait croire inexpiables. Dans un avenir plus ou moins lointain, il n'en ira plus de même, à moins que l'afflux de l'étranger non seulement compense notre déficit, mais aussi fasse progresser la population.

Retenons encore que nous allons de plus en plus devenir une nation de vieillards. La gérontocratie a l'avenir devant elle, surtout en présence des progrès incontestables de l'hygiène et de la médecine.

Nos calculs sont, à cet égard, entachés d'une incertitude de plus. Nous nous sommes basés sur la mortalité actuelle; mais rien ne dit que la vie humaine ne pourra être prolongée encore. S'il en était ainsi, les échéances que nous venons de fixer seraient retardées; elles demeureraient cependant inévitables.

Quoi qu'il en soit, voici comment, à vingt ans de distance, se présentera le nombre de personnes âgées de plus de 65 ans:

HABITANTS ÂGÉS DE PLUS DE 65 ANS

1920	..	..	..	..	.. 487,000
1940	..	..	..	..	.. 780,000
1960	..	..	..	..	.. 965,000
1980	..	..	..	..	.. 1,058,000

Bref, ces personnes âgées, au lieu de représenter $6\frac{1}{2}$ pour cent comme en 1920, arriveront un jour à constituer 16 pour cent de la population.

III. Le mouvement migratoire que nous sommes amenés à considérer comme probable doit être placé dans un cadre d'une amplitude insoupçonnée. Il est la répétition de ces grandes invasions dont la lointaine histoire a gardé le souvenir. L'Europe Occidentale en a été maintes fois le théâtre; à plusieurs reprises des invasions, pacifiques ou guerrières, ont fait affluer sur son sol des populations originaires de l'Est.

Nous avons l'habitude de considérer les Gaulois comme les premiers habitants des régions situées à l'ouest du Rhin. Les historiens des derniers temps assurent, au contraire, que les Gaulois seraient en réalité les quatrièmes occupants dont on a retrouvé la trace. D'après Camille Jullian,* il a existé d'abord une race constituée par des tribus de chasseurs; une race dite de "Cro-Magnon," plus intelligente et plus robuste, lui a succédé. "Dans le cours des derniers millénaires avant notre ère," une nouvelle invasion est signalée, probablement non

* De la Gaule à la France.

pacifique; une population plus rude et vivant de l'agriculture s'établit dans nos régions. Ce ne serait qu'en quatrième lieu, environ deux mille ans avant notre ère, que sont arrivées les populations appelées indo-européennes, auxquelles appartenaient les Celtes, dont les Gaulois faisaient partie.

Il y eut ensuite la conquête romaine, qui ne fut pas à proprement parler une migration, puis les invasions germaniques, au Ve siècle surtout. Depuis lors, l'Europe Occidentale est restée relativement stable, et a même fourni d'appréciables contingents d'émigrants. Mais depuis le début du XIXe siècle, on notait déjà qu'en Europe la rang des pays latins se maintenait péniblement, pendant qu'au contraire les Slaves progressaient. D'après M. Kuczynski, les pays latins, qui représentaient 37 pour cent de la population, sont revenus à 25 pour cent du commencement à la fin du XIXe siècle, pendant que les Slaves passaient de 25 à 37 pour cent, prenant exactement la place des premiers.

Depuis quelques années, le mouvement s'est accéléré. C'est la Pologne qui a joué le rôle principal, en choisissant pour champ d'émigration la France et la Belgique, alors que précédemment elle s'intéressait plus à l'Amérique et à l'Allemagne. Mais les États-Unis restreignent fortement l'immigration et l'Allemagne a présentement de la main-d'œuvre en excès, outre que des difficultés politiques rendent les Polonais moins désirables.

A l'heure présente, il semble y avoir quelque 50,000 Polonais en Belgique, d'après les services consulaires de leur pays d'origine, contre 5,300 recensés en 1920; en France, d'après la même source, il y en aurait 700,000 au lieu des 45,000 accusés par le recensement de 1921.

Le mouvement, on le voit, n'est nullement négligeable; la crise économique le ralentira, mais le déficit de main-d'œuvre se fera de nouveau sentir rapidement, en France du moins.

Parmi les 50,000 Polonais qui se trouvent en ce moment en Belgique, un certain nombre travaillent dans les mines. Mais il y en a beaucoup dans l'industrie diamantaire d'Anvers, et dans le commerce; la proportion de Juifs y est assez forte.

Nous ignorons si la natalité polonaise sera suffisante à repeupler le Centre et l'Ouest de l'Europe devant la carence des habitants actuels. D'autre part, la Pologne nourrit la legitime ambition de donner du travail à tous ceux qui aujourd'hui sont forcés de s'expatrier. Il n'est pas douteux que ce pays, pleinement mis en exploitation, pourrait avoir une population de 50 millions au lieu de 30. Mais il réduira aussi un jour sa mortalité enfantile, ce qui accroîtra sensiblement ses excédents de naissances sur les décès.

Quoi qu'il en soit, si la Pologne suivait les autres nations sur le chemin de la dénatalité ou retenait chez elle sa population, pour éviter le dépeuplement et la décadence de l'Europe Occidentale, c'est la Russie peut-être qui devrait faire l'appoint; ses excédents actuels de naissance sont formidables.

La situation particulière de la Russie confère à cette question un intérêt capital. Certes, nous ignorons où en seront les Soviets dans vingt ou cinquante ans, et il est possible que l'on n'en parlera plus alors. Mais supposons que le régime ait duré et qu'en face d'une Russie surpeuplée, comptant 300 millions d'habitants, jeunes, fanatisés, se croyant investis d'une mission rédemptrice, on ne puisse opposer qu'un ensemble morcelé, comptant une population à peu près équivalente, mais vieillie, engourdie par la prospérité et au surplus manquant d'unité de commandement—souvent déchirée de dissensions intestines —que ne peut-on craindre?

Si la migration russe doit être pacifique et se faire sous l'égide d'un autre régime que celui des Soviets, le dommage sera moindre. Il restera que l'Europe serait colonisée par les peuples de l'Est. Ceux-ci pourraient, il est vrai, se trouver un jour atteints eux-mêmes par la dénatalité; la chose est possible, mais ces nations ont des chances d'y résister plus longtemps. Elles n'ont pas le culte de leurs aises, l'excès de calcul et de prévoyance qui sont les causes principales de la dépopulation de nos pays. En tous cas, les peuples auxquels nous appartenons, subiraient les conséquences de la politique qu'ils pratiquent en ce moment; ils sont probablement condamnés à disparaître, ou à se laisser absorber par les nouveaux venus.

Il subsiste d'ailleurs une grosse incertitude en ce qui concerne cette migration. Les éléments slaves seraient-ils assimilés par les populations actuelles, comme le furent souvent les peuples envahisseurs? En ce qui concerne la France, c'est assez probable; ce pays a assimilé déjà tant d'étrangers sans difficulté que vraisemblablement il gardera en bonne partie son individualité actuelle. Ce n'est pas aussi sûr pour les autres, et notamment pour la Belgique surtout si, comme tout tend à l'indiquer, c'est surtout dans le Nord-Est du pays, partie à peu près exclusivement flamande, que ces étrangers s'établissent.

Mais, dira-t-on, n'y a-t-il pas de chance que la natalité de nos pays se relève? Nous craignons qu'il n'y ait que peu d'espoir à concevoir à cet égard, encore qu'il ne faille n'en négliger pour y parvenir. Il faut prévoir au contraire que certains îlots de résistance devront encore capituler, ce qui abaissera la moyenne. Un certain facteur de relèvement peut être aperçu dans la sélection que voici: les familles comptant un nombre relativement élevé d'enfants laissent derrière elles des continuateurs, alors que les ménages sans enfants ou avec peu d'enfants ne laissent rien. La population comptera donc une plus forte proportion de gens issus de milieux où les traditions familiales et la non-limitation des naissances étaient en honneur. Toutefois, il faut compter avec les transfuges.

Du reste, nous ne trouvons aucun exemple de natalités qui se soient relevées d'elles-mêmes. On ne les rencontre, à notre connaissance, que lors de la christianisation de populations jusqu'alors païennes. Mais normalement ce sont les immigrants qui, en apportant leurs mœurs et leurs traditions, relèvent la natalité.

Les historiens des prochains millénaires écriront sans doute, en parlant de notre époque, qu'elle vit la cinquième grande invasion de l'Ouest de l'Europe, et ils en situeront les débuts à la guerre mondiale. Vu de Sirius, ce chapitre éventuel de l'histoire de l'humanité ne manque pas d'être intéressant.

APPENDICES

I. MOUVEMENT DE LA POPULATION

CHIFFRES PRINCIPAUX

	Naissances	Décès	Mariages	Proportions par 1,000 habitants		
				Naissances	Décès	Mariages
Belgique:						
1900	194,000	129,000	57,700	29·0	19·3	8·6
1910	176,000	113,000	58,800	23·7	15·2	7·9
1928	147,000	106,000	71,500	18·4	13·2	8·9
1929	146,000	121,000	71,800	18·1	15·0	8·9
1930	151,000	107,000	71,600	18·6	13·2	8·8
France:						
1901*	858,000	785,000	303,000	22·0	20·1	7·8
1910*	774,000	703,000	308,000	19·6	17·8	7·8
1928	745,000	675,000	339,000	18·2	16·5	8·3
1929	729,000	741,000	334,000	17·7	18·0	8·1
1930	749,000	649,000	343,000	18·1	15·7	8·3
Allemagne:						
1900†	1,996,000	1,236,000	476,000	35·6	22·1	8·5
1910†	1,925,000	1,046,000	496,000	29·8	16·6	7·7
1928	1,182,000	740,000	589,000	18·6	11·6	9·2
1929	1,147,000	806,000	590,000	17·9	12·6	9·2
1930	1,127,000	711,000	562,000	17·5	11·0	8·7
Italie:						
1896–1900†	1,085,000	732,000	228,000	33·9	22·9	7·1
1910†	1,144,000	682,000	269,000	32·9	19·6	7·8
1928	1,078,000	646,000	285,000	26·2	15·8	7·0
1929	1,040,000	664,000	288,000	25·2	16·1	7·0
1930	1,085,000	579,000	297,000	26·0	13·7	7·1

* Non compris l'Alsace-Lorraine, donnant actuellement 35,000 naissances, 26,000 décès et 15,000 mariages.
† Anciennes frontières.

II. POPULATION PROBABLE DE LA BELGIQUE*

D'Après les Naissances et les Décès à Prévoir

Nombre d'habitants	1910	%	1920	%	1930	%	1940	%
De moins de 10 ans ..	1,525,000	20·6	1,153,000	15·7	1,359,000	17·1	1,210,000	15·0
De 10 à moins de 20 ans ..	1,429,000	19·2	1,424,000	19·2	1,120,000	14·2	1,300,000	16·0
De 20 à moins de 30 ans ..	1,238,000	16·7	1,287,000	17·4	1,370,000	17·3	1,070,000	13·1
De 30 à moins de 40 ans ..	1,078,000	14·5	1,092,000	14·7	1,220,000	15·5	1,290,000	15·9
De 40 à moins de 50 ans ..	840,000	11·3	965,000	13·2	1,030,000	13·0	1,140,000	14·2
De 50 à moins de 60 ans ..	614,000	8·3	726,000	9·7	880,000	11·1	930,000	11·4
De 60 à moins de 70 ans ..	424,000	5·7	469,000	6·3	600,000	7·5	710,000	8·8
De 70 ans et plus ..	276,000	3·7	290,000	3·8	349,000	4·3	460,000	5·6
	7,424,000	100·0	7,406,000	100·0	7,910,000	100·0	8,110,000	100·0

Nombre d'habitants	1950	%	1960	%	1970	%
De moins de 10 ans ..	980,000	12·4	1,000,000	13·0	875,000	12·1
De 10 à moins de 20 ans ..	1,160,000	14·6	940,000	12·3	955,000	13·2
De 20 à moins de 30 ans ..	1,240,000	15·6	1,100,000	14·4	900,000	12·4
De 30 à moins de 40 ans ..	1,000,000	12·7	1,170,000	15·2	1,040,000	14·3
De 40 à moins de 50 ans ..	1,200,000	15·2	940,000	12·2	1,090,000	15·0
De 50 à moins de 60 ans ..	1,030,000	13·0	1,080,000	14·1	845,000	11·6
De 60 à moins de 70 ans ..	750,000	9·5	850,000	11·1	899,000	12·3
De 70 ans et plus ..	550,000	7·0	600,000	7·7	666,000	9·1
	7,910,000	100·0	7,680,000	100·0	7,255,000	100·0

* Ces chiffres ne comprennent ni la population d'Eupen-Malmédy (62,000 habitants), ni l'excédent des immigrés à partir de 1920.

Fifth Session

GENERAL POPULATION

Chairmen: (*a*) PROFESSOR JENS WARMING
(*b*) DR. S. D. WICKSELL

Papers read:

PAPER No. 20

THE STRUCTURE OF A GROWING POPULATION

By Dr. ALFRED J. LOTKA

(*Metropolitan Life Insurance Company, New York*)

TABLE OF CONTENTS

THE STRUCTURE OF A GROWING POPULATION

INTRODUCTION

FOR the sake of brevity, and to avoid technical terms, I have chosen for my title "The Structure of a Growing Population." I should state at the outset, however, that I propose to deal expressly with the characteristics of a population growing according to the logistic law.

As is well known, the logistic curve of growth has been found to fit certain populations rather well. One of the best, and, for us at any rate, the most important example of this, is the population of the United States, which, at the recent Census of 1930,* fell within 400,000, or less than one-third of 1 per cent., of the calculated figure. I may say that we shall not here be concerned with a forecast, and therefore the question whether the population of the United States will continue to grow according to the logistic does not arise. We are here solely concerned with the fact that it has closely followed the logistic in the past, and this is established beyond possible dispute.

Now, such a population, which has for an extended period of time been following the logistic law, has a definite pattern. Its demographic characteristics are not fortuitous or capricious, but conform to a type or model determined by the logistic law of growth itself. It is my purpose on this occasion to present a view of some of these typical characteristics of a logistic population, and to show how the model compares with the actually observed population. We want to know, for example, what is the typical trend, in such a population, of the birth-rate, the net fertility, the death-rate, the distribution by age and sex, the discrepancy between the "true" or "inherent" rate of natural increase, and the observed excess of the birth-rate over the death-rate.

In the treatment of the problem the following plan will be followed: We shall first of all examine the situation as it presents itself in a simplified or conventionalized case, namely, that of a population in which the life table remains unchanged and in which immigration and emigration are negligible.

* Pearl, R., *Science*, 1930, vol. 72, p. 399. The forecast of the population of the United States for 1930 by the logistic curve of Pearl and Reed was 122·4 millions. The actual enumeration at the Census was 122·8 millions.

Upon the results obtained for this simplified case we shall then build a representation of the more general case, corresponding to actual conditions, in which the life table is subject to a secular drift, and in which immigration and emigration form a notable part of the changes in the number of the population.

ARGUMENT

Consider the process by which the existing age distribution has come into being. Persons who are now ten years old were born ten years ago. Of the persons born at that time a certain fraction, determined by the life table, survives to the present day and forms the ten-year-old contingent of the existing population. A similar statement applies to every individual year of life.

FUNDAMENTAL EQUATION

Our fundamental formula, therefore, is

$$N(t) = \int_0^\infty B(t-a)p(a)da \quad . \quad . \quad . \quad . \quad (1)$$

This states that the total number $N(t)$ of persons living at time t is the sum of the survivors to every age a of $B(t-a)da$ persons born at time $t-a$ in a small interval of time da. The symbol $p(a)$ denotes the probability, at birth, of living to age a,* that is, the fraction, out of a given large number born, that survive to age a. The formula applies to an "isolated" population, in which immigration and emigration are negligible.

APPLICATION TO LOGISTIC POPULATION: ANNUAL BIRTHS†

If we apply this fundamental equation to the case of a population growing according to the logistic law we have

$$\int_0^\infty B(t-a)p(a)da = \frac{N_\infty}{1 + e^{-rt}} = N_\infty(e^{rt} - e^{2rt} + e^{3rt} - \ldots) \quad . \quad (2)$$

where N_∞ is the ultimate population.

* In actuarial notation $p(a)$ would be written l_x/l_0.
† A preliminary and partial account of the development set forth in this section has been given by the writer in the *Proceedings*, National Academy

Making the trial substitution

$$B(t) = U_1 e^{rt} - U_2 e^{2rt} + \ldots \qquad \cdots \quad (3)$$

we find that this satisfies the fundamental equation provided that

$$U_k = \frac{N_\infty}{\displaystyle\int_0^\infty e^{-kra} p(a)\,da} \qquad \cdots \quad (4)$$

We will write

$$b_k = \frac{1}{\displaystyle\int_0^\infty e^{-kra} p(a)\,da} = c_0 + c_1 kr + c_2 k^2 r^2 + \ldots \quad \cdots \quad (5)$$

The coefficients c are readily found by expanding the exponential function under the integral sign; denoting by L_n the nth moment of the function $p(a)$, that is, putting

$$\int_0^\infty a^n p(a)\,da = L_n \qquad \cdots \quad (6)$$

Science, 1929, vol. 15, pp. 793–798. An analysis of a population in which the annual births (not the population) follow a logistic curve has been given by E. Zwinggi, *Beiträge zu einer Theorie des Bevölkerungswachstums*, 1929.

The problem here solved has been referred to by U. Yule (*Journal of the Royal Statistical Society*, 1925, vol. 88, Part I, p. 35) in these words: "I see no general method of effectively attacking this problem at present, and have contented myself with working out a couple of cases as illustrations." Yule sets up an initial population with an arbitrarily given age distribution (namely, in one example a life table age distribution, in his other example a Malthusian age distribution), and then computes step by step the ensuing age distributions and death-rates, hence birth-rates.

It is to be noted that in the development set forth in the present communication no hypothesis of any kind is made regarding any initial age distribution. The problem is found to be entirely determinate without any such hypothesis, the logistic law defining its own age distribution for all time from $-\infty$ to $+\infty$. This, therefore, furnishes the answer to Yule's perplexity (loc. cit., p. 55): "I was at first puzzled how to arrive at the population at $t = -4$ (of Yule's units) . . . without a good deal of troublesome approximation." Yule then cuts the Gordian knot by assuming initially a Malthusian age distribution, a step which is pragmatically justified by the fact that logistic growth in its early stages is very nearly Malthusian. But in the method here set forth the perplexity of an initial age distribution does not arise at all.

we find

$$c_0 = \frac{1}{L_0}; \quad c_1 = \frac{L_1}{L_0^2}; \quad c_2 = \frac{L_1^2}{L_0^3} - \frac{L_2}{2L_0^2};$$

$$c_3 = \frac{L_1^3}{L_0^4} - \frac{L_1 L_2}{L_0^3} + \frac{L_3}{6L_0^2};$$

$$c_4 = \frac{L_1^4}{L_0^5} - \frac{3L_1^2 L_2}{2L_0^4} + \frac{L_1 L_3}{3L_0^3} + \frac{L_2^2}{4L_0^3} - \frac{L_4}{24L_0^2};$$

$$c_5 = \frac{L_1^5}{L_0^6} - \frac{2L_1^3 L_2}{L_0^5} + \frac{L_1^2 L_3}{2L_0^4} + \frac{3L_1 L_2^2}{4L_0^4};$$

$$- \frac{L_2 L_3}{6L_0^3} - \frac{L_1 L_4}{12L_0^3} + \frac{L_5}{120L_0^2}.$$

$$\qquad \cdot \quad \cdot \quad (7)$$

Substituting these expressions for b_k in (3), and rearranging terms by collecting according to ascending powers of r instead of ascending powers of e^{rt}, we find

$$B(t) = N_\infty e^{rt} \left\{ \frac{c_0}{(1 + e^{rt})} + \frac{c_1 r}{(1 + e^{rt})^2} + \frac{c_2 r^2 (1 - e^{rt})}{(1 + e^{rt})^3} \right.$$

$$+ \frac{c_3 r^3 (1 - 4e^{rt} + e^{2rt})}{(1 + e^{rt})^4} + \frac{c_4 r^4 (1 - 11 e^{rt} + 11 e^{2rt} - e^{3rt})}{(1 + e^{rt})^5}$$

$$+ \frac{c_5 r^5 (1 - 26 e^{rt} + 66 e^{2rt} - 26 e^{3rt} + e^{4rt})}{(1 + e^{rt})^6} + \ldots$$

$$\left. + \frac{c_j r^j}{(1 + e^{rt})^{j+1}} \sum_{n=1}^{n=j} (-e^{rt})^{n-1} \sum_{\omega=0}^{\omega=n-1} (-1)^\omega \binom{j+1}{\omega} (n - \omega)^j + \ldots \right\}$$

$$\qquad \qquad \qquad (8)$$

$$= N_\infty \left\{ c_0 e^{rt} f(t) - \sum_1^\infty c_j f^j(t) \right\} \quad . \quad . \quad . \quad . \quad . \quad . \quad . \quad (9)$$

where

$$f(t) = \frac{1}{1 + e^{rt}} = \tfrac{1}{2} - \tfrac{1}{2} \tanh \frac{rt}{2} \quad . \quad . \quad . \quad (10)$$

and $f^j(t)$ denotes the jth derivative of $f(t)$ with respect to t. Or, writing

$$\phi(t) = \frac{1}{1 + e^{-rt}} = \tfrac{1}{2} + \tfrac{1}{2} \tanh \frac{rt}{2} \text{ and noting that then } f^n(t) = (-1)^n \phi^n(t)$$

we effect a slight simplification, namely,

$$B(t) = N_\infty \left\{ c_0\phi(t) - \sum_1^\infty (-1)^j c_j \phi^j(t) \right\} \quad \cdots \quad (11)$$

Computation is greatly facilitated by expressing $f(t)$ and $\phi(t)$ in hyperbolic tangent form.

TRANSFORMATION OF ORIGIN

The expression (8) for $B(t)$ can be simplified by the introduction of a new set of parameters b' and a shift of the origin of t, the time scale.

TRANSFORMATION OF COEFFICIENTS c

In analogy with the constants b_k defined above (5), let us introduce a new set of constants

$$b'_k = \cfrac{1}{\int_0^\infty e^{-kr(a-\tau)}p(a)da} \quad \cdots \quad (12)$$

$$= \cfrac{1}{e^{kr\tau}\int_0^\infty e^{-kra}p(a)da} \quad \cdots \quad (13)$$

$$= e^{-kr\tau}b_k \quad \cdots \quad (14)$$

Now it is evident from (5) that

$$c_j = \left(\frac{1}{j!}\frac{d^j b_1}{dr^j} \right)_{r=0} \quad \cdots \quad (15)$$

and similarly, in terms of the primed parameters

$$c'_j = \left(\frac{1}{j!}\frac{d^j b'_1}{dr^j} \right)_{r=0} \quad \cdots \quad (16)$$

Thus, for example,

$$c'_1 = \left(\frac{db'_1}{dr} \right)_{r=0} = \left(-\tau e^{-r\tau}b_1 + e^{-r\tau}\frac{db_1}{dr} \right)_{r=0} \quad \cdots \quad (17)$$

$$= -\tau b_0 + c_1 = c_1 - \tau c_0 \quad \cdots \quad (18)$$

and similarly for higher coefficients. We thus find

$$
\left.
\begin{aligned}
c_1' &= c_1 - \tau c_0 \\[1em]
c_2' &= c_2 - \tau c_1 + \frac{\tau^2}{2!}c_0 \\[1em]
c_3' &= c_3 - \tau c_2 + \frac{\tau^2}{2!}c_1 - \frac{\tau^3}{3!}c_0 \\[1em]
c_4' &= c_4 - \tau c_3 + \frac{\tau^2}{2!}c_2 - \frac{\tau^3}{3!}c_1 + \frac{\tau_4}{4!}c_0 \\[1em]
c_5' &= c_5 - \tau c_4 + \frac{\tau^2}{2!}c_3 - \frac{\tau^3}{3!}c_2 + \frac{\tau^4}{4!}c_1 - \frac{\tau^5}{5!}c_0
\end{aligned}
\right\} \quad . \quad . \quad (19)
$$

or in general

$$
c_n' = \sum_{k=0}^{k=n} \frac{(-\tau)^{(n-k)}}{(n-k)!}c_k \cdot \quad . \quad . \quad . \quad . \quad (20)
$$

These formulæ apply quite generally for any value of τ. If, in particular, τ is the mean λ_1 defined by

$$
\lambda_1 = \frac{\displaystyle\int_0^\infty a p(a)da}{\displaystyle\int_0^\infty p(a)da} = \frac{L_1}{L_0} \quad . \quad . \quad . \quad . \quad (21)
$$

then the formulæ (19) reduce to very simple functions of the Thiele seminvariants of the function $p(a)$, as follows:

$$
\left.
\begin{aligned}
c_0'' &= \frac{1}{L_0} \\[1em]
c_1'' &= 0 \\[1em]
c_2'' &= -\frac{\lambda_2}{2!L_0} \\[1em]
c_3'' &= \frac{\lambda_3}{3!L_0} \\[1em]
c_4'' &= -\frac{1}{4!L_0}\{\lambda_4 - 3\lambda_2^2\} \\[1em]
c_5'' &= \frac{1}{5!L_0}\{\lambda_5 - 10\lambda_2\lambda_3\}
\end{aligned}
\right\} \quad . \quad . \quad . \quad . \quad (22)
$$

Shifting of Origin of Time

Of particular interest is a simultaneous shifting of the origin of time to $t - \lambda_1$ and the introduction of the parameters b', with $\tau = \lambda_1$. Let us consider how this will affect our fundamental equation. The fundamental equation (1) can indifferently be written

$$\int_0^\infty B\{(t - \tau) - (a - \tau)\}p(a)da = N(t) \quad \cdots \quad (23)$$

$$= N_\infty\{e^{rt} - e^{2rt} + \ldots\} \quad (24)$$

Make the trial substitution

$$B(t) = U_1 e^{r(t+\tau)} - U_2 e^{2r(t+\tau)} + \ldots \quad \cdots \quad (25)$$

This gives

$$U_1 e^{rt}\int_0^\infty e^{-r(a-\tau)}p(a)da - U_2 e^{2rt}\int_0^\infty e^{-2r(a-\tau)}p(a)da + \ldots$$

$$= N_\infty(e^{rt} - e^{2rt} + \ldots) \quad \cdot \quad (26)$$

so that the trial is effective provided that

$$U_k = \frac{N_\infty}{\int_0^\infty e^{-kr(a-\tau)}p(a)da} \quad \cdots \quad (27)$$

$$= N_\infty b'_k \cdot \quad \cdots \quad (28)$$

It is clear from this, that all the formulæ developed with reference to the origin of time and age at zero are directly applicable when referred to the origin of time $-\tau$, provided that we understand the coefficients c to be those defined above as c', and that the symbol t in the right-hand member of (8) is understood to denote t', the time reckoned from $-\tau$ as origin, remembering that primarily the origin of time was taken at the centre of the logistic curve $N(t)$.

In particular, when shift of origin is made to time $t - \lambda_1$, the formula for $B(t)$ becomes especially simple in view of the formulæ (22) for the coefficients c''. We then have

$$B(t) = \frac{N_\infty}{L_0}\left\{\phi(t') + \frac{\lambda_2}{2!}\phi^{ii}(t') + \frac{\lambda_3}{3!}\phi^{iii}(t') + \frac{\lambda_4 - 3\lambda_2^2}{4!}\phi^{iv}(t') \right.$$

$$\left. + \frac{\lambda_5 - 10\lambda_2\lambda_3}{5!}\phi^{v}(t') + \ldots\right\} \quad \cdot \quad (29)$$

where $t' = t + \lambda_1$.

For purposes of computation it will be convenient to give this formula *in extenso*, as it appears when $\phi(t)$ is expressed in terms of the hyperbolic tangent:

$$
\begin{aligned}
B(t)=\frac{N_\infty}{L_0}\Bigg\{ &\left(\tfrac{1}{2}+\tfrac{1}{2}\tanh\frac{rt'}{2}\right)+\frac{\lambda_2 r^2}{2\,!4}\left(\tanh\frac{rt'}{2}-\tanh^3\frac{rt'}{2}\right) \\
&-\frac{\lambda_3 r^3}{3\,!8}\left(1-4\tanh^2\frac{rt'}{2}+3\tanh^4\frac{rt'}{2}\right) \\
&-\frac{(\lambda_4-3\lambda_2^2)r^4}{4\,!4}\left(2\tanh\frac{rt'}{2}-5\tanh^3\frac{rt'}{2}+3\tanh^5\frac{rt'}{2}\right) \\
&+\frac{(\lambda_5-10\lambda_2\lambda_3)r^5}{5\,!8}\left(2-17\tanh^2\frac{rt'}{2}+30\tanh^4\frac{rt'}{2}-15\tanh^6\frac{rt'}{2}\right) \\
&-\dots\Bigg\}
\end{aligned}
\tag{30}
$$

NUMERICAL EXAMPLE

The computation has been carried out on the basis of the United States life table 1919–20 (white females*) and the logistic curve of growth of the American population. The resulting curve of computed annual births is shown as a fully drawn line in the first panel of Fig. 1. The components corresponding to successive terms in the series (30) are shown in the first and second panels of Fig. 1. It will be seen that the fundamental component

$$
\frac{N_\infty}{L_0}\left(\tfrac{1}{2}+\tfrac{1}{2}\tanh\frac{rt'}{2}\right) \quad\dots\dots\dots \tag{31}
$$

accounts alone for nearly the entire contingent of births. The higher terms would hardly appear at all on the scale of the first panel in Fig. 1, and have therefore been plotted separately on a scale twenty-five times greater in the second panel. A feature of special interest is that the third and the fifth term, whose presence disturbs the skew-symmetry of the resultant curve, are relatively very small; in consequence the

* Since we are dealing with a model population it is, in principle, immaterial what life table we use. Nevertheless it is desirable to use one corresponding as far as possible to the concrete existing conditions; see also footnote on p. 262.

resultant curve is very nearly skew-symmetric, resembling the simple logistic.

The curve takes its course between two asymptotes, the lower corresponding to a vanishingly small population and number of births,*

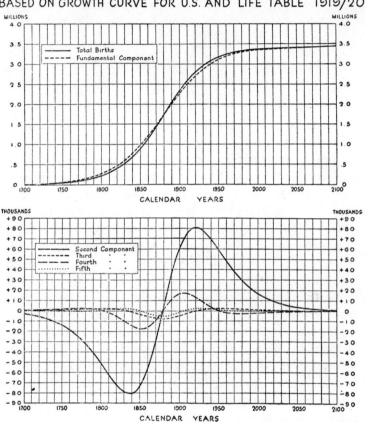

ANNUAL BIRTHS IN LOGISTIC POPULATION
BASED ON GROWTH CURVE FOR U.S. AND LIFE TABLE 1919/20

FIG. 1

the upper corresponding to the ultimate population N_∞ and a stationary birth-rate equal to the reciprocal of the mean length of life. A point of special interest is that the half-way point of the curve of annual births

* Although population and births vanish for $t = -\infty$, the birth-rate per head has a definite value, namely, 0·0419.

is reached earlier than the half-way point of the population growth by a period very nearly equal to λ_1, the "mean age of the living in the life table population." This follows from the fact that the odd components* of the series (29) are very small (as already mentioned), and that the even components have, by the shift of origin, all been made to have their centre of skew-symmetry at the point $t = -\lambda_1$, i.e. at a date thirty-five years prior to the centre of skew-symmetry of the population growth curve.

RELATIVE IMPORTANCE OF HIGHER TERMS IN SERIES (29) AND (30), AND APPROXIMATE COMPUTATIONS

A glance at the diagram Fig. 1 shows at once that the fundamental component alone gives a very fair approximation to the curve of annual births. To this degree of approximation, therefore, the annual births require for their computation a knowledge only of the first two moments L_0 and L_1 of the life curve. The moment L_0 is nothing else than the mean length of life or expectation of life at birth, and therefore requires no computation at all, since it is one of the fundamental data given in all life tables. Thus the only life table characteristic that actually has to be computed for this approximation is the moment L_1, the average age of the living in a life table population. This computation is very easily made.

If a closer approximation is wanted than that given by the first component alone, we can still help ourselves in the following manner, and greatly reduce the labour required, provided that the curve of annual births has been computed for one typical life table. Inspection of panel two, Fig. 1, shows that the higher components (shown there on twenty-five times the scale of the first panel) are relatively very small. Even rather roughly approximate values of the coefficients c_2'', c_3'', . . . are therefore quite sufficient to give the total sum of the components with a very good degree of approximation. This suggests the following simple expedient: Determine the coefficients c_2'', c_3'', . . . for any suitable standard life table, and then use these unchanged when computing the annual births on the basis of any other life table. It goes without saying that it is desirable to use life tables not too widely divergent, but the latitude permissible is very considerable.

* i.e. components containing odd derivatives of ϕ.

Numerical Example

The following example shows with what very satisfactory degree of accuracy it is permissible to use coefficients c_2, c_3, . . . from a previously employed life table, in computing the annual births (in a logistic population) on the basis of a new life table, thus saving the labour of computing new values of these coefficients, only the moments L_0 and L_1 of the new life table being actually required.

Table I

ANNUAL BIRTHS IN LOGISTIC POPULATION, COMPUTED ON BASIS OF GROWTH CURVE FOR UNITED STATES AND LIFE TABLE 1919–1920

Year	All Coefficients, C_k, accurately determined for 1919–20 Life Table	Only Moments L_0 and L_1 accurately determined for 1919–20 Life Table. Higher Coefficients, c_2, c_3, . . ., taken from 1910 Life Table
1800	218,695	218,654
1850	890,975	890,880
1900	2,330,669	2,330,740
1950	3,164,261	3,164,439
2000	3,373,610	3,373,512

Note.—The reader should be reminded that we are here dealing with a model population having the same logistic growth curve as the United States, but growing entirely by excess of births over deaths (that is, without immigration), and with a fixed life table.

Birth-rate per Head

Having found the annual births $B(t)$, the birth-rate per head follows immediately as

$$b(t) = \frac{B(t)}{N(t)} \quad \cdot \quad \cdot \quad \cdot \quad \cdot \quad \cdot \quad \cdot \quad (32)$$

It will be seen from the graph of $b(t)$ in Fig. 2 that this is a nearly skew-symmetric curve resembling an inverted logistic.

Inspection of the curve (Fig. 2) shows that in the early stages of the development of a logistic population the birth-rate declines at first very slowly, then more rapidly. Then follows a period of rather rapid decline, giving way finally to a period of slow decline towards a final stationary level. The point of mid-level is, in this case, reached in the year 1902, about twenty-two years later than the mid-level of the total births (1880), but about twelve years before the mid-level of the population 1914).

BIRTHRATE AND DEATHRATE IN LOGISTIC POPULATION
COMPUTED FOR UNITED STATES, 1700-2100
BASED ON GROWTH CURVE FOR U.S. AND LIFE TABLE 1919/20

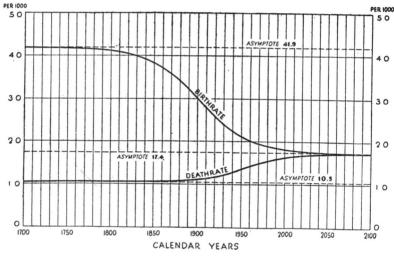

FIG. 2

DEATH-RATE PER HEAD

The birth-rate having been determined, and the rate of increase being given by the logistic curve of growth, the death-rate immediately follows by subtraction as rate of increase minus birth-rate. The figures thus computed for the case of a fixed life table are represented graphically in Fig. 2 together with the birth-rate curve. The detailed discussion of this curve may with advantage be deferred to a later section, where comparison will be made with the corresponding curve as computed on the basis of a fluent life table.

Age Distribution

Given the annual births and the survival function $p(a)$, the age distribution follows at once; for the persons which at any particular moment are between a and $a + da$ years old are the survivors of those born at time $t - a$ in a time interval da, that is to say

$$N(t)c(a)da = B(t - a)p(a)da \quad . \quad . \quad . \quad . \quad . \quad (33)$$

$$c(a) = \frac{B(t - a)}{N(t)}p(a) \quad . \quad . \quad . \quad . \quad . \quad (34)$$

The curves of age distribution for successive quarter centuries have been computed on the basis of the United States life table 1919–20 and of the logistic curve for the United States, and are shown as a solid model in Figs. 3 and 4. The former presents a view of the model as seen from the face corresponding to the early stages of development, the latter a view from the "late" face.

The upper edge at the back of the surface representing the age distribution corresponds to age zero, and therefore represents the curve of birth-rate per head which thus appears as a repetition of the birth-rate curve in Fig. 2. Birth-rate and age distribution are closely interrelated and interdependent, the persons of age zero being the newly born, so that the first point in the curve of age distribution represents the birth-rate per head.

In the early stages the curve of age distribution is concave upward throughout its extent, and exhibits a high birth-rate, and a high proportion of young persons (see Fig. 3). In the late stages (see Fig. 4) the age distribution is convex upward over a considerable range of ages; birth-rate and proportion of young people are low. At intervening stages the age distribution passes through transitional types, giving rise to the "warped" surface of the diagram. It will be worth while to give a little closer consideration to these two extreme types and to the transitional type of age distribution.

Stable or Malthusian Age Distribution

It will be remembered that in its early stages the logistic law of growth coincides nearly with the Malthusian law of geometric rate of increase (compound interest law). Accordingly, the age distribution in the early stages of the growth of a population is very nearly the Malthusian (or "stable") age distribution corresponding to the fertility and mortality which prevail at the time, and which at this stage change very slowly, that is, are nearly constant. The form of this Malthusian or stable age distribution is

$$c(a) = be^{-ra}p(a) \quad . \quad . \quad . \quad . \quad . \quad . \quad (35)$$

AGE DISTRIBUTION IN LOGISTIC POPULATION
SHOWING TRANSITION FROM MALTHUSIAN TO STATIONARY TYPE *

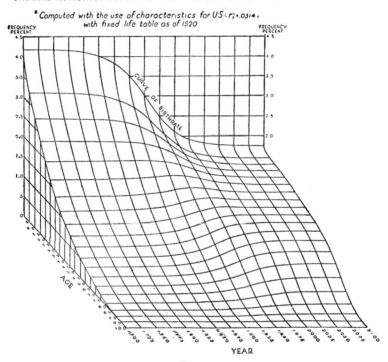

FIG. 3

where $c(a)$ is the coefficient of age distribution, such that $c(a)da$ gives the proportion, in the total population, of persons whose age is comprised within the limits a and $a + da$; the symbol b denotes the birth-rate per head per annum; $p(a)$ is the probability,* at birth, of reaching age a, and r is the incipient rate of increase per head per annum, which for the United States has a value of 0·0314.

* Commonly denoted in actuarial notations by l_x/l_0, or simply by l_x if it is understood that the radix of the life table is unity at age zero.

STATIONARY OR LIFE TABLE AGE DISTRIBUTION

In its terminal stages a population following the logistic curve of growth approaches a stationary state. The age distribution is then not only

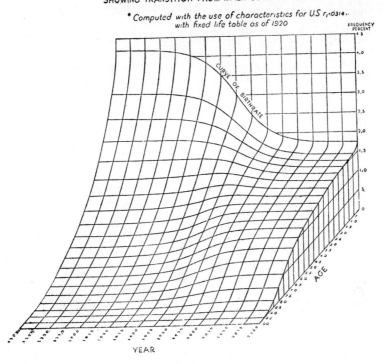

AGE DISTRIBUTION IN LOGISTIC POPULATION
SHOWING TRANSITION FROM MALTHUSIAN TO STATIONARY TYPE*

*Computed with the use of characteristics for U.S. r_1 .0314 .. with fixed life table as of 1920

FIG. 4

stable, but conforms directly to the life table, since the formula (35) above, when $r = 0$, reduces to

$$c(a) = b_0 p(a) \qquad \ldots \qquad \ldots \qquad (35a)$$

where b_0 is the stationary birth-rate per head, and is equal to the reciprocal $\dfrac{1}{L_0}$ of the mean length of life.

AGE DISTRIBUTION: PLANE DIAGRAM

Another representation of the trend of the age distribution in a logistic population is shown in the "plane" diagram Fig. 5, which brings out certain important points with particular clarity. As regards the general character of the diagram, it is to be noted first of all that for the younger ages the trend of the proportion of persons of a given age is systematically downward, in the form of an inverted S. When we come to the age

AGE DISTRIBUTION FOR LOGISTIC POPULATION GROWTH
COMPUTED FOR THE UNITED STATES, 1850-2000
ON BASIS OF LIFE TABLE 1919-1920

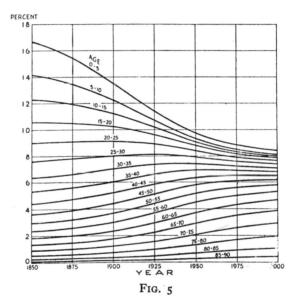

FIG. 5

group 20 to 25, we have a transitional type of curve which begins with a slight upward gradient and then ends in an inverted S. For the higher age groups, the upward gradient at the beginning becomes more and more marked, and at the same time the inverted S becomes transformed into an S in its natural position, so that the general trend for the curves of the higher ages is upwards. This is quite characteristic—the lower age groups diminish proportionally and the higher age groups increase, so that the population on the whole becomes older. If we look at that part of the diagram which corresponds about to the present date, 1930, we observe the following facts: Age groups 0 to 5, 5 to 10, 10 to 15, 15 to 20, 20 to 25, are on a downward grade. Age group 25 to 30 is just at the turning-point from an upward to a downward grade. Essentially the same is true of the next age group, 30 to 35, while higher age groups are on an upgrade, and will remain so until they flatten to a horizontal, when a stationary population is reached.

COMPARISON OF MALTHUSIAN WITH LOGISTIC AGE DISTRIBUTION

While the age distribution in a logistic population is practically identical with the Malthusian in the early period of development, in its charac-

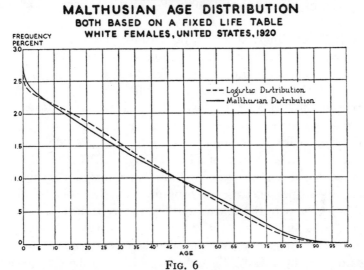

FIG. 6

teristic form, corresponding to the transitional period, the logistic age distribution differs from the Malthusian in certain important respects. This is shown in Fig. 6, in which there are plotted on one diagram, (a) the logistic age distribution computed for the 1920 population on the basis of a fixed life table (as of 1919–20); and, (b) the Malthusian age distribution, computed on the basis of the same life table, but for a constant rate of increase per head $r = 0 \cdot 014$, the value given by the logistic curve for the year 1920.*

* Equation (35) gives the Malthusian age distribution for a special case, namely that in which the rate of natural increase has the incipient value $r = 0 \cdot 0341$.

The important point to note is that logistic age distribution rises above the Malthusian for early adult life (ages 10 to 45), but falls below it at ages above 45. It is this characteristic of the logistic age distribution that gives the population a natural rate of increase momentarily greater than that actually corresponding to existing fertility and mortality, as discussed in a later section below.

THE SECULAR DRIFT IN FERTILITY

Since in the preceding development the mortality (life table) of the population has been considered constant, the continually diminishing rate of increase per head r characteristic of the logistic law of growth is referable to a diminishing fertility. We may, therefore, inquire what is the law of this diminishing fertility.

Now, speaking quite generally, the fertility cannot be defined by a single figure, since it represents the resultant of age-specific fertilities integrated over the entire period of reproduction. A given rate of increase can therefore arise, with a given life table, from a variety of different fertility curves. To make the problem determinate, some restricting assumption must be made regarding the mode of variation of the fertility curve. The simplest assumption, and the only one which shall here be used as a basis of discussion, is that the curve of fertility as a function of age (for females)* changes in amplitude only, while keeping its shape otherwise unchanged. With this assumption it is possible to compute the relative fertility at any instant as compared with the given fertility (1920) standard. For, if we denote by $m(a, 1920)$ the maternity frequency (counting daughters only) at age a in the standard year, 1920, and by $m(a,t)=k(t)m(a, 1920)$ the corresponding maternity frequency at time t, then we have, evidently,

$$B(t) = k(t)\int_0^\infty B(t - a)p(a)m(a, 1920)da \quad . \quad . \quad . \quad (36)$$

A Malthusian age distribution can, of course, also be computed for any other rate of natural increase, such as r_t, the rate corresponding to the logistic at time t. See Appendix, equation (60).

* It is most convenient to carry out the entire computation on the basis of the female population, because the period of reproduction of females has a more definite and earlier termination than that of males. In the equation (36) the symbols $p(a)$ and $m(a)$ are therefore to be read as referring to the female population.

This equation defines $k(t)$ in terms of quantities known or determined above.

The values of $k(t)$, the *relative fertility* (in terms of the standard fertility of 1920), computed for a succession of calendar years, are set forth in Table II below, together with the corresponding ratio $R(t)$ between the total births in two successive generations. This ratio $R(t)$ itself is a sort of measure of net fertility, and has the advantage that it automatically assumes the value unity for a stationary population. It is not, however, a complete measure of net fertility because it is expressed in terms of a vague unit of time, namely, the "mean length of a generation."

Having ascertained the fertility coefficient $k(t)$ as a function of the time, we can at once proceed to derive therefrom two other demographic characteristics of interest, namely, (1) the "true" or "inherent" rate of natural increase, and (2) the average size of families per wife, or, if the proportion of sterile marriages is known, per mother.

THE TRUE OR INHERENT RATE OF NATURAL INCREASE: COMPARISON WITH EXCESS OF BIRTH-RATE PER HEAD OVER DEATH-RATE PER HEAD

It has been shown elsewhere* that the true or inherent rate of natural increase r_0 is given by the real root of the equation

$$ 1 = \int_0^\infty e^{-ra}p(a)m(a)da \quad . \quad . \quad . \quad . \quad . \quad (37) $$

where $m(a)$ is the maternity frequency per head of female population of age a, counting births of daughters only. It is to be noted that the inherent rate of increase so defined is a definite measure of the net fertility of the population, reckoned no longer in the vague unit of a generation, but in the common unit of time, i.e. per calendar year.

In the present case $m(a)$ is a function of the time, and, according to the assumption made in the preceding section, we write

$$ m(a, t) = k(t)m(a, 1920) \quad . \quad . \quad . \quad . \quad (38) $$

* *Phil. Mag.*, 1911, vol. 21, p. 436; *Journal American Statistical Association*, 1925, vol. 3, p. 329.

where $m(a)$ now refers specifically to the standard maternity frequency, i.e. in this case that of 1920. Thus we have

$$1 = k(t)\int_0^\infty e^{-ra}p(a)m(a, 1920)da \quad \cdots \quad (39)$$

Solving (39) explicitly for r, we find*

$$\mu_2\frac{r^2}{2} - \mu_1 r + \log_e k(t)R_0 = 0. \quad \cdots \quad (40)$$

$$r = \frac{\mu_1 - \sqrt{\mu_1^2 - 2\mu_2 \log_e k(t)R_0}}{\mu_2} \quad \cdots \quad (41)$$

$$= F(t) \quad \cdots \quad (42)$$

where

$$\mu_1 = \frac{R_1}{R_0} \quad \cdots \quad (43)$$

$$\mu_2 = \frac{R_2}{R_0} - \left(\frac{R_1}{R_0}\right)^2 \quad \cdots \quad (44)$$

and where R_k is the kth moment of the function $p(a)m(a, 1920)$.

Fig. 7 shows the graph of the function $F(t)$, the "true rate," and side by side with it the graph of the observed rate of natural increase, i.e. the excess of the birth-rate over the death-rate. It will be noted that throughout the history of a population growing according to the logistic law, the true or inherent rate of natural increase falls systematically below the excess of birth-rate over the death-rate, but these two quantities approach each other more and more as we pass either to the extreme right or to the extreme left of the diagram. Thus in the early stages of the development of a population growing according to the logistic, where this law of growth is nearly identical with the compound interest law, the excess of birth-rate over death-rate, and the true rate of natural increase practically coincide; and they again practically coincide in the last stages, when the population is nearly stationary and the age distribution is nearly a life table distribution.

* For the method of solution, see *Journal of the American Statistical Association*, 1925, pp. 331–332. For values of r such as occur in practice terms of higher than second degree in r are negligible and have here been omitted.

COMPARISON OF TRUE RATE OF NATURAL INCREASE
WITH
EXCESS OF BIRTHRATE OVER DEATHRATE
For Logistic Population Growth

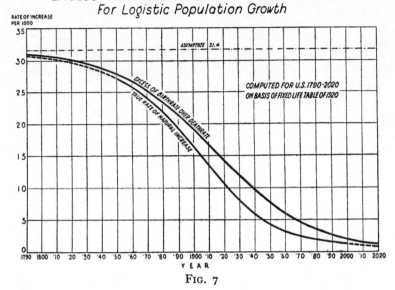

FIG. 7

Throughout the intervening period the "true" or inherent rate of natural increase falls below the excess of the birth-rate over the death-rate.*

SIZE OF FAMILIES: NUMBER OF CHILDREN PER MOTHER

The ratio of total female births in two successive generations is evidently given by

$$R(t) = \int_0^\infty p(a)m(a, t)da = k(t)\int_0^\infty p(a)m(a, 1920)da \quad . \quad . \quad (45)$$

$$= k(t)R(1920) \quad . \quad . \quad . \quad . \quad (46)$$

If M is the proportion of all women born who eventually marry (i.e.

---

* In reading this diagram it must be remembered that it relates to an ideal population growing entirely by natural increase; i.e. the immigration-rate is here included in the birth-rate, and the space between the two curves represents only qualitatively the divergence between the true rate of natural increase and the excess of the birth-rate over the death-rate in the actual population.

the proportion "ever married"), then evidently the average number of daughters per wife is $\dfrac{R(t)}{M}$, and the number of children* per *wife* is $\dfrac{2\cdot057R(t)}{M}$.

If, further, the proportion of wives that for any reason whatever† bear no children ("gross" sterility) is s, then the average number of children per *mother* is

$$C = \frac{2\cdot057k(t)R(1920)}{(1-s)M} \qquad \cdots \qquad \cdots \qquad (47)$$

NUMERICAL DATA

The sterility s and the proportion "ever married" have no doubt undergone considerable changes in the course of past decades and centuries. We are, however, at this stage considering a conventionalized model population with a fixed life table and growing entirely by natural increase, i.e. without immigration or emigration. For the present we will, therefore, merely substitute constant values for these coefficients, namely, the values prevailing in the United States in 1920: $s = 17\cdot1$ per cent., $M = 78\cdot2$ per cent. We then find for C, the number of children per mother, the figures set forth in Table II. The actual figures for earlier calendar years must have deviated from those here shown as follows: (1) A deduction must be made on account of net immigration, the effect of which is here tacitly included in the births. (2) A further deduction must be made on account of a lower sterility in the past. (3) It is somewhat uncertain whether the correction for proportion of married should be positive or negative. (4) A positive correction would have to be made on account of the much less favourable life table at earlier dates. (5) There has undoubtedly occurred a change in the profile, as well as the amplitude, of the age-fertility curve.

It should be remarked that in the case of the year 1920, the standard at the basis of this computation, the second and third corrections

---

* In the United States the sex ratio at birth (male : female) has been fairly constant at 1·057 for years past.

† That is to say, either from inherent (true) sterility, or through premature disruption of marriage by death of wife or husband, or by divorce. See A. J. Lotka, *Proceedings of the National Academy of Science*, 1928, vol. 14, p. 99.

TABLE II

NET FERTILITY IN LOGISTIC POPULATION COMPUTED ON BASIS OF GROWTH CURVE FOR UNITED STATES AND FIXED LIFE TABLE, WHITE FEMALES, AS OF 1919–1920

	Year									
	1800	1825	1850	1875	1900	1920	1925	1950	1975	2000
Ratio, $k(t)$, of fertility to standard (1920)	2·011	1·951	1·836	1·639	1·371	1·162	1·119	0·971	0·911	0·886
Ratio, $R(t)$, of total births in two successive generations	2·329	2·260	2·127	1·899	1·588	1·346	1·296	1·125	1·056	1·027
Number of children per mother (with 17·1 per cent. gross sterility)	7·40	7·18	6·76	6·03	5·05	4·28	4·12	3·57	3·35	3·26
"True", or "Inherent" rate of natural increase r_0	0·0304	0·0293	0·0271	0·0229	0·0165	0·0105	0·0092	0·0042	0·0019	0·0009
Rate of increase according to logistic curve, r_l	0·0306	0·0296	0·0277	0·0243	0·0191	0·0143	0·0131	0·0077	0·0040	0·0020

NOTE.—In studying the figures in the table it must be borne in mind that they refer to a model population, having the same total rate of increase per head as the logistic curve for the United States at the same date, but growing solely by excess of births over deaths. In other words, the net immigration has been, as it were, included in the birth-rate. So, for example, the reason why the figure 1·162 for $k(t)$ in the standard year (1920) is not unity is that it refers to the *model* population in which population growth takes place wholly by natural increase; whereas the standard fertility is that actually observed in the *real* population in 1920.

Again, in reading the figures for dates later than 1925, it must be understood that these have been given merely in order to complete the model, *not by the way of a forecast.*

enumerated above drop out, and the chief remaining correction is that for net immigration. As a matter of fact, a separate determination of the size of families for that year, by the direct method which does not involve immigration, gives 3·68 children per mother.*

The difference between this figure of 3·68 and the 4·3 shown in the table indicates at least approximately how much greater the average family would have had to be in 1920 in order to produce the actual rate of increase without the aid of immigration.

The Sex Ratio

Just as the logistic population has a characteristic age distribution, so also the distribution according to sex is definite at each stage in the growth of the population. The ratio of males to females in the total population (all ages) is simply given by

$$\frac{N_m}{N_f} = \frac{B_m}{B_f} \times \frac{b_f}{b_m} \quad \cdots \cdots \quad (48)$$

$$= 1 \cdot 057 \frac{b_f}{b_m} \quad \cdots \cdots \quad (49)$$

where the subscripts m and f denote that the quantities to which they are affixed refer respectively to the male and the female population considered separately.

For obvious reasons the sex ratio so computed varies within rather narrow limits. Thus computation gives the following sequence of figures (on the basis of the United States Life Tables for white males and females 1919–20, and a sex ratio at birth of 1·057 males per one female).

The ratio actually observed in 1920 among the native white population was 1·0173. In view of the fact that the computation was carried out on the basis of fixed life tables and without regard to immigration, only a qualitative agreement with the observed figure could here be expected.

Influence of Changing Mortality

So far the discussion has been conducted on the basis of a fixed life table, the reason for this being that this case admits of a direct and

* *Journal American Statistical Association*, 1925, p. 325.

exact mathematical treatment for a logistic population. As was pointed out in the Introduction, we can now proceed, upon the results obtained for the simplified model population, to build a method for treating the more general case, corresponding to actual conditions, with a fluent life table, and with allowance for immigration. The procedure is best explained by the aid of the diagram Fig. 8.

On this diagram will be seen a number of birth-rate curves drawn in lines of dashes. Each of these was obtained by computation in precisely the same manner as the curve appearing at the top of Figs. 3 and 4, except that a different life table was used for each of the dashed curves. The lowermost curve, corresponding to most recent conditions, is

TABLE III

SEX RATIO IN LOGISTIC POPULATION COMPUTED ON BASIS
OF GROWTH CURVE FOR UNITED STATES, AND FIXED
LIFE TABLES AS OF 1919–1920

Calendar Year	Ratio of Males to Females in White Population	Calendar Year	Ratio of Males to Females in White Population
1800	1·0282	1920	1·0219
1850	1·0276	1950	1·0188
1900	1·0245	2000	1·0172

based on a life table for 1927, which was the latest available at the time this diagram was made. The next previous in order is based on the United States life table for 1919–20, the last official life table published by the Census Bureau. Prior to these are shown the curves based on the life tables of 1910 and 1901. Earlier than this we have no American life table, and it was necessary to employ English life tables corresponding to the earlier dates. A reasonable justification for this is found in the fact that English life tables generally closely resemble ours, and in the further fact that the results as plotted were quite harmonious with those based on later life tables.*

* As pointed out in a previous section, the birth-rate curve based on a fixed life table is almost completely determined by the first two moments of the life table alone. Minor differences in the general outline of the English and the United States life tables are therefore inconsequential.

On each of these inverted S-shaped curves a ten-year segment is drawn in a heavy line, this segment representing the ten years centred at the calendar year to which the life table primarily applies. When mortality is actually undergoing the secular changes corresponding to the successive life tables, the curve truly representing the relation between the birth-rate and the time in calendar years must pass through these heavily drawn segments approximately at their midpoint. In fact, we may think of the true curve as being formed by each of these heavily

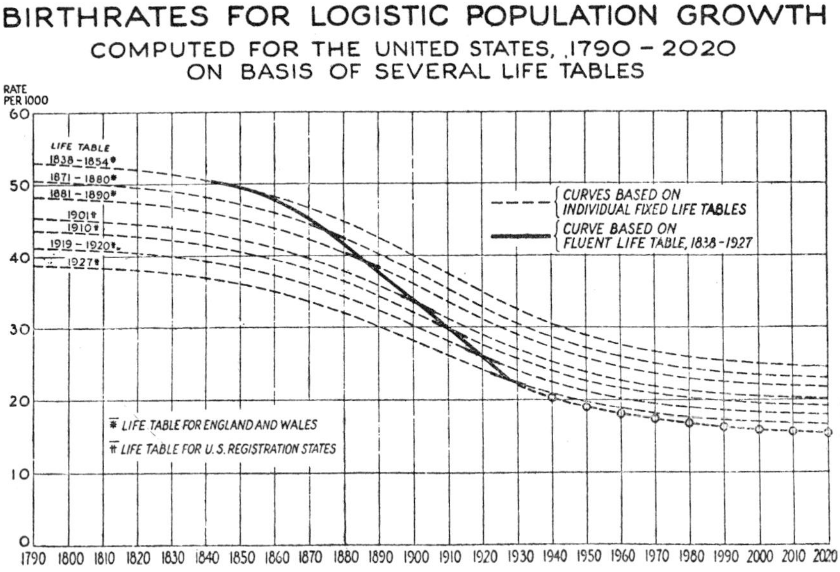

BIRTHRATES FOR LOGISTIC POPULATION GROWTH
COMPUTED FOR THE UNITED STATES, 1790 – 2020
ON BASIS OF SEVERAL LIFE TABLES

Fig. 8

drawn segments being turned around until they form a continuous curve; that continuous curve has been drawn through in a heavy line, and represents essentially the course of the birth-rate under the conditions of changing mortality to which the diagram relates.

Remembering that we are here speaking of a model population, and not attempting a forecast, we can say that if the population were to continue to grow according to the logistic law, then the birth-rate would have to follow a curve closely similar to that shown in dashes and circles at the right-hand lower portion of Fig. 8, which is drawn with the New Zealand life table in mind (expectation of life, sixty-five

years). The picture would not be very greatly altered if we assumed a
slightly better mortality such as may in time be achieved.

It will be seen that, on the assumption of a continued growth according
to the logistic law and with a fluent life table, the course of the birth-rate
is again represented by an inverted S-shaped curve, as it was when
computed on the basis of a fixed life table, but now with a much
steeper middle limb.

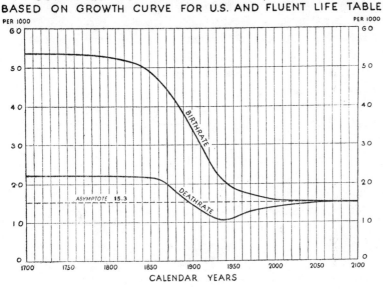

BIRTHRATE AND DEATHRATE IN LOGISTIC POPULATION
COMPUTED FOR UNITED STATES, 1700-2100
BASED ON GROWTH CURVE FOR U.S. AND FLUENT LIFE TABLE

CALENDAR YEARS

FIG. 9

DEATH-RATE

It is interesting to compare the general character of the death-rate
curve as computed for a fluent life table (Fig. 9) with that as computed
for a fixed life table (Fig. 2), as there is a very decided difference between
the two.

For a fixed life table the death-rate curve takes the form of a very
flat S, starting from a lower asymptote of 10·5 per 1,000 per annum
(as computed on the basis of the 1919–20 life table), and turning upwards
to seek finally the level of the upper asymptote at 17·4, where it joins
the birth-rate that approaches the same asymptote from above.

The curve computed on the basis of a fluent life table is quite different in character. After remaining nearly level for a considerable period, it presently turns downward, following the general course of the birth-rate until about the year 1930 or 1940, after which it turns up again and approaches the common asymptote on which birth-rate and death-rate unite to the level corresponding to a stationary population for the life table that has been selected as the ultimate life table.

A characteristic feature of this death-rate curve is a descending portion between the years 1850 to 1930. This is the result of the improving mortality which finds expression in the fluent life table, and which, of course, is not brought to expression when a fixed life table is used as the basis of computation, so that this descending portion is absent from the curve in Fig. 2. In the computation with the fluent life table, the final optimum life table was assumed to come into force at 1950, so that after this there is no further improvement in mortality and the death-rate curve from here on takes an upward course, as in the case of a fixed life table, as is only natural, for from here on the life table *is* fixed.

The initial condition for the curve based on the fluent life table differs, of course, materially from the initial conditions with a fixed life table. According to the fluent life table the initial birth-rate is in the neighbourhood of 53 per 1,000 and the initial death-rate in the neighbourhood of 22 per 1,000. This corresponds to the early life table of 1838 to 1854, which was applied as representing approximately conditions at this early period. The early part of the curve of death-rates is very flat, partly because here the growth curve of the population is itself rather flat, and partly because a constant life table (England and Wales, 1838–54) was here used as basis, no attempt being made, for lack of suitable life tables, to allow for higher mortalities prior to this period.

AGE DISTRIBUTION WITH ALLOWANCE FOR CHANGING MORTALITY

Having learned how to allow for the secular changes in mortality in computing the annual births, we can go back to the computation of the age distribution on the basis of a fluent life table and of the corresponding birth-rates. This more exact computation has been carried out for the age distribution in the year 1920.

Method of Using Fluent Life Table in Computing the Age Distribution

Consider a block of persons a years old in 1920, for example. They were born in the year $1920 - a$. In the year of their birth they were subject to a mortality corresponding to a life table for the year $1920 - a$. We shall assume that this life table is computed with sufficienct accuracy by linear interpolation between the two nearest actually available life tables between which $1920 - a$ lies. For example, if a is less than 10, we shall use a survival factor

$$p(a, 1920 - a) = p(a, 1910) + \frac{(1920 - a) - 1910}{1920 - 1910}$$
$$\{p(a, 1920) - p(a, 1910)\} \quad . \quad (50)$$

and similarly for values of a for which the year of birth lies between any other two nearest available life tables.

In this way, for persons of each age a, a life table corresponding to the year of birth was used.*

With this method of establishing a fluent life table, we now employ a modification of the age distribution formula (34), namely,

$$c(a, t) = \frac{B(t - a)}{N(t)} p(a, t - a) \quad . \quad . \quad \cdot \quad \cdot \quad (51)$$

where $B(t)$ is computed by the special method set forth above with use of a succession of life tables.

It is understood that there is a distinctly empirical element in these methods. Their justification is to be seen largely in the results, as will appear in the sequel.

Comparison of Various Types of Age Distribution

In a previous paragraph and diagram (Fig. 6) comparison was made between the age distribution in a logistic population, as computed on the basis of a fixed life table (1920), and the corresponding Malthusian

---

* An alternative and more refined procedure would be to apply to each age class a mortality (probability of dying within one year) $q(a, t)$ obtained by interpolation between the two nearest available life tables. The application of this method would be excessively laborious.

age distribution. A similar comparison can now be made between the logistic age distribution computed on the basis of the fluent life table, and the Malthusian distribution. This comparison is shown in Fig. 10. It will be noted that in general character this diagram closely resembles the one previously constructed on the basis of a fixed life table, but that the characteristic features pointed out in the former diagram reappear in accentuated form: there is an excess of persons below the age of 45

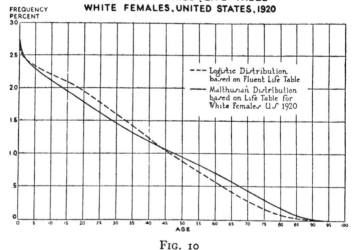

FIG. 10

and a deficiency of persons above that age, in the logistic, as compared with the Malthusian age distribution.

Another comparison of particular interest is that between the logistic age distribution, computed on the basis of the fluent life table, and the *actually observed* age distribution. This comparison is made in Fig. 11. It will be noted that the native* white female population of the United

* The "native" population was chosen for comparison in order to eliminate at any rate in some degree the influence of immigration. A still further elimination of the effect of immigration is secured by making the comparison with the "native white of native parentage." It was found that this additional precaution had very little influence on the resulting picture.

States conformed rather closely to the logistic age distribution thus computed.

ALLOWANCE FOR IMMIGRATION

Lastly, there remains to be considered the influence of immigration on some of the demographic characteristics as here computed.

"Birth-rates" computed as described, from the growth curve of the

AGE DISTRIBUTION IN LOGISTIC POPULATION
COMPARED WITH
NATIVE WHITE FEMALE POPULATION OF U.S. 1920

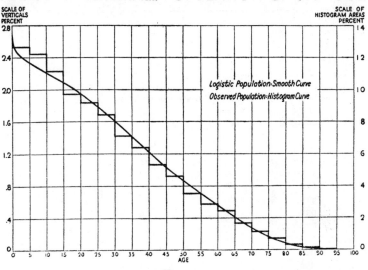

FIG. 11

population, include a contingent which is actually supplied not by births, but by net immigration. From the resulting series of birth-rates it is therefore necessary to make a subtraction to correct for the fact that the actual growth included the effect of immigration. It was found that by making a constant subtraction of three per thousand per annum, a set of figures was obtained which agreed very fairly with the observed birth-rates, as shown in Table IV. This correction of three per thousand harmonizes well with the observed facts that during the period 1915 to 1928 the net female immigration was 2·4 per thousand per annum, and during the period 1908 to 1913 it was about five per thousand per annum. We may, if we please, regard this procedure merely as an empirical method of obtaining a series of birth-rates, a method which is justified by its results over that period over which observed data for comparison are available.

TABLE IV

COMPARISON OF BIRTH-RATE COMPUTED ACCORDING TO LOGISTIC GROWTH CURVE AND OBSERVED BIRTH-RATE

UNITED STATES, WHITE FEMALES, SINCE 1915, PER THOUSAND

Year	Birth-rate *		Observed
	Computed		
	Uncorrected for Immigration	Corrected for Immigration	
(1)	(2)	(3)	(4)
1915	28	25	25
1916	28	25	25
1917	27	24	24
1918	27	24	24
1919	26	23	22
1920	26	23	23
1921	26	23	24
1922	25	22	22
1923	25	22	22
1924	24	21	22
1925	24	21	21
1926	23	20	20
1927	23	20	20
1928	22	19	19
1929	22	19	19

* The birth-rates here shown were actually computed on the basis of statistics for white females born per white female population. After the completion of the computation, decimals have been dropped, and to this degree of approximation it would be futile to retain a distinction between the rate "white female births per white female population" and the general birth-rate in the form in which it is commonly stated.

COMPARISON OF POPULATION AS COMPUTED (*a*) BY THE LOGISTIC CURVE
AND (*b*) BY SUMMATION OF THE SURVIVORS INTO EACH AGE OF LIFE

Method of Checking

The convergence of the series developed in preceding pages and
employed in the computations has not been subjected to a theoretical
investigation, nor has a theoretical estimate been made of the magnitude
of the remainder term when only a finite number of terms of the series
are retained. Instead of such a theoretical investigation, an empirical
arithmetical test has been made by comparing together the figures
obtained for the *total population* (*a*) directly by the logistic formula,
and (*b*) by summation of the survivors into each year of life resulting
from the annual births in accordance with the fundamental formula (1)

$$N(t) = \int_0^\infty B(t-a)p(a)da \quad \cdots \quad \cdots \quad (1)$$

or its modification applicable to a fluent life table

$$N(t) = \int^\infty B(t-a)p(a, t-a)da \quad \cdots \quad \cdots \quad (52)$$

The check in this form was applied separately to the case of a fixed
life table, and also to the case of a fluent life table. The results obtained
are shown below.

1. *Check of Computation with Fixed Life Table*

TABLE V

COMPARISON OF POPULATION AS COMPUTED BY (*a*) LOGISTIC
FORMULA, (*b*) SUMMATION OF AGE DISTRIBUTION

Year	Population Computed by		Per Cent. Error $100\frac{(a)-(b)}{(a)}$
	(*a*) Logistic Curve	(*b*) Summation of Age Distribution	
1850	23,245,464	23,255,366	− 0·04
1875	44,713,034	44,756,896	− 0·10
1900	77,220,510	77,254,191	− 0·04
1925	115,495,009	115,365,520	0·11
1950	149,206,157	149,104,610	0·07
1975	172,104,490	172,245,474	− 0·08
2000	185,049,703	185,136,134	− 0·05

The very good agreement shown in the figures of the table above represents, of course, merely an arithmetical check showing that the computation has been correctly conducted, and that the higher terms omitted in cutting off the infinite series at a finite term would make only a negligible contribution.

2. Check of Computation with Fluent Life Table

For the case of a fluent life table only one comparison of the total population computed by methods (a) and (b) was made, namely, for the year 1920, as the computation becomes very laborious when a fluent life table is used.

The "fluent" life table was made by the method described in a previous section, interpolating the requisite values of $l_{x,t}$ between the tabular values as given in the following life tables:

- (a) England and Wales, Females .. No. 3, 1838–54.
- (b) England and Wales, Females .. No. 4, 1871–80.
- (c) England and Wales, Females .. No. 5, 1881–90
- (d) United States White Females, Original Registration States, 1901.
- (e) United States White Females, Original Registration States, 1910.
- (f) United States White Females, Twenty-Seven States and D.C. 1919–20.

Using the figures for the total births $B(t)$ obtained as described in a previous section by the use of successive life tables, and applying to these figures survival factors corresponding to the "fluent" life table as explained above, comparison was made between the total population computed by the summation formula (52), and by the logistic formula.

For the year 1920 this comparison gave the following result:

United States Population Computed by		Discrepancy, Per Cent
Summation Formula	Logistic Formula	
105,212,000	107,875,000	2·5

There is here a discrepancy of $2\frac{1}{2}$ per cent., which, considering the somewhat empirical nature of the method employed, and its admittedly approximate character, may be regarded as satisfactory.

APPENDIX

ALTERNATIVE EXPRESSION FOR ANNUAL BIRTHS

The curve of annual births in a logistic population, under a fixed life table, is also capable of representation by an alternative formula which has certain advantages in combining a certain simplicity with a high degree of approximation. It is more exact than the use of a fundamental component alone of the exact formula given in an earlier section, and is simpler to use than the full series. It disregards, however, the slight asymmetry of the true curve.

The details of the development of this formula will here be omitted. The formula is

$$B(t) = \frac{GB_\infty}{1 + e^{-r(t-\eta-\theta)}} \quad \cdot \quad \cdot \quad \cdot \quad \cdot \quad (53)$$

$$B(t) = B_\infty \left\{ 1 - \frac{G}{1 + e^{r(t-\eta+\theta)}} \right\} \quad \cdot \quad \cdot \quad \cdot \quad (54)$$

The formula (53) is to be used for values of t less η, and the formula (54) for t greater than η, the origin of t being as before the centre of the population growth curve and the symbols η, θ, G, and B_1 being given by

$$\eta = \frac{1}{2r} \log_e \frac{\beta_1}{b_1} \cdot \quad \cdot \quad \cdot \quad \cdot \quad \cdot \quad \cdot \quad (55)$$

$$\theta = \frac{1}{r} \{ \log_e b_0 - \log_e (2\sqrt{b_1\beta_1} - b_0) \} \quad \cdot \quad \cdot \quad \cdot \quad (56)$$

$$G = \frac{\sqrt{b_1\beta_1}}{2\sqrt{b_1\beta_1} - b_0} \quad \cdot \quad \cdot \quad \cdot \quad \cdot \quad \cdot \quad (57)$$

$$\beta_1 = \frac{1}{\int_0^\infty e^{ra}p(a)da} \quad \cdot \quad \cdot \quad \cdot \quad \cdot \quad \cdot \quad (58)$$

GEOMETRIC MEANING OF THIS REPRESENTATION

According to this mode of representation the curve of annual birth consists of two fragments of separate logistic curves pieced together.

One of these logistics has its lower asymptote at zero, its upper asymptote at GB_∞, and its centre at $t = \eta + \theta$. The other has its lower

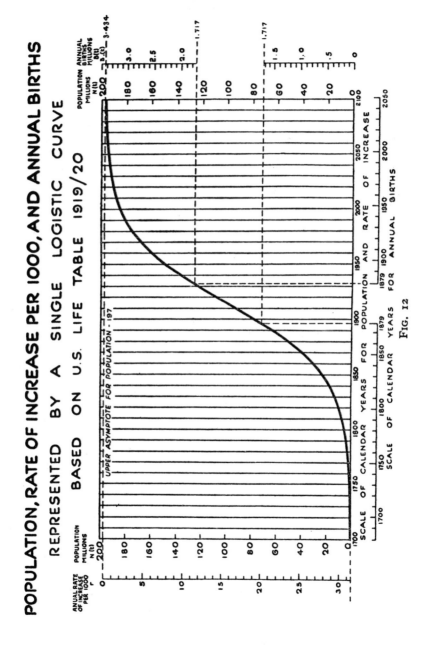

POPULATION, RATE OF INCREASE PER 1000, AND ANNUAL BIRTHS REPRESENTED BY A SINGLE LOGISTIC CURVE BASED ON U.S. LIFE TABLE 1919/20

FIG. 12

asymptote at $(1 - G)B_\infty$, its upper asymptote at B_∞, and its centre at $t = \eta - \theta$. The numerical values of the several constants, as computed for the United States, on the basis of the life table for 1919–20, are as follows:

$$
\begin{aligned}
GB_\infty &= 4\cdot685 \text{ millions} \\
B_\infty &= 3\cdot434 \text{ millions} \\
\eta &= -35\cdot5 \text{ years zero (at } 1914\cdot6) \\
\theta &= 17\cdot5 \text{ years} \quad . \quad . \quad . \quad . \quad . \quad . \quad . \quad . \\
b_0 &= 0\cdot0174 \\
b_1 &= 0\cdot0419 \\
\beta_1 &= 0\cdot00449 \\
r &= 0\cdot0314
\end{aligned}
\qquad (59)
$$

SINGLE DIAGRAM TO REPRESENT TOTAL POPULATION, ANNUAL RATE OF INCREASE PER HEAD, AND ANNUAL BIRTHS

It can easily be shown that the rate of increase $r(t)$ per head of a population growing according to the logistic law follows an inverted logistic curve

$$
r(t) = r_i \left(1 - \frac{N_t}{N_\infty} \right) \quad . \quad . \quad . \quad . \quad . \quad (60)
$$

where r_i is the incipient rate of increase per head, which throughout the preceding sections has for brevity been written simply r without subscript.

It has also been shown that the annual births $B(t)$ can be represented as two pieces of logistic joined together. This suggests that curves for all three of these demographic characteristics can be represented on a single diagram. This has been done in Fig. 12. The basic feature of this diagram is the logistic curve for the population itself, $N(t)$. Values of this are read in the ordinary manner, the time scale running horizontally and the population scale vertically. To read values of the rate of increase per 1,000 a separate scale is shown at the extreme left, and since this rate of increase follows an inverted logistic, this scale reads from above downwards.

To read values of the annual births $B(t)$ a split scale is used shown at the bottom of the diagram for the time scale and on the extreme right for the scale of births. The diagram practically explains itself and further comment seems unnecessary.

PAPER No. 21

SOME ASPECTS OF HUMAN BIOLOGY

By J. A. FRASER ROBERTS

(*Department of Animal Genetics, Edinburgh University.*)

SOME ASPECTS OF HUMAN BIOLOGY

Iᴛ is with much hesitation that I venture to open a discussion upon one or two applications of biology to human affairs, and I trust that you will forgive me if I intrude a note of personal explanation. For some time I have been engaged in animal experimentation, and through the kindness of Professor Crew I am now enabled to undertake studies in human biology. At this moment, before becoming involved in that new work, I feel that it is a very great privilege to be permitted to suggest to this audience one or two subjects for discussion, relating more particularly to the problem of differential fertility, in the hope that criticism will be forthcoming.

In the first place, it seems to be clear that in the present state of our knowledge new principles in biology must emerge from the results of animal experiments, and as far as we can see at the present time it is very unlikely that any new biological principle, founded on direct observations on man, will be forthcoming. The task of the human biologist, therefore, is to examine the body of biological knowledge that has been accumulated and to devise tests in order to discover how far that knowledge is applicable and how it can be related to practice.

If we examine the knowledge that has been accumulated during recent years on the mechanism of heredity, and at the same time study the practical results that have been obtained in the improvement of breeds of animals of economic importance, a rather remarkable contrast presents itself. On the one hand, a breed such as the Shorthorn breed of cattle has been changed out of all recognition in a relatively small number of generations. It is true that this progress has not always been continuous, and that there have been set-backs, but the feat that has been accomplished is a remarkable one. Even the bad Shorthorn of to-day is a vastly different animal from its unimproved ancestors. On the other hand, if we consider a single factor difference such as the occurrence of reds in black breeds of cattle, we see that the measure of selection that has been relatively so effective in the case of general conformation has been, during the same period, relatively far less effective in the case of the simple Mendelian difference. I have some personal knowledge of a small flock of Merino sheep in which black lambs still cropped up after a hundred years of close inbreeding, during the last forty of which no single introduction of outside blood of any kind was made. And yet we are sometimes asked to believe that the selection for more general, unanalysable characteristics is based upon very many hundreds of such simple Mendelian differences, that the process that is only relatively efficient in the case of a single factor becomes in some mysterious way rapid and effective if only there are many factors.

How can this apparent discrepancy be explained? Is it not possible that although dominance is a common phenomenon in the case of simple qualitative differences in coat colour, or in the case of the presence or absence of clearly defined defects, it may be that it is of relatively uncommon occurrence in connection with ordinary quantitative differences? Not being a mathematician I speak with great diffidence on this point, but is it not correct to state that if dominance is not involved in any particular case the effects of artificial selection are produced far more rapidly? It may be that the secret of the rapid improvement that has followed selection in the case of domesticated breeds of animals is a reflection of the fact that dominance has been largely absent in the case of those quantitative characteristics that have formed the basis of the selection. Prepotence is often referred to dominance, and exceptions to the generalization that "like begets like" are equally often referred to the same cause; but may not prepotence be more an expression of homozygosis, and the difference in breeding results between two animals of apparently equal phenotypic merit also, equally easily, be a reflection of the fact that one is more homozygous for its good qualities than the other?

It seems to me that this very simple point has an important bearing on all the problems connected with differential fertility in man. At the present time for all practical purposes the only form of selection possible is mass or phenotypic selection, and it becomes of the utmost importance to determine how far changes can be produced in a single generation, and then to form some estimate as to whether further progress is to be expected if selection is continued in subsequent generations. The point would appear to be an extremely obvious one, but when one reads the literature one wonders whether its implications are usually grasped. There seems to be a tendency to base a prediction upon theoretical calculations instead of upon *ad hoc* observations of parents and offspring in selected groups of all kinds and in various environments.

Starting from the assumption that, as regards most quantitative inheritance, dominance is a relatively uncommon feature, the efficacy of mass selection is affected by a number of considerations. In the first place it is affected by the amount of heterozygosity involved. If dominance is absent the mean of parents will coincide with the mean of offspring, however many factors are involved, but the variability of offspring will depend upon the number of factors involved and upon the amount of heterozygosity of the parents. Homozygosity is greatly desired in the breeding of domesticated animals, but in the case of man it is hardly necessary to elaborate the argument that heterozygosity is desirable. We shall not be surprised, therefore, to find great variability amongst the offspring of any group, however it is selected, but we shall look for a close correspondence between the mean of parents and the mean of offspring. If selection is practised we shall anticipate a shift of the mean with each generation. We shall deduce that mass selection will be effective to limits beyond our present horizon, but we shall recognize the practical difficulty involved in the variability. There may be a reluctance to discriminate between groups even if mean performance shows a definite difference, but if at the same time the curves overlap to a considerable extent. That practical difficulty, however, would appear to be the concern of the statesman rather than of the biologist.

In the second place we may expect a certain amount of interaction in the expression of complementary factors, modifying factors, and the like. This interaction will, to the extent that it occurs, increase the time during which mass selection must operate to produce a given effect.

In the third place, there is the perennial question of nature versus nurture. Of course, an organism without an environment is as unthinkable as one without a heredity, but in practice we deal with individual differences. In the case of defined groups and given limits of environment the distinction can be drawn if the methods of analysis are sufficiently refined. Studies to determine the effectiveness of mass selection will often resolve themselves into a determination of how far environmental variability swamps the expression of genetic variability. We may sometimes find that under the actual conditions of existence the efficiency of mass selection is so reduced on this ground that it could not be advocated as a practical procedure. In other cases we may find that the existing variability of environment has little effect upon the expression of inborn potentialities.

It is unfortunately the case that the discussion of these problems rouses much social and political prejudice. The function of the biologist ceases when he has examined and expounded the effects of any procedure. The consideration of its merits lies entirely outside his province. He should not, therefore, be at all concerned with these repercussions. It seems to me, however, looking at the matter quite from the outside, that some reconciliation is not impossible, and that the atmosphere of prejudice that surrounds much of the discussion of these problems is possibly based on mistaken ideas. We see only too often the association of opinion inclining to the left in politics with an environmentalist standpoint, while opinion inclining to the right makes use of theories of rigid hereditary determinism. It seems to me, however, that curiously enough both sides appear to use the wrong arguments. Surely it should be the environmentalist who hails with satisfaction studies tending to show that there is a large and sharp distinction between the offspring of different social classes, while the advocate of hereditary determination should triumphantly counter by pointing out notable exceptions. One would have imagined that the social reformer would point out with the utmost satisfaction that the children of the very rich were of high average merit. He would use this as an argument for equalization and the raising of the standards of the masses. One would have imagined that the extreme advocate of hereditary determination would become lyrical over the appearance of talent and of genius in the face of appalling social obstacles. Curiously enough, however, these arguments would appear to be commonly used by the wrong side and the wrong way round, and one can only hope that some acceptance of this view, even if it is a specious one, might temporarily abate the flames of controversy and permit a dispassionate investigation of the facts.

To return to the main argument. The layman appears to demand information as to the effect of selection in a single generation. He would like to know how the offspring of particular groups do, in fact, differ and why they differ. It seems to me that this demand is a perfectly reasonable one, and that upon the answers given depends the hope of progress. It would also seem to be the sound biological approach. The layman would like to know, for example, what the reduction would be in the number of aments in the country in a single generation if no aments were allowed to have children. Instead of this he is assured that heredity plays a large part, or is offered estimates based upon theoretical considerations that may, but probably do not, bear any relation to the facts. He is tacitly informed that the scientist is far too busy investigating other considerations relative to this problem, of much greater theoretical interest. The one thing he is not given is a straight answer, and that answer could certainly be provided by suitable investigations.

In conclusion I should like to mention one consideration which seems to me fundamental as regards the application of science to human affairs. There seems to be a widespread tacit assumption, both on the part of the biologist and of the layman, that science deals with certainties, and that it is necessary to know a great deal more before any application of biology to human affairs is possible. Is not this based upon a misconception? The results of science do not lead to certainty, but to probability, and it is probably this fact that explains the extreme irritation produced in the mind of the layman by the expert scientific witness. If certainty is demanded before any application to human affairs is made, the problem as to whether any application is possible will still be in process of discussion thousands of years from now. The existing political and legal mechanisms are certainly not free from error, and it must not be assumed that the hypotheses based upon scientific experiments and applied to specific practical problems will be free from error either. Needless to say, no sensible person would wish to suggest a far-reaching and revolutionary change except upon the basis of a probability of an extremely high order, but with regard to many of the problems raised by differential fertility the choice is not of this type. Decisions are being continually taken which have a bearing on this subject, and are being taken, as far as one can see, with little reference to the teachings of biology. Even if the probability of a particular hypothesis being correct is only moderate, it is a factor that should be taken into consideration. If progress is to be achieved, the layman must not be surprised at discovering the scientist occasionally in error; nor must the scientist, however much he will regret and deplore it, feel overwhelmed with shame if he makes an honest mistake.

I fear that I have roamed over a wide field in rather a general way, and, without at all venturing to suggest what lines any discussion should take, I do feel that there are one or two points on which discussion and criticism will be very welcome. First of all, the explanation of the rapid effects of mass selection in domesticated animals. In the second place, the importance or otherwise of dominance in relation to mass selection; and in the third place, the proper conduct of investigations designed to measure the resemblances and differences between parents and offspring and the best methods for referring those resemblances and differences to their underlying causes.

DISCUSSION

Professor F. A. E. CREW said that it could be imagined with what satisfaction he heard this confession of faith on the part of his friend and colleague, Mr. FRASER ROBERTS. It was indeed the case that that which man had done for his domesticated animals he was expected to do for mankind, but manifestly, it was a very difficult matter to apply the lessons learned in the stable and on the farm to human affairs. One of the reasons for this was that though many males are born, but few were chosen to be the sires of succeeding generations. Professor CREW thought that the reason why the physical conformation of the domesticated breeds had been changed so remarkably in such short periods of time was because the breeder was not controlling the transmission of hereditary factors recognized by him as such, but rather, by selection, was increasing the rates and modes of development processes. Indeed, it could be said of the breeder that he was an experimental physiologist, mainly interested in the endocrine system. The breeder has been mainly concerned with the phenomena of growth, sexual maturity, and reproduction, all of which are profoundly influenced by the glands of internal secretion. It would seem that he has been unconsciously collecting into the hereditary constitutions of his breeds those genes which affect the rate of functioning and the time of onset of functioning of various members of the endocrine system, and, at the same time, those which influence the responses of the bodily tissues to the hormones elaborated thereby. It is probable that this is the reason why careful and continued selection towards an ideal type has been so successful.

In the case of mankind it is not improbable that those qualities known to be inherited and of importance socially are of the same kind, being end-results of the developmental processes concerned with growth, sex, and reproduction. If this is so, then in a study of human genetics, formal genetics will not be enough, for the principles of developmental physiology and endocrinology must also be considered, since it may become possible to compensate for the possession of an undesirable factor by controlling developmental processes by the administration of appropriate endocrine extracts or chemical substances.

PAPER No. 22

A. THE SIGNIFICANCE OF BLOOD-GROUPING
IN ANTHROPOLOGY

By Dr. TAGE KEMP

(*Denmark*)

A. THE SIGNIFICANCE OF BLOOD-GROUPING IN ANTHROPOLOGY

IT should be unnecessary to point out the importance of anthropology in the scientific investigation of population problems. It forms a scientific basis for race biology, eugenics, and social hygiene; and by its standards one may investigate and estimate the physical and mental properties of a population.

In the anthropological estimation of a population, attention is especially directed towards characteristics present in the whole population or in a part of it, large or small, and which are easily definable and hereditary. There are actually few characteristics that meet these requirements—such, for instance, as the colour of eyes and hair, the cephalic index, and other so-called racial characters. There are particularly few isolated characters that are refractory to environmental influences and developmental conditions whose inheritance is simple and easy to trace. These are the characteristics of the blood-groups, and they are therefore of great significance in anthropology.

Our knowledge of the blood-groups dates from the beginning of this century when Landsteiner, of Vienna, discovered them. He demonstrated that with the isohæmagglutination test all human beings may be divided into four groups: O, A, B, and AB. Serum of type O agglutinates the red corpuscles of the other three groups; serum of type A agglutinates corpuscles B and AB; serum of type B agglutinates corpuscles A and AB; and serum of type AB does not agglutinate any type of corpuscles.

The corpuscles of the various groups (or types) are equipped with special biochemical structures—receptors—which make them agglutinable. Recent investigations have demonstrated that this type character is not limited to the red corpuscles, but also applies to all the other cells of the body and its fluids—such as serum, saliva, tears, urine, and other secretions and excretions of the body which have the same type character as is found in the corpuscles of the respective individual. Thus it would really be more correct to speak of the serological types rather than of the blood types into which all mankind can be divided into blood-groups. These properties of blood type may be demonstrated throughout life—from the earliest days of fœtal existence to death—and they do not change in quality.

As has finally been demonstrated by Bernstein, in 1925, the characters of blood type are hereditary, and the inheritance follows simple rules: there are three genes of blood type—*O*, *A*, and *B*—which are allelomorphic, and so constituted that both *A* and *B* are dominants and dominate over *O*. The relative distribution of blood types remains constant in a population that is not invaded to any great extent by foreign elements. The study of the blood-groups that has to be carried out with the technique of modern serology, if it is to be done properly, has been of very great importance to surgery in the matter of blood transfusion, to forensic medicine in questions of paternity, and to anthropology.

The anthropological significance of the blood types was investigated on a large scale first by Ludwig Hirzfeld and Hanna Hirzfeld among the coloured troops on the Macedonian border during the Great War, and since then many authors claim to have confirmed their results. It has been found that the four blood-groups occur in every nation of the world that has been examined so far, but their distribution differs widely in the various peoples. It is supposed that group *A* is most widespread amongst the nations of Central and North Europe, with a lower frequency towards the East and South, concurrent with an increase in the frequency of group *B*. In the English, for instance, there is approximately 45 per cent. *A*, and only 10 per cent. *B*. Almost a similar proportion is found in the French, Italians, Germans, and Austrians, whereas the proportion is altogether different in negroes, Mongolians, and Hindus. Some authors suppose that *A* represents especially the Nordic elements, *B* the Central Asiatic, and *O* the Mediterranean elements.

In Denmark we find the following distribution of types amongst about 7,500 normal individuals, of which a large part have been examined by arrangement of the Danish Anthropological Committee:

O	*A*	*B*	*AB*
43 per cent.	43 per cent.	10·5 per cent.	3·5 per cent.

During the past 3 or 4 years, however, our knowledge of the serological types has been extended considerably in some essential respects, partly through the continued studies of Landsteiner and his collaborators, but also through some Danish investigations carried out by Oluf Thomsen and his collaborators. These recent investigations have added considerably to the anthropological significance of the blood types and thus to their importance in population problems. This is the reason why I venture to read this paper before the General Assembly.

It has long been known that there are sub-groups under the four original groups, but the recent investigations of Thomsen, Friedenreich, and Worsaae have shown that group A can be divided into two well-defined sub-groups, A^1 and A^2, which can always be distinguished from each other. The proportion of these sub-groups to the main groups is such that A^1 makes about 80 per cent. of the original group A, and A^2 about 20 per cent. A^1 dominates over A^2. Thus we have six groups instead of four.

Further, in 1927–29, Landsteiner and Levine demonstrated that the red corpuscles of some individuals are equipped with special receptors —"immune receptors," M and N—which are not revealed by the usual blood typing, as they can be demonstrated only by means of serum from rabbits immunized with human corpuscles. A third immune receptor—P—has been demonstrated in negroes, but it is of very rare occurrence in Europeans. All human individuals examined so far have either M or N or both M and N, so there is a possibility of three types: M, N, and MN. These three type characters are independent of the first known types, and there is no correlation between M and N on one hand, and A and B on the other. Thomsen and Clausen have examined 442 normal individuals in Copenhagen, and in this material they found the following distribution of M and N:

M in 74·7 per cent. N in 70·1 per cent. MN in 44·6 per cent.

The distribution agrees in the main with the findings of Landsteiner in the United States, and of Schiff in Berlin, whereas Wiener found a much smaller percentage of N in the North American Indians.

Family examinations have shown that M and N are to be interpreted as two hereditary, mutually independent, dominant properties, developing through two allelomorphic genes.

On the basis of family examinations, Thomsen has advanced the hypothesis that the development of the blood types demonstrable with isoagglutinins hinges on four allelomorphic genes, and not on three, as assumed by Bernstein. We may then replace the following scheme:

3 genes: $O \quad A \quad B$

4 types: $O \quad A \quad B \quad AB$ as $\left.\begin{array}{l} OA \\ AA \end{array}\right\} = A \quad \left.\begin{array}{l} OB \\ BB \end{array}\right\} = B$

by the following:

4 genes: $O \quad A^1 \quad A^2 \quad B$

6 types: $O \quad A^1 \quad A^2 \quad B \quad A^1B \quad A^2B$ as $\left.\begin{array}{l} A^1A^2 \\ OA^1 \\ A^1A^1 \end{array}\right\} = A^1 \quad \left.\begin{array}{l} A^2A^2 \\ OA^2 \end{array}\right\} = A^2 \quad \left.\begin{array}{l} OB \\ BB \end{array}\right\} = B$

And for the three serological types depending on the presence of immune receptors:

2 genes: $M \qquad N$

3 types: $M+\ N+ \qquad M\div\ N+ \qquad M+\ N\div$

A large number of observations have now been published which make it highly probably that this system is correct. But it should be stated most emphatically that the correct diagnosis of these blood types is by no means always a simple matter, and that it requires a great deal of care and serological experience; when carried out on a large scale, which is always essential in anthropological investigations, this work will naturally be rather expensive. It should further be mentioned that no certain correlation has been demonstrated between the characteristics of blood type and certain other characteristics such as, for instance, racial characters or constitutional predisposition to disease or other physical or psychical hereditary propensities.

Since these studies have so far demonstrated the existence of six types with regard to receptors reacting with isoagglutinins, and three types with immune receptors, and as these two systems are independent of each other, it is obvious that at present all mankind may be divided into eighteen groups with regard to blood-type properties, according to the following scheme, where each square gives one of the eighteen types (see table on opposite page).

This division is based on an exact scientific foundation. The properties employed for criteria are hereditary qualities, depending for their development upon a single gene; and the presence or absence of these qualities can be settled in every instance.

It goes without saying that such a classification of a population by serological types is of great importance in anthropological estimation, be it for the sake of comparison between two groups of

O	A^1	A^2	B	A^1B	A^2B
M	M	M	M	M	M
O	A^1	A^2	B	A^1B	A^2B
N	N	N	N	N	N
O	A^1	A^2	B	A^1B	A^2B
MN	MN	MN	MN	MN	MN

people of different geographical regions, or for a comparative study of the same group in different periods. Naturally, there have been as yet only very few and limited investigations of this kind, but it is to be hoped that in the near future opportunities may be found to continue and extend them.

DISCUSSION

Dr. EUGEN FISCHER said he had been greatly interested in this paper, but he must emphasize what Mr. KEMP had said, that there was no real relation between these new groups and the other anthropological race characteristics, and it must be remembered that the same blood-groups were found in the anthropoid apes and the gorilla. The chimpanzee had the same blood-groups in the same percentage as man, and therefore it could not be taken at present that blood-groups were a very reliable means of differentiating the races of mankind. Dr. FISCHER said he had been interested in the preparation of a paper now in the press on investigations into the blood-groups of identical and non-identical twins. The blood had been tested by Dr. Schiff of the Sociological Institute, and it had been found that in all cases of identical twins the blood-groups were identical, and in non-identical twins in

50 per cent. of the cases they were the same as those found in brother and sister.

Professor RUGGLES GATES thought Professor FISCHER had raised an interesting question. He had referred to the fact that anthropoid apes had blood-groups of *A* and *B*. It seemed still possible that the differences of blood-groups in different races might be genetically surveyed. It would be necessary to assume that the blood-groups in anthropoids had arisen independently of the blood-groups in man. There was a certain amount of evidence in favour of such a view. The North American Indians and the Eskimo were practically all zero, and another interesting point in that connection was that the Australian natives were known to be high *A*. The late Dr. Bernstein had agreed that *A* was older than *B*, *B* being of more recent native origin. There was a certain amount of evidence for a comparison of the races in North America with those now occupying Mongolia, where the percentage of *B* was very high.

All these facts and a good many others did fit together with a genetical view if one assumed that blood-groups in man had arisen independently of animals.

Professor CREW believed the blood-groups were also found in certain domesticated animals. There were certainly suggestions of blood-groupings in sheep. He had hoped that Dr. KEMP would leave solid fact and wander into speculation in this connection. Undoubtedly there existed a certain amount of anxiety lest the blood-groups of the Australian blacks should in any way be similar to those of the whites. Why should one try to read into blood-groups a suggestion that they were not to some extent indicative of racial origin? If one looked at the origins of those who spoke with such assurance of race, the characteristics which were held to distinguish race from race seemed often rather frivolous, and he did not see any reason for appealing to blood-groups to reinforce one's prejudices. It seemed to him that the manner of using a knife and fork was more significant than the curl of the hair or shape of the nose.

Mr. FRASER ROBERTS asked Dr. KEMP whether he was satisfied from the evidence he had obtained that in the case of *A* and *B* the inheritance depended upon a separate factor?

Professor RUGGLES GATES said that Dr. KEMP had referred to differentiations of *A*, to types A^1 and A^2. The possibility approached that the *A*, which was present in high degree in the Australian native, might be one of those types, and the *A* in Europeans might be of the other type. There was no evidence of this at the present time, but he merely suggested it as a possibility.

Dr. KEMP said it had been very interesting for him to hear what Professor FISCHER and the other speakers had said in the discussion, and he could agree on many points with what had been said from the different sides. He understood quite well that this character of the blood types was not in any way correlated with the other characters that from old time had been called racial. The old racial characters are rather inexact and unsatisfactory to work with. One can, however, depend perfectly on the blood-group characters.

One could be quite certain at the present time that the hypothesis of Bernstein was right. It was a very interesting thing that all human beings could be divided into eighteen groups which in one direction or another differed from each other. It would be very important if in different populations all the world over an investigation could be made to define how the population was divided into these eighteen groups. It would certainly be found that there was a great difference in different populations of the world. When this work was done it would be time to discuss the subject more adequately.

B. REPORT ON THE STUDIES OF MM. DEGERBÖL AND NYBÖLLE ON THE SHEDDING AND ERUPTION OF TEETH IN COPENHAGEN SCHOOL CHILDREN

During the last year one great work has been published by the Danish Anthropological Committee (*Meddelelser om Danmarks Antropologi*, vol. iii, 2), which forms the original National Committee for Denmark of the International Union.

It is:

Magnus Degerböl: *On the Shedding and Eruption of Teeth Among Copenhagen School Children*. Compared with that of the other Primates.

And

H. Cl. Nybölle: *Calculation of the Average Age of Shedding and Eruption of Teeth*.

The foundation on which this publication is based is an investigation made in the year 1913, with a material of 11,190 children attending Copenhagen Municipal Schools, all between the ages of 7 and 15 years.

The work is published in the Danish language, but is supplied with a very complete summary in the English language.

PAPER No. 23

A NEW ASPECT OF POPULATION THEORY

By Professor HENRY PRATT FAIRCHILD
(*New York University, U.S.A.*)

A NEW ASPECT OF POPULATION THEORY

THE contribution to population theory made by Thomas R. Malthus was so unparalleled and so comprehensive that there has been a tendency to regard it as the final word on the subject. Those who have accepted it have felt the necessity of defending it *in toto*, and have been unwilling to concede the necessity or the possibility of any important modifications, while those who have attacked it have assumed that if they could disprove any portion of it they would thereby overthrow it entirely, and that to overthrow the Malthusian system was to overthrow the whole of population theory.

The position of the opponents of Malthusianism has been strengthened by many occurrences of the nineteenth century which Malthus did not foresee and could not foresee, and therefore could not include in his system. The basic fears which gave Malthus's analysis such a gloomy tinge do not seem to have been realized. Not only has the population of the world increased during the years since Malthus by a much larger figure than during the whole previous span of man's existence, but the general standard of living has improved simultaneously. The pressure of population on the supporting power of the land seems to have been less than ever before.

This seeming refutation of the Malthusian doctrine, however, has been specious rather than real, temporary rather than permanent. Every scientific theory is predicated upon the existence of certain conditions, and presumes to hold good only so long as those conditions persist. The really significant scientific theories are those based upon such fundamental conditions that their central conclusions continue to hold good, even though many superficial alterations in conditioning factors may take place. A careful consideration of the Malthusian theory shows it to be of this character.

The central propositions of the Malthusian theory are first, that the natural capacity of the human species to reproduce is so great that it is always capable of exceeding man's ability to get subsistence from the land, and second, that the forces back of reproduction are so powerful and insistent that they continually drive population to press upon the means of subsistence, causing perpetual misery of a greater or lesser degree, according to whether the positive checks or the preventive checks are brought into operation.

About the former of these propositions there can be no reasonable doubt. The record of the United States alone is sufficient proof. From 1790, when the first Census was taken, to 1930 the population increased from about 4,000,000 to nearly 123,000,000, or nearly thirty-one-fold in one hundred and forty years. Even allowing, for purposes of argument, the dubious assertion that foreign immigration has been largely responsible for this increase, this growth still indicates a fecundity which no one could possibly believe to be capable of being cared for over the world at large for any extended period of time.

The really serious criticisms of the Malthusian theory raise the questions whether in fact this potential fecundity does strive to realize itself to such a degree as to cause a real pressure on the means of subsistence, with resulting misery. To many persons the history of the nineteenth century seems to disprove this contention.

The whole answer revolves around the point as to whether the conditions of the nineteenth century are permanent, and represent possibilities for human increase that can be duplicated in the twentieth century, and again in the twenty-first, and so on indefinitely.

The truth is, as the briefest consideration of the facts will suffice to indicate, that the nineteenth century was unique in human history, and will probably remain so. During that century there came to fruition the combination of three great improvements in the supporting power of the earth—the discovery of the Western Hemisphere, and the Industrial and Commercial Revolutions. These gave the human species a new chance such as it had never experienced before, and the phenomenal population increase of the century was the answer. There is not the slightest hope that such a combination of fortunate circumstances can ever be repeated. Whatever technical advances may still be in store, there will never be added to them another hemisphere.

But even in spite of this unprecedented good fortune, nothing actually happened during that pregnant period that was contrary to the Malthusian theory. The increase in population of the world as a whole was immeasurably below the rate of doubling every twenty-five years, which he admitted as a reference point, and even in the United States the rate was distinctly lower than this. And as to misery, he would be an optimist indeed who, in the face of present conditions, would deny that there has been misery even in the most thinly populated and prosperous countries. Even in the phenomenal nineteenth century there is abundant evidence of population pressure and its resultant evils.

The outstanding fallacy in the criticism of Malthus is the habit of judging his theory by the one century that followed its statement, rather than by the hundreds of thousands of years that preceded it. We are all of us liable to fall into this error, particularly in our use of vital statistics. Since there are practically no reliable vital statistics antedating the nineteenth century, all our curves and charts and formulæ are limited to an exceptional epoch in population history. Yet we are very much inclined to treat them as if all the years before 1800 were on the whole similar to those that followed it. In short, we are likely to assume that any population curve that we are able to construct from such data as we have might be extrapolated backward according to the indicated trend just as we undertake to extend it forward.

In other words, we are prone to fall into the error of assuming that increase at a rather rapid rate has been characteristic of the human species during its entire existence. Nothing could be more fallacious. If there are about two billion people in the world to-day, and if man has existed for about one million years, that means an average increase of the species as a whole of only about two thousand a year. Of course, this is a very liberal use of a simple average to cover a very wide range, but it will suffice to indicate how very slow has been the actual increase of mankind, particularly when we recall that about two-thirds of this total has been added in the last one hundred and thirty years. We should cease to be alarmed at the prospect of a very slowly increasing, or even a stationary, population. On the contrary, this should be regarded as the normal state of affairs.

There is just one important factor which has come into wide operation since Malthus wrote his essay, which requires any serious modification in his theory. This is the extensive spread of contraceptive ideas and practice. Malthus assumed that births in marriage would occur on an essentially biological basis. This was fundamental to his theory as he stated it. He talked about the "permanence of the passion between the sexes." He took it for granted that the gratification of this passion would result in offspring in about the numbers dictated by Nature. There is abundant evidence that he knew about birth control, but he disdained to give it a place in his system.

But birth control can no longer be ignored. It has become, in many lands, the characteristic, if not the dominating, element in the determination of the size of the typical family. This involves, not an abandonment, but an amplification, of the Malthusian doctrine. Contraception is simply another preventive check, to be added to those that Malthus enumerated.

But it is an addition of the very highest importance. The introduction of the voluntary control of childbearing into family life has required an entire restatement of the overt phenomena of population growth, though it has not vitiated any of the fundamentals of population theory as set forth by Malthus. It is the specific applications and implications of theory that must be altered.

One of the best illustrations of the sweeping character of the changes introduced by the voluntary limitation of reproduction is furnished by the relation between migration and population growth. The theory held by practically all contemporary scientific students of the problem is that under ordinary conditions migration of the modern type does not decrease the size of population of an overcrowded country, nor reduce the evils of over-population, nor does it increase the rate of growth of the population of the receiving country after it has passed through the primary stages of under-population. But this theory is predicated upon the existence of population pressure. If this pressure is removed, or if there is a possibility of its being removed, by voluntary contraception, then the whole implications of migration are modified, if not actually reversed.

Perhaps the most significant change introduced by birth control is that it has made population a manageable factor in human welfare, to be manipulated on the same basis of reason, forethought, and self-control as any of the other great human interests. This gives it an entirely different aspect from that visualized by Malthus. He thought of population as a great, menacing force, ever brooding over humanity, ever threatening it with a burden of misery, which the best of man's devices could never eliminate, but at most only alleviate. To-day, we are able to contemplate population as another of the great forces of nature that has been partially, and can be much more generally, harnessed and made to serve human purposes.

In this brief paper I have used the word "population" in its conventional quantitative sense, the use encouraged by Malthus. I cannot resist this opportunity to register an emphatic protest against this practice, and to urge a more systematic and scientific terminology. "Population" ought to be a big, inclusive term, comprehending both the qualitative and the quantitative aspects of the subject. We already have a word, "eugenics," commonly accepted as designating the study of the qualitative side. It has been the lack of a similar specific word to indicate quantitative study which has caused the word "population" to acquire a more and more limited numerical significance. This is a tendency that ought to be checked before it is too late. For this reason, I have recently ventured to suggest a new word to cover the scientific study of the quantitative aspects. This word is "larithmics," derived from two Greek words meaning "people" and "number." The adoption of this particular word is not important if a better one can be found. But it is highly important first, that we recognize the existence of a distinct field of study—the quantitative aspects of population—and second, that this field be given an accepted name, so that "population" itself may stand where it belongs, including the whole field, and signalizing the fundamental interrelationship and inseparability of the quantitative and qualitative aspects.

DISCUSSION

Miss M. C. BUER said the question had been raised as to the cause of the increase of population in the eighteenth and nineteenth centuries. She happened to have done some work on this subject with reference to Great Britain, and a similar piece of work on rather different lines had been done by Mr. W. R. Griffiths; the results of the investigations were published almost simultaneously (although they worked independently and unknown to each other), and they arrived at almost the same conclusion, which was that the rate of increase was due to a very dramatic fall in the death-rate. Mr. Griffiths thought there was a slight rise in the birth-rate, but Miss BUER was not at all convinced of that. They had agreed on the main theme, that that fall in the death-rate was not to any great extent a fall of the general death-rate; it was mainly a fall in the infantile death-rate. The reason for that could be divided into two—the improvement in infant welfare and the improved food supply. The improved food supply decreased the incidence of rickets and other malnutrition diseases.

It was extraordinary to realize that there was actually in London in 1816 an institution which was in effect a modern baby Clinic to which poor mothers could take their children and receive advice. There was a copy of a little pamphlet, now in the British Museum, issued by this Clinic containing advice to mothers, which was extraordinarily modern. There was evidence that such advice, coupled with the introduction of vaccination, led to a great improvement in the infant mortality-rate. In England and Wales that improvement went on until 1820; from that date there was a slight rise, probably due to economic conditions resultant upon the Napoleonic War. There was then a static death-rate over births for some years, and then a static birth-rate. It was difficult to prove anything about the birth-rate definitely for that period because registration was unsatisfactory. About 1875 there was another period of fall in the adult-rate, and in the twentieth century another dramatic fall in the infantile death-rate.

The static condition of the death-rate appeared to be due to a period of great economic and social change. Miss BUER said she had only done a slight amount of work outside her own country, but such reading as she had done pointed to the fact that the course of events for other parts of Europe was much the same, and that the same factors were at work.

Dr. DUBLIN said he was definitely of the impression that the view expressed by Professor FAIRCHILD carried with it, if not clearly and openly, at least in an implied form, certain points of view which he believed to be unjustifiable and which he believed to be quite disproved. For that reason he wished to try to wrench the discussion out of what he believed to be the false direction it had taken, and to consider the subject along other lines.

Professor FAIRCHILD had called attention to some of the errors that Malthus made; he had called attention to the fact that Malthus made no provision for the force of birth control which had been so powerful in this century; he also referred to Malthus's guess as to the capacity of man to raise sufficient food to meet the population's needs, and also to the first phase of Malthus, that man would increase disproportionately. In all those points it had been shown that Malthus was quite wrong, he could not have been more so; and yet Professor FAIRCHILD went back, and by a clear twist assumed that essentially Malthus was right. Dr. DUBLIN felt as sure as he could be that Malthus was quite wrong, and that his influence was likely to become increasingly harmful. His reasons for saying this were (1) because the last century had proved that the world's capacity to produce food had not yet begun to be measured, and (2) because the whole tendency of the last century had been in the direction of man's loss of natural fertility. If there was anything that was perfectly clear it was that in civilized society families did not reproduce themselves now to the same extent as formerly, and that more and more of the material of humanity came into the category that not only did not, but could not, reproduce itself. Sixteen per cent. of the families of the United States were sterile; only eighteen years ago that figure had been 6 per cent. It would be very important, if it were possible, to know whether the proportion of sterile families reported from other countries were naturally sterile or not. Man was not peopling the world. Whether it was the effect of the use of poisons or the combined effect of altered psychology, advanced age of marriage, or additional educational processes—whatever the factors, the end result went to disprove thoroughly that man was a breeding animal in the present stage of his development.

It would be a pity for the Conference to close on the note that Malthus's was essentially a correct doctrine. In the doctrine of Professor FAIRCHILD's speech there was a very definite implication that Malthus was right throughout the age, whereas in Dr. DUBLIN's opinion he was wrong all the time.

Professor GLOVER held that Malthus was right in this respect—that man left alone would reproduce; he felt the time had come when that force had been controlled. Professor FAIRCHILD had given an analogy of a great force which man had learnt to control.

Mrs. HOW-MARTYN thought the great new factor in this question was the emergence of the emancipated woman who looked upon motherhood in quite a different way; her thoughts and her views had not been sufficiently taken into account. If every woman in the country could be offered, on condition that they passed a medical examination, £1 or £2 a week for every child they had between the ages of 1 to 16, the problem would be what to do with the population, even if the women could select the fathers and not be driven by the necessity of having to get a bread-and-butter ticket for life.

Professor FAIRCHILD said that if there was any criticism implied at all in what he had said, it was levelled at the psychologist and not at the biologist or statistician. He had tried to impress the tremendous importance of research, and the almost complete dearth of research in the sociological aspect of the problem.

With reference to the application of new contraceptive devices, he had not passed any judgment, but had simply said that a new factor had come into population theory. Since, however, the question of desirability had been raised, he wished to say that his sole interest in contraception was that the increase of the human species should be subjected to the same reason, care, intelligence, and foresight as were applied to any great aspect of human life. If that point of view once became established, and if it became socially desirable in any group to increase the rate of production, there would have been already placed in the hands of the community the instruments for bringing that about; a system would have been set up which would eventuate in an increase rather than a decrease.

Professor FAIRCHILD said he had been tremendously pleased to see that in the Birth-Control Clinics in Great Britain the feature of providing help for those who wanted more children was stressed, as well as rendering assistance to those who wanted less. He had urged that principle for many years past, and he thought a move was beginning to be made in that direction in America; because birth control ought to be controlled in both senses, upwards and downwards.

Dr. CHADDOCK thought the attention of the Assembly had been diverted to a discussion on birth control from certain fundamental considerations vastly more important. The things that ought to be considered were the underlying factors which caused the decline of the birth-rate, the distribution of wealth, urbanization of the population, and such things. Birth control and contraceptive devices were a means to an end.

REPORTS OF RESEARCH COMMISSIONS
AND NATIONAL COMMITTEES

Reports read:

1. A. PROBLEMS IN THE FIELD OF COMMISSION I ON POPU-
   LATION AND FOOD SUPPLY. By Dr. J. D. BLACK.
   B. REPORT OF COMMISSION I. By Dr. J. D. BLACK.
2. REPORT ON THE WORK OF COMMISSION II. By Dr. F.
   A. E. CREW.
3. ACTIVITIES OF THE DUTCH NATIONAL COMMITTEE IN
   THE FIELD OF COMMISSION I. By Dr. H. W. METHORST.
   *FOR THE REPORT OF THE DUTCH NATIONAL COMMIT-
   TEE IN THE FIELD OF COMMISSION II, see Paper No.* 10,
   p. 137. *"RESEARCH ON INCOME, NATALITY AND
   INFANT MORTALITY IN HOLLAND."*
4. THE WORK OF THE SWEDISH NATIONAL COMMITTEE.
   By Dr. S. D. WICKSELL.
5. REPORT OF THE STUDIES OF DR. SANDERS ; THE
   WORK OF THE DUTCH NATIONAL COMMITTEE. By
   Dr. G. P. FRETS.
6. REPORT ON THE ACTIVITIES OF THE BELGIAN SOCIETY
   FOR THE SCIENTIFIC STUDY OF POPULATION PROB-
   LEMS. By N. EUGÈNE DUPRÉEL.

A. PROBLEMS IN THE FIELD OF COMMISSION I
ON POPULATION AND FOOD SUPPLY

By Dr. J. D. BLACK

(Harvard University, U.S.A.)

As indicated in the formal report which accompanies this discussion, the major undertaking of Commission I thus far has been to map out its field of research and discover what its important problems are. The objective has been to make a complete logical outline; hence subjects have been included upon which little or no research has thus far been done, and also subjects upon which it would be untimely to undertake research.

This outline is not to be understood as a programme of research to be undertaken, but only as a basis for selecting projects in research to be undertaken.

It is also to be used at this stage as a basis of taking an inventory of the research which has thus far been done or is under way in the field of Population and Food Supply, and of the people now engaged in research in this field. An attempt will be made in the next year or so to get someone in each country to prepare a bibliography of the literature relating to the different topics in the outline, together with a statement of major content and conclusions, and of the principal available sources of data relevant thereto.

The outline as presented in the following embodies the suggestions made by members of the Commission and reported by Professor East, the first Chairman of Commission I, in the *Bulletin* of the Union, the responses up to the time of this Assembly of members of the Commission and others to the tentative form of the outline circulated by the present Chairman in mimeographed form, and also the suggestions made during the meeting of the Assembly. It will no doubt need further revision as suggestions come in from other members of the Commission.

I. Definition and Content of the Field

First to be made clear in this outline is that it is to furnish the basis for an international programme of research. This means that it must provide for all the circumstances relating to population that are found in any country, and that those phases of the subject that are of international significance are particularly to be stressed.

No definitive statement of what is to be included in the field of Commission I is possible until research in population is considered as a whole and its various sub-fields are chosen and defined in the manner indicated in one of the resolutions passed by the 1931 General Assembly. The sub-fields designated are certain to overlap each other at many points and to be closely interrelated. Nevertheless, each will have a central theme of its own. It is well to state this for Population and Food Supply at the outset. Malthus set over against each other two rates of increase, that of the population and that of the food supply. The field of Commission I relates to the latter.

We cannot, of course, look upon rate of increase in food supply in the same manner as did Malthus. Population is pressing upon food supply, it is true, in much the manner Malthus indicated, over a considerable portion of the earth's surface. Probably, so far as numbers go, a large majority of the population of the earth is now subject to this form of population pressure. But over most of the Western world new developments, including changes in the technique of production, in the last century have profoundly altered the outlook, so that the population of the earth has more than doubled since then, and at the same time the population as a whole is better provided with food and the other means of living than in Malthus's time.

Food-supply problems are of course especially important in those countries where the population is pressing upon food supply. They are important there not only from the standpoint of the welfare of these countries themselves, but from the standpoint of peaceful relations between these countries and their neighbours and the rest of the world.

In those countries where the plane of living is now well above the subsistence level, and destined to remain there so far as the best judgment of mankind can foresee, the food supply is worth studying from the standpoint of the welfare of these countries at least in proportion to the relative importance of food in the family budget, and from the world standpoint in so far as the food supply of the country enters into international trade either as import or export.

No doubt there are intermediate countries where the food supply may be a matter of more consequence in the future than at present, or where there is sufficient possibility of this to make the matter one of much concern.

Much of the literature written on the subject of population and food supply, even in the last decade, has accepted as highly probable an increase in population for the world as a whole such as will press with growing strength upon the food-producing powers of the earth. The recent analyses of population increases, which show that the present population of the United States and North-Western Europe is scarcely sustaining itself when adjustments are made for the abnormally large percentages of persons of child-bearing age in the existing populations, raise doubt as to whether it can longer be accepted as probable that world population will press increasingly on food supply. The recent developments in expanding food production contribute further to this doubt. Nevertheless, taking the world as a whole, food is likely indefinitely to constitute the largest single element in living, and hence to be that part of it which is most worth studying from the standpoint of population well-being.

But the problem cannot safely be considered as if the world were a unit. Nationalism is a tremendous force in world affairs—of late an increasing force. This means that national Governments are prone to look upon the nation as the unit in food production and food consumption, and to consider such eventualities as being isolated in war-time and forced to rely upon their own food resources; as being deprived by tariff barriers of an outside market for the manufactured goods that they are now exchanging for food; and as being deprived by immigration barriers of outlets for their still growing numbers. Let any Government base its national policy upon such eventualities as these, and food supply becomes a matter of major importance to its well-being. Pressure upon food supply may under such conditions develop at any time. It is now very evident in some of the countries pursuing such national policies. An international programme of research in population and food supply must therefore take cognizance of these national aspects of food problems. In order to understand food-supply problems internationally, one must therefore study them in considerable part by nations as units.

Of equal importance even from an international standpoint is the unequal distribution of food-buying power between different areas within a country and between different social classes and individuals. There may be so much food in a country such as the United States that the principal concern may be how to dispose of it, and yet at the same time definite shortage of food in some areas (the Southern Appalachians in the United States, for example), or among some large groups of factory workers in cities. Possibly as high a fraction as a fourth of the population of the United States is under-fed in a normal year. Thus in almost any country there may be enough of a group living at or near the subsistence margin, and suffering keenly every crop failure or slackening in business, to produce internal disturbances with international consequences.

Food supply may be increased in several ways, as follows:

(1) By bringing more land into food production.
(2) By applying more labour, etc., to the existing land.
(3) By substituting mechanical for animal power.
(4) By improving the organization of the productive resources of agriculture —getting the right crops on the right land, combined with the right management and labour, etc.
(5) By improving the art of agricultural production—introducing better cultural or breeding practices, improving breeds and varieties, etc.
(6) By shifting to food products yielding higher nutritive values per acre.

If occasion arises for decreasing the food supply, as may easily happen to a nation, it will normally come about through Numbers 1, 2, and 6 of the above.

But there is more involved in the food supply of a nation or the world than mere production. It is estimated that the *per capita* consumption of food in the United States has decreased one-fourth in the last forty years. Utilization may at times play as large a rôle as production. The changes in utilization that may occur are as follows:

(1) In the amount of nutrients consumed *per capita*.
(2) In the relative proportions of starch, protein, etc.; or of cereals, meat, etc.
(3) In the proportion between direct human food production and feed production for livestock.
(4) In the proportion of the product which is saved for human use—of the kernel of wheat, for example.
(5) In the amount of wastage of food in processing and consumption.
(6) In practices as to preservation and storage.

Food production and food consumption also interact upon each other and are interrelated in various other ways, all of which must be taken into account.

Both food production and food consumption are in turn inter-related with population increase. On the one hand, the extent to which the remaining food-producing resources of the world are utilized depends greatly upon whether or not the population produces the numbers to develop them. On the other hand, food may be so difficult to produce at the intensive margin of cultivation that the natural increase in population is held in check thereby. These interrelations also need to be explored somewhat.

Analysis along the foregoing lines involves both the natural and the social sciences. It is characteristic of population research that it cuts across all the accepted disciplines. This is nowhere more true than in its food supply phases. With population living at or near the margin of subsistence, no doubt natural science considerations are principally concerned.

The farther a population gets above this margin, the more important the social science considerations become. No longer is the question one of determining how much food could be produced from a given territory, but instead how much it will choose to produce (using the term *choose* in its very loose sense); no longer how much food a population needs to maintain itself, but instead, how much it will choose to consume, and of what types of food its diet will consist. The economic phenomena of value and price figure largely in all such determinations; likewise the social interactions of the members of the groups into which the population becomes organized.

It is important at this point to indicate that the research programme of Commission I must not undertake to explore thoroughly all the inter-relations between food and the processes involved in human reproduction and natural increase. To do so would take it into domains of research that only specialists in the natural sciences are equipped to explore. Population science is co-ordinating in character. It takes the results of researches in basic natural and social sciences and focuses them on the problems of population change, deriving therefrom a set of generaliza-tions relating especially to population.

The foregoing has made no distinction between the numbers of the population and the quality of it. Interest is shifting more and more to the latter. In those parts of the research here outlined where the effects of food production and consumption on population are involved, it is important to consider quality as well as numbers as a resultant and as a cause. Even in the best-fed countries of the earth the distribution of ability and earning power is such that large numbers suffer in quality from malnutrition.

It would seem advisable to separate clearly the secular from the cross-section approach to food-supply analysis, since much confusion has arisen in the past from failure to do so. The cross-section approach assumes in effect all other conditions as they are now except for the one which is varied. The secular approach attempts to combine with this the effects of whatever changes in related conditions we may assume are likely to occur as the years go by—such changes as improvement in the arts of food production and the possible depletion of soil fertility through continuing cropping or erosion. Of these secular changes, the one last mentioned—the conservation aspect of agricultural production— would seem to be the most important. In practice, of course, the secular and cross-section type of analyses are combined in the same problem. The issues are really such as whether the fertility of the soil can be maintained with heavier and heavier cropping as population increases; and whether or not the needed supplies of fertilizer can be provided indefinitely; and whether or not it is going to be necessary to keep large acreages in timber or grass in order to prevent erosion and dissipation of the soil resources.

Finally we come to the question of how strictly the field of Commission I should be restricted to food. Surely all of agricultural production must be included in the analysis, particularly the production of cotton, flax, wool, and hides for clothing. These products are as much needed almost as food at the margin of subsistence, and maintain their relative importance more nearly than food products as standards of living rise. Furthermore, they use land in production in the same manner as food. Food supply should therefore be interpreted to include the supply of all agricultural products.

Almost as good reasons exist for including forest products as textile products, and surely some consideration must be given to them in the research programme. Very clearly, also, one cannot avoid bringing production and supplies of power, fuel, and minerals into the discussion at various stages. Power is becoming increasingly important in agricultural production. But the field of Commission I is broad even when restricted as much as possible. It will be well, therefore, to focus attention on strictly agricultural products, and to consider the others only when they become involved.

II. Objectives in Research in Population and Food Supply

Following is a list of possible objectives in research relating to population and food supply:

1. To determine the relation between food supply and population changes as a basis for forecasting future population—numbers, quality, food supply, etc.
    (a) In order to plan facilities and institutions for them more intelligently, even to plan the food supply itself. This will be a significant objective only in so far as food supply affects population changes. It can apply to an area or a city as well as to a nation.
    (b) In order to forestall the undesirable consequences of population changes. This objective will be particularly important in regions now over-populated or in danger of being so. It is important for the rest of the world because of the international complications involved.
2. To determine the relations between food supply and population changes in order to control population changes through immigration and emigration policy, education, dissemination of pertinent information and otherwise.
3. To determine the relations between food supply and population conditions in terms particularly of areas where undesirable population conditions exist in order to furnish a basis for improving these conditions—that is, to lay the foundations for programmes of remedial measures.

By the term "changes" in the foregoing is intended to be designated both decreases and increases in numbers, and also changes for the worse or better in quality.

Before any of the foregoing results can really be put to use, a body of facts relevant to existing population conditions is needed. It is the business of research to assemble such facts as well as to discover relationships.

It will be noticed that the actual formulation of population policies is not included as an objective. This is excluded by statute from the work of the Union. It is a function of Government rather than of research agencies.

In most of population research thus far, the emphasis has been upon forecasting. Malthus, no doubt, gave population study this bent. If it were followed, the major objective of Commission I would be to forecast the food supply of nations and the world, and relate it to the population numbers forecasted by Commission II. It should be apparent that such forecasting is highly worth while. But forecasting food supply with even reasonable certainty is not easy. The forecasts will be highly conjectural at best, or based on assumptions so academic that the conclusions will be unreal. It would therefore seem wise to turn more attention than usual to the second and third objectives, particularly to objective No. 3 in the work of Commission I.

III. OUTLINE OF RESEARCH TOPICS

The following, it needs to be repeated, is not a programme of research, but an outline upon which a programme may be based, or from which particular topics may be selected for development at any time.

A. RESEARCH BY COUNTRIES OR REGIONS

Although the unit is the country or region, the projects undertaking should fit into an international programme. This will commonly mean that similar projects will need to be conducted in different countries.

A'. PRODUCTION

1. *Physical, chemical, and biological factors.*

(*a*) Determining the various physical upper limits of food production, all natural factors combined.

(*a'*) For a new country, such as Australia.

(*b'*) For an old one, such as France.

Research under this head will consider the various natural factors and their relation to the growth of various species of crops and livestock, and to yields and production.

(*b*) Determining the effect of particular natural factors on yields and production in a country.

(*a'*) Soil, topography, and drainage

(*b'*) Rainfall and humidity.

(*c'*) Sunlight.

(*d'*) Winds and storms.

(*e'*) Diseases and pests.

(*c*) Estimating the rate at which the plant food is being used up by cropping, erosion, etc.—including studies of the effect of particular practices or factors on rate of soil depletion.

(*a'*) Continuous single-cropping as practised in the country.

(b') Continuous grazing as practised in the country.

(c') The crop rotations followed.

(d') The combined crop and livestock systems followed.

(e') Woodlot and timber production.

(f') Use of artificial manures as supplements.

(g') Varying degrees of intensity of cultivation (measured as output per acre).

(d) Estimating for the country the supplies of artificial manures and the possibilities of adding plant foods to the soil to make up for depletion.

(e) Estimating the possibilities of conserving plant food by substituting mechanical power for animal and human power. This must take into account the available and potential supplies of power.

(f) Estimating the possibilities of increasing output by more intensive cultivation of crops—

    (a') In general.

    (b') In terms of particular factors of production.

        (a'') Fertilizer.

        (b'') Irrigation water.

        (c'') Labour employed in working the soil—ploughing or equivalent, fitting of seedbed, weeding and stirring of soil around plants, etc.

        (d'') Labour employed in harvesting operations.

        (e'') Seed or stand of plants.

(g) Estimating possibilities of increasing output by more intensive feeding of livestock—

    (a') Feed lot or stall-feeding.

    (b') Grazing.

The relationships involved in (f) and (g) are those expressed in the so-called static principle of diminishing outputs, which assumes a given production year or period, a given set of production factors, and a given cultural practice, and merely varies the proportions in which these factors are combined. In research with respect to this principle, if any time variation enters its effect must be eliminated. Such circumstances as the gradual using up of the plant food in the soil and means of offsetting this do not enter into the problem. The two research approaches to the problem are the experimental one of varying the input of one or more factors —seed, fertilizer, tilth, etc.—on identical plots of land, with the same plant food available in them, the same rainfall, temperature, and sunlight, etc.; and the statistical one of letting the amounts of the factors of production vary, but measuring all these amounts, and endeavouring by mathematical means to reduce them to constants. Obviously the analysis by either method is simplified if the records used are all from the same year. This does not mean, however, that the results of experiments or statistical studies in different years and in different areas cannot be used inductively to build up a body of general quantitative relationships.

The principle of diminishing physical outputs may be stated in terms of (a) the total output resulting, (b) the additional or marginal output resulting, (c) the average output per unit of the increasing input factor, (d) the average inputs of the several production factors per unit of output, and (e) the additional inputs per unit of output. These statements are capable of being converted into each other by simple mathematical processes. The part of the curve of diminishing physical outputs which is most significant, because explaining most actual production, begins somewhat beyond the point of diminishing average output for the major production factors and ends considerably this side of the point of diminishing total outputs; but from the standpoint of population and food supply the curve is significant before its point of inflection as well as after, and clear to the point of diminishing total outputs and beyond. The early parts of the curve help explain the numbers of population giving a maximum standard of living, and the late parts the maximum population with the lowest possible standard of living.

Such analysis should not stop with mere statement of input-output relations in numerical or other mathematical terms; it should seek for an explanation of the behaviour of the curves in terms of the chemistry and physics of plant growth, etc. But this reaches beyond the field of population research as such.

2. *Economic and other social factors.*

(a) To determine the economic limits of agricultural production for a country or region, all economic factors combined, assuming given population numbers.

(a') For a new country.

(b') For an old country.

(b) Research under this head will consider the probable value of the natural resources involved, and of the labour, capital, etc., when utilized in turning out other than agricultural products. This will involve such detailed analysis as listed under the following heads:

(a') Trends in expansion of various lines of production competing with agriculture.

(b') Trends in returns to labour and capital in agricultural and competing lines of production—measured as indexes or relatives.

(c') Trends in the composition of family budgets, as indicating changes in relative demand for agricultural and other products. (See "Consumption.")

(d') Trends in the balance between urban and farm population.

(e') Trends in imports and exports of agricultural products and other products competing with them, as evidence of changing comparative advantage in production.

(f') Trends in land utilization.

(g') Effect on the real income in economic well-being of the nation of expanding or contracting its agriculture in various ways. It is here assumed that effect on real income is the economic criteria of advantage; income not, however, being defined in the narrow sense of pecuniary income.

(c) To determine the limits of agricultural production, taking account of existing population trends. These trends may seem to indicate, as in the United States at present, that population numbers will be a major factor in determining the economic limits of agricultural production.

(d) To determine the limits of agricultural development of the nation which represent greatest advantage, taking into account other objectives than economic well-being, such as—

(a') Political and military.

(b') Religious and ethical.

(c') Aesthetic.

3. *Measuring and interpreting changes in agricultural production in a given period, such, for example, as from 1930 to date.*

B'. CONSUMPTION.

1. Determining the diet of the population of a country, with variations in the same geographically, by social groups, income classes, etc.

2. Determining variations in diets in a country due to difference in age, sex, weight, occupation and task, rate of work, climate, clothing, working conditions, individual variations, etc.

3. Determination of the adequacy of the various diets of a country from a physiological standpoint.

4. Comparison of the diets of families living at subsistence, adequacy, and higher levels.

5. Measuring changes in diets of a country, particularly for a recent period, such as since 1900, and interpreting these changes.

6. Forecasting changes in the diets of a country.
7. Analysis similar to No. 1 to No. 6 for clothing.
8. Analysis of consumption budgets as a whole with a view to determining variations in proportions represented by agricultural products and other goods and services, and accounting for these variations.

C'. INTERRELATIONS OF PRODUCTION AND CONSUMPTION.

1. Analysis of effects of inadequate consumption upon human productivity in the country.
2. Effect on population-supporting power of the country of adjusting diets to types of foods most advantageously produced in the region. The parallel effect of adjusting the food production of an area to the types of food needed for a balanced diet.
3. Effects of the opposite tendency, as with a so-called "rising" standard of living.
4. In particular, the effects of shifting from cereals to meats and livestock products and the reverse of this.
5. Secular aspects of the foregoing—effects of changing food habits, etc.

D'. DIRECT EFFECTS ON POPULATION CHANGE.

1. Relation to the population increase of the country of—
   (a) Different kinds and degrees of labour in production.
   (b) Diets of varying degrees of adequacy and luxury.
2. Determination of the point of balance between the marginal output of food and the marginal inputs of energy and food required to supply it, the reproduction process and sustenance of growing children being taken into account.
3. Secular changes in these relationships in the country.

B. RESEARCH INCLUDING THE WORLD AS A WHOLE

A'. PRODUCTION.

1. *Physical, chemical, and biological factors.*
   (a) Determining the physical limits of world production of food and other agricultural products.
   (b) Estimating the rate at which the world supplies of plant food are being used up.
   (c) Estimating world supplies of artificial manure and possibilities of their effective use.
   (d) Estimating the world possibilities of substituting mechanical power for animal and human power, and the effect of this on food supply. This must consider potential supplies of power in the world.
   (e) Estimating the possibilities of increasing the world food supply by more intensive applications of labour, fertilizer, etc. Same for feed and livestock.

(*f*) Estimating the possibilities of increasing world output by breeding more productive plants and animals.

(*g*) Estimating the effect of diseases and pests on future production of food and clothing.

(*h*) Estimating the possibilities of synthetic production of food.

2. *Economic and other social factors*—as outlined for an individual country above.

(*a*) The economic limits.

(*b*) The limits as affected by population changes.

(*c*) The limits based on other considerations than economic well-being.

(*d*) Relation to the foregoing of transportation and international trade in food and clothing; also of trade restrictions.

B′. CONSUMPTION ON A WORLD BASIS.

(*a*) Variations in diet between various countries and reasons therefor.

(*b*) Changes in world diets and reasons therefor.

(*c*) Forecasting world changes in diets.

(*d*) Same as (*a*) to (*c*) for clothing.

(*e*) Proportioning of consumption in the world between agricultural products and other goods and services.

C′. THE EXTENT OF ADJUSTMENTS OF PRODUCTION AND CONSUMPTION TO EACH OTHER IN THE WORLD AS A WHOLE, AND TRENDS IN THE SAME, AND EFFECTS.

D′. THE EXTENT AND IMPORTANCE IN THE WORLD AS A WHOLE OF THE EFFECTS OF LABOUR AND DIET ON POPULATION CHANGES; AND SECULAR CHANGES IN THE SAME AND THEIR EFFECTS.

C. RESEARCH RELATING TO AN AREA WHERE POPULATION CONDITIONS ARE UNDESIRABLE

A′. ASCERTAINING THE FACTS AS TO THE AREA, UNDER SUCH HEADS AS THE FOLLOWING:

1. Composition of population.
2. Density—ratio to land and resources.
3. *Per capita* production.
4. Income and purchasing power.
5. Diets—composition, adequacy, effects.
6. Living budgets.
7. Population movements.

B′. DISCOVERING TRENDS IN THE FOREGOING.

C′. ACCOUNTING FOR THE FOREGOING CONDITIONS.

COMMENTS ON THE OUTLINE

There remains only the need for further discussion of some of the tenets or assumptions upon which the outline is based. The first of these is that relating to the importance of food supply in present-day population analysis. We are told by many that the food supply is no problem at present, that rather we are living in a period of agricultural surpluses. Yet if you will examine the literature on the population question that has appeared in the past decade, you will find that most of the writers envision a menace of a population pressure even within the present century that will seriously disturb the peace of the world.*

Of course, population pressure is a very elusive indefinite term. According to one concept, population pressure develops whenever a population group finds itself unable to live at the level which it has come to accept as its "standard." The definition of a standard of living which such a statement assumes is *a way of living which a group feels deprived of if it does not have it, and which it makes a somewhat unusual effort to attain.* It acquires this feeling of deprivation commonly either from having had it, by the processes of habit or custom or tradition, or from contact with others who now have it. Once a population group finds itself unable to support its existing members according to its standard as above defined, it will begin to manifest evidence of population pressure. It will, in the Western world, in the first instance strike for higher wages or demand legislation that will lower prices of goods purchased. If it is a farmer group, it may demand legislation that will raise prices. When these emergency measures fail, as they almost always will if a real increase in population ratio is at the basis of the situation, the population often begins to shift to other industries, and migrate to other areas, often to other countries. A nation of peoples so beset stirs itself to provide for its surplus population by colonization, by spreading into new territory, as in Manchuria in the last decade, by developing new industries, and new foreign outlets for its products, by insisting upon freedom of ingress of its emigrants into other lands. These

---

* I am troubled as I read this literature with the fear that many of the writers have unconsciously assumed that the whole world is working toward a common level of near-subsistence living such as now prevails over considerable areas of the earth's surface. I know that a good many of these writers would disclaim any such belief; but their logic betrays them at point after point.

efforts breed friction between nations, and even downright aggression, if history is to repeat itself in this particular.

If population pressure is thus defined, it obviously may exist in any part of the world at any time as a result of certain changes in production; it has developed since 1920 over a large part of the rural area of America, and especially in the Southern States. According to this definition, population pressure is most acute not necessarily where food is the scarcest, but where the population has gained upon it most rapidly of late, or where the *per capita* productivity of the people has most seriously declined, relatively if not absolutely.

Population specialists, however, think of population pressure as somehow associated with a subsistence or near-subsistence level of living, and as being most acute where the living level is nearest to a subsistence basis, manifesting itself in high death-rates and the like. This is merely another concept which happens to be called by the same name. It would be well to separate clearly the two meanings of the term. They are surely confused in the literature of the subject.

If population pressure is defined according to the first meaning, one must concede that it will appear in many portions of the world well within the present century, perhaps within a decade or two; furthermore, that it will appear in countries where it is inimical to the peace of the world to have it appear. Even in the United States, the period from 1895 to 1918 was one of rising food prices, accompanied by much agitation about the rising cost of living. These conditions were paralleled in many other countries. No doubt the phenomena of this period will be repeated within the lives of many of those present.

If the United States could isolate itself completely from the rest of the world, however, such population pressure would probably not appear, if we accept the forecasts of Thompson and Whelpton of a maximum of 150,000,000 or less within the present century. Increasing efficiency in production, consumption, and distribution would give to the individual a larger and larger income in goods and services. But since America is not thus isolated, it must share in the experience of the world. If world population expands, so that world production of food and clothing is less *per capita*, then prices of these products will rise, and America will expand its production of them for export, and at the same time its own people will pay more for them than at present, and agricultural products will absorb a larger proportion of incomes.

Under such circumstances, population pressure as above defined would appear even in the United States, although not, of course, in as acute a form as in those countries where the population was still increasing at the same time.

A rational belief is that, taking the world as a whole, the food supply, and with it the supply of fibres for clothing, is not as vital a matter as was believed not only in the time of Malthus, but even in the period from 1900 to 1920. There is abundant evidence of the ability of food production to expand along with population increase, and equally convincing evidence of a tendency for populations to decrease their rate of expansion. The history of the human race has been a history of escape from subsistence living. This trend is continuing. The greatest cause for alarm is the possible exhaustion of certain elements of soil fertility, and of cheap sources of fuel and power. But these are not immediate causes for alarm. The situation at present is that, taking the world as a whole, the supplies of food and other agricultural products are pressing on the population. I have not the slightest doubt that if prices of agricultural products were to rise 10 per cent. above their level of 1925 to 1929, and stay there, a steady rise in their volume would develop and continue for a few decades. Developments in scientific agriculture are principally responsible for this. We have only made a good start in utilizing the developments of science in this field. Dairy husbandmen believe that three-fourths of the cows in the United States are underfed, that is, that a heavier rate of feeding would give a more advantageous ratio of output to input. A nearly similar statement could be made for other forms of livestock. Most cotton growers in the United States use much less fertilizer than is at present economical. Somewhat similar statements can be made for some other crops. A somewhat similar situation maintains in other important food- and fibre-producing countries. The success of Germany, Denmark, and other European countries in increasing yields in the last half-century suggests important possibilities even in the older portions of the globe.

In view of the foregoing circumstances, one seems scarcely justified in going as far in stressing food supply as a factor in population as some of the recent writers on population problems. But though this may be true, there are still important problems for research in the field of food supply in relation to population. Most of them arise from the circumstance that the different nations of the earth represent greatly varying ratios of population to the land and other natural resources. These differences exist even within a country so large as the United States; as, for example, between our own North and South, and East and West. The other important factor in these problems is the wide disparity in income and food-buying power of different social groups within any country. Such being the case, it is important to shift our attention somewhat away from forecasting and more to determining present relationships, on the theoretical side, and toward improvement of the population situation on the applied side. If there be any part of the earth where the ratio of the population to food and other natural resources is such as to produce conditions that most rational persons would declare undesirable—and surely we do not need to look far to find such conditions in any country one might name—could we not outline a programme of research for it that would give us an explanation of these conditions and lay the foundation for a way of escape from them? Could we not outline an international programme of research directed at explaining such conditions wherever they occur? or singling out particular relationships prevalent in various situations and endeavouring to understand their nature more precisely? Such research would, of course need to collect the facts as to the various situations as well as discover the relationships, because the facts are needed before the results of the research can be applied.

The facts and relationships which are needed in accounting for various population conditions, or delineating various relationships that are basic to improving population conditions in various parts of the earth, centre around changes in population numbers and quality on the one hand, and on changes in the supplies of food and clothing on the other. The conditions of peoples can be improved both by increasing or improving the supplies of food, fibres, etc., and their utilization in consumption, and by adjusting the numbers of population to the supplies of the foregoing. Research relating to the latter belongs outside the field of Commission I. Research relating to the former, belongs wholly within the sphere of Commission I.

The relationships in which we are interested exist in a wide range of degrees and circumstances in various areas and countries. They need to be studied over the whole of these ranges. The best unit for a particular study of many of them is likely to be a country or group of countries, partly because many of the significant related variables are more likely to be more uniform within one country than between countries, and partly because the nation or some subdivision of it is likely to be the unit that will undertake the ameliorative measures that will be based on the research. But no study sponsored by the Union should be planned particularly with the thought of furnishing a basis for remedying a situation in an individual country. The results obtained must be such as will fit into relationship structures of broad international significance.

To illustrate the foregoing, such a problem as the relations between labour input and output of a product needs to be studied under conditions of intensive hand labour as in India, and also under the varying degrees of intensivity that are found in different countries clear to wheat production with tractor combines in the United States or Australia. Similarly the relation of under-consumption to labour effectiveness in agricultural production must be studied under various conditions. Competition between divisions of the budget needs to be studied at various income levels. The significance of food is very different in Italy and in New Zealand.

The outline as presented excludes the natural resources other than those of the soil or used in growing crops. But this does not mean that these can be neglected in population analysis. Some other Commission should eventually be set up to handle them. Many of them are so closely linked up with food production that they cannot be kept altogether out of the field of Commission I. There is good reason, for example, for believing that, in case of long-continuing population growth, power would prove a more limiting factor on expansion of population than soil resources. Dr. Alonzo Taylor, of the Food Research Institute of Stanford University, thinks that in case world population continues to expand, our stored-up resources in fuel will eventually be exhausted, and that we shall have to depend upon vegetable matter as a source of alcohol for our power, in which case the competition between power and direct production of human food would take on a new form, similar to that in the case of animal power and human food to-day, but vastly more important.

Whatever form the power-supply problem may take in the distant and uncertain future, there can be no doubt that power supply is a real factor in food production in many countries to-day. Dr. O. E. Baker has advanced the thesis that lack of power causes large acreages of land in China not to be utilized for cultivated crops. The use of power is being advocated as a way of converting the heavy lands of Eastern England back to arable land again. Power machinery has certainly made cultivable large areas of semi-arid wheat land in the United States, Russia, Australia, etc. Power is also needed to manufacture fertilizers, farm machinery, and the large volume of manufactured foods, clothing, and other goods that figure so largely in modern life. Its part in fertilizer production is especially significant.

Of the minerals, those that are needed for fertilizers, for nitrates, phosphates, and potash, are of most importance from the standpoint of our present problem. Most authorities envision a relatively early shortage of phosphate supplies, or their production from low-grade deposits at great expenditure of power.

On the consumption side, the competition between needs for food, fibres for clothing, fuel for warmth, and timber products for shelter and other uses, needs only to be mentioned to be appreciated at its full significance. Vast acreages of land, even at the level of mere subsistence which so many population students so carelessly unconsciously assume, must be taken out of food production to grow the cotton, flax, wool, hides, and timber that mankind needs. At the levels of consumption which we may more reasonably expect for most of the world, these acreages may amount to a considerable fraction of the land product of the earth.

It would appear from the foregoing, therefore, that any analysis of population and food supply which was strictly limited to production of human food would be academic and unreal. The other items that have been mentioned must be included not only in their bearing on food supply, as increasing or decreasing it, but also in their own right as making up part of what the *living* of the population comprehends.

In similar relation, I could mention the industry and commerce of the world. These not only play their part in making food, fuel, clothing, etc., available by bringing them from the areas where they are most easily obtainable to the places where they can be most advantageously utilized, thus actually enlarging in effect the supplies available for consumption; but they also themselves provide a considerable part of the goods and services that go to make up present-day living. The balance between industry and trade and agriculture in any country together with the nature of its imports and exports, must be considered in any statement concerning the adequacy of its food supply or its resources. The same is true for the world as a whole. And if some nations will set up tariff barriers and force their peoples into manufacturing when otherwise they would be producing food and fibre for the rest of the world and trading these for manufactured goods, thus decreasing the productivity of these people, this circumstance must be taken into account also.

In conclusion, let me indicate how large and important the field of research in population and food supply is by saying that we are very far from knowing at the present time: (1) How much the yield of a given crop from an acre can be increased. One writer claims that yields of present varieties of wheat can be increased to 172 bushels per acre. (2) How far yields can be increased economically under the conditions existing in different countries. (3) How much plant and animal breeding may yet add to the yields of crops and livestock. Some recent developments in the United States in which effort has been concentrated upon the unit character productivity suggest that more rapid progress is possible in this field. Neither do we have very good information as to the actual food consumption of different nations and social groups. The available estimates for some countries vary as much as 25 per cent. We do not know how ratios of consumption have changed with changes in working and living conditions. The boasts of some geographers to the contrary, we know relatively little as to the food-producing possibilities of the relatively undeveloped sections of the earth.

B. REPORT OF COMMISSION I ON POPULATION AND FOOD SUPPLY

By Dr. J. D. BLACK

(*Harvard University, U.S.A.*)

WHILE Professor East was Chairman of Commission I its activities were as follows:

1. Enlargement of the membership of the Commission beyond that originally specified, until it includes the following:

Great Britain	..	.. 2	Belgium ..	..	.. 1
Italy	.. ..	.. 4	Argentina	..	.. 1
France ..	..	.. 3	Germany	..	.. 1
Denmark	..	.. 2	Holland ..	..	.. 1
United States	..	.. 5			

2. Correspondence between members of the Commission to obtain suggestions from them as to lines of research worth promoting; also consultations directed to the same end.

3. The initiating of a research project on the methods of collecting, summarizing, and analysing the statistics on population and food supply of the various countries. There is a progress report on this project in the last number of the *Bulletin* of the Union. It is under the direction of the present Chairman of the Commission who was not a member of the Commission at the time the project was begun. It is being financed by a grant from the Bureau of International Research of Harvard University and Radcliffe College.

The present Chairman has been obliged to proceed rather slowly with the task of organizing the work of Commission I, partly because of conflict with other demands on his time holding over from prior commitments, and partly because of unfamiliarity with the objectives and plans of procedure of the Union. The work undertaken thus far has mostly related to the preparation of an outline of the scope and content of population and food supply as a subject for research, and the taking of an inventory of the research done or under way and the workers engaged on it. This has seemed highly necessary as a step preliminary to selecting particular projects for research and getting someone to work upon them; also to passing on the merits of any proposal for research that may be brought before the Commission. We must know the research which has already been done or is under way to prevent us from duplicating effort, even from undertaking projects for support that others are already working upon. For example, the Chairman has found since embarking on the project on international statistics of population and food supply that work closely related to it that might easily be duplicated is being done by the United States Department of Agriculture, the International Institute of Agriculture, the International Statistics Institute, Professor Huntington of Yale, and several other agencies or persons. Arrangements have already been made to co-operate with most of these agencies.

Proceeding upon the foregoing lines, the Chairman has thus far prepared a preliminary outline of the scope and content of the field, with a considerable list of research subjects, and has circulated this among the members of the Commission, asking for their suggestions as to changes and additions. The members of the Commission have also been asked to indicate any work which is being done on any of these projects in their countries. The outline is based on the suggestions that were made to Professor East, on additional suggestions received since from members of the Commission, and upon a review of a considerable volume of the literature on the subject. The Chairman has been assisted in this since last September by a part-time secretary, who is an advanced graduate student at Harvard University.

The work in the mind of the Chairman for the coming three years is as follows:

1. A revision of the outline on the basis of suggestions received and further review of literature.
2. Securing a careful summary statement of research done and results obtained on each of the subjects named in the revised outline, for each of the countries adhering to the Union. This statement should also indicate the data that are available. It is proposed to have this done by or through the members of the Commission in each of the countries. It is intended that these statements will be published in full or in abstracts as seems wise in the *Bulletin* of the Union or elsewhere.

3. Carrying out a similar programme for other countries, preferably following the setting up of national committees in these countries. Where the Union is unable to arrange for setting up such national committees in the near future, the Commission will ask informed students in these countries to render the service not as members of the Union.

4. Selecting projects from time to time from the outline and asking for grants for research upon them in various countries, either directly from the Executive Committee or with its approval from outside sources.

5. Encouraging national committees to propose projects for their countries that come within the scope of the field.

This statement of plans has been approved by the members of Commission I in attendance at the meeting of the General Assembly in London in June 1931, and is presented to the Executive Committee for its approval.

The Commission could be assisted in its work in the following ways:

1. By the setting up of national committees in a number of countries where problems of food supply are especially important—such as Japan, China, India, and Russia.

2. By more support from the National Committees and members of the Union in developing the outline of the field above described, and in securing a record of work done or under way on the various subjects within the field.

3. By suggestions from National Committees and members of the Union as to projects in need of prosecution and persons to work upon them.

4. By more adequate financial support for its activities. The sums thus far received are not sufficient even for carrying out the programmes of obtaining a record of current and completed research in its field. Extensive research projects of an international character will no doubt need to be financed on the basis of grants by foundations or other agencies especially for this purpose. But the Committee should, by the end of another year, have still further funds to be used for subventions to individuals in the various countries for pieces of research fitting into the general programme, these funds to be used to pay the

expenses of clerical assistance, for the use of research equipment, for research materials, and for necessary travel and field expenses. It is suggested that $5,000 should be available for 1933, and $10,000 for 1934.

A rough summary of the finances of Commission I for the period since its creation up to and including the present meeting of the Assembly is as follows. (An exact account will be rendered at the end of the fiscal year.)

RECEIPTS		$2,500
EXPENDITURES:		
Salary of Secretary and Clerical Assistance..	$950	
Travel	450	
Printing, Supplies, and Postage	75	
Cablegrams, etc.	25	
	——	$1,500
Balance		$1,000

(*Signed*)   JOHN D. BLACK
Chairman

REPORT ON THE WORK OF COMMISSION II
(DIFFERENTIAL FERTILITY)

By Professor F. A. E. CREW
(*Chairman of Commission II of the Union*)

PROFESSOR F. A. E. CREW (Chairman of Commission II on Differential Fertility, Fecundity, and Sterility) took the chair, briefly opened the session, and called upon the Hon. Secretary of the Commission, Mr. Eldon Moore, to read an account of progress.

Mr. ELDON MOORE, on behalf of the Chairman and himself, said that the pressure of papers in their subject—the most crowded of any— had decided both of them to refrain from making any original contributions. He therefore proposed only to give as brief a joint report as possible of the work of the Commission.

Interim reports had already appeared in the *Bulletin* of the Union of January 1930, May 1930, and March 1931. Since the last, three more studies had been organized and financed by the Commission:

1. A Study of Differential Fertility in Spain, by Professor Almansa, to whom a grant of £35 had been made at the request of Professor Aznar, Vice-Chairman of the Commission and Chairman of the Spanish National Committee.

2. A Study of the Anthropological and Physiological Characteristics of Large Families in Italy, by Professor Sergi, to whom a grant of £60 had been made at the request of Professor Gini, a member of the financial executive of the Commission and the Chairman of the Italian National Committee.

3. The third application, Mr. Moore said, could best be explained by reading the letter of application from Mr. D. Caradog Jones, of the School of Social Science of Liverpool University and Director of the Social Survey of Merseyside.

"The University of Liverpool is at present engaged upon a survey of social conditions in Merseyside, somewhat similar in character to the Booth Survey which is being repeated in

London. Our survey is conducted from the School of Social Science, and Professor Carr-Saunders himself is Chairman of the Committee concerned with it.

"There is a great deal of research we should like to do, but the amount is naturally limited by the funds we have at our disposal.

"The work so far undertaken will give a fair picture of fertility in a large urban population, its correlation with age, housing, unemployment, economic conditions, social class, industry, and so on. So far, however, attention has been confined to the normal types in the community, since expense has made it necessary to disregard certain well-defined abnormal types. It is now proposed, if financial assistance is granted, to round off the whole Survey by making a study of fertility among the following types living in the district studied:

Those born deaf.
Those born blind.
Those born physically defective.
Those born mentally defective.
Those in constant receipt of relief from Public Assistance Committees and charitable agencies.

"Besides showing how, if at all, the reproductive activities of these people differ from those of their normal neighbours already included in the Survey, the study will answer the following questions:

"Are these different classes all separate and distinct, or is there some close correlation between them? Are the people who compose them spread uniformly over any large area, or are they found thickly grouped in certain definite patches? Are they producing large or small families of children? Do most of their children survive, or do many die off at an early age?

"It should be noted, in particular, that the whole study will provide an answer to an important and much vexed question, the correlation between fertility and child mortality, and indirectly throw light upon the voluntary factor.

"It is hoped that in this way it will be possible to compare the reproductive rates and other factors of the various subnormal elements in the community with the same factors of the normal population as a standard or control group.

"Much data on these questions has already been collected in the course of the Survey, but it awaits classification and analysis, and certain further studies will be needed to complete it."

This application was endorsed by Sir Bernard Mallet, Chairman of the British National Committee, and Professor Carr-Saunders, a member of the Commission. At their request a grant of £100—the first to any British student—was made to Mr. Caradog Jones.

Mr. MOORE next reminded the Assembly that the Commission, having surplus funds at the end of its first financial year, had decided, at the Chairman's and his own suggestion, to devote them to a bibliography of differential fertility, the need for which had become acute. Three members of the Commission had volunteered to supervise different sections of the work: Professor Mahaim, Chairman of the Belgian National Committee, the French section; Mr. R. R. Kuczynski, of the German and American National Committees, the German section; and the speaker himself the references in the English language. The work was now complete up to the beginning of that year (1931); Professor Mahaim's worker, Mlle Racine, having sent in about 180 references, ranging from 1838 to 1929; Dr. Kuczynski's worker, Dr. J. P. Kuczynski, about 200 since the War and up to 1930; and Mr. Moore's own worker, Mrs. Betty Fraser, just 700 references to English and American literature from 1798 to 1931.

After outlining certain technical details in the Bibliography, the speaker pointed out that its publication would lay the foundation for some much needed work. But it would be worth little, he said, unless advantage were taken of it by workers in each language to make an expert analytical survey of the data. What was needed was a monograph on the work in each of the three languages, a monograph which would also indicate the principal points requiring further research.

ACTIVITIES OF THE DUTCH NATIONAL COMMITTEE IN THE FIELD OF COMMISSION I

Dr. H. W. METHORST
(*Chairman Dutch National Committee*)

THE Commission met in April 1930, in order to discuss the well-known letter received from Dr. East.

The discussions, conducted with perfect understanding among the members present, showed that each of the members was very willing to take his share in the activities of the Commission, but did not know in what way this could be done. The results of the investigations indicated in Dr. East's letter gave promise of no great expectations. For this reason it was decided not to give any directions on methods to be followed, but to wait for possible indications of results from the International Commission. Dr. Black, who is Dr. East's successor, was accordingly informed to this effect. Subsequently a more definite programme was received from the first International Commission.

There are no objections to this programme, although the Commission could hardly adopt it as its own. The subjects included are not suitable for treatment by an International Commission. For this reason we only see the possibility of perhaps inviting from time to time an expert to study a particular question, or to collect the results of former investigations—or to have these collected—so as to put them at the disposal of all countries.

Finally, the first Commission for the Netherlands has formulated the following proposition for the International Commission.

Owing to the progress of science and technology, the production of food for human consumption has increased to such an extent that supposing a further normal development of the world-situation, a shortage of food need not be feared, even in the remote future. However, there are several indications that during the last few decades, the consumption as well as the production of food has changed considerably.

So it seems probable—

1. That in several countries the consumption of carbohydrates per head of the population has decreased, whereas the consumption of proteins has increased, and also changes have taken place in the consumption of different kinds of animal and vegetable fats.

Indications which make this probable are:

(a) The decrease of the muscular labour required in consequence of the extension in the use of machinery;
(b) The increase of that part of the population occupying itself chiefly with intellectual labour;
(c) The general increase of food-production.

2. That the production of cereals, used for direct human consumption (chiefly wheat), has increased less than the production of animals foodstuffs, dairy produce, sugar, vegetables, vegetable oils, etc.

Although different studies have been undertaken within the sphere of these problems, the Netherlands Committee is of opinion that insufficient facts are available to form an exact idea of the real situation.

Therefore this Committee urges the International Union for the Scientific Investigation of Population Problems to stimulate National Committees to undertake investigations into the changes which have occurred in the production and the consumption of foodstuffs since 1900.

RAPPORT DE LA PREMIÈRE COMMISSION NATIONALE NÉERLANDAISE

Le Dr. H. W. METHORST
(*Président*)

LA Commission s'est réunie au mois d'avril 1930 pour la discussion de la lettre bien connue du Dr. East.

Le résultat des discussions qui ont fait preuve de l'accord parfait des membres présents, était qu'on a pu constater que chacun des membres ne demande pas mieux que de coopérer aux activités pour lesquelles la Commission a été créée, mais qu'on ne savait pas encore de quelle manière ce serait possible. On ne s'attendait pas à de bons résultats des recherches signalées par la lettre du Dr. East. Pour cette raison il a été décidé de ne faire aucune indication en ce qui concerne la méthode à suivre, mais d'attendre pour voir, si des indications venant peut-être de la part de la Commission Internationale promettent quelque résultat.

Une communication relative à ces points a été faite au Dr. Black, successeur du Dr. East.

En suite, un programme plus définitif de la premiére Commission Internationale a été reçu.

Il n'y a pas d'objections à ce programme, bien qu'il ne puisse guère être le programme de la Commission elle-même. Les sujets signalés ne se prêtent pas aux activités d'une Commission internationale. La Commission devra donc se borner à inviter quelqu'un peut-être de temps à autre à faire des recherches relatives à un point déterminé et à réunir ou à faire réunir les résultats de recherches antérieures, afin de les mettre à la disposition des divers pays. Enfin la première Commission pour les Pays-Bas a formulé la proposition suivante pour la Commission Internationale.

Par suite du progrès de la science et de la technologie, la production des matières alimentaires destinées à la nourriture de l'homme a augmenté à un si haut point, qu'on n'aura pas à craindre, même dans un avenir éloigné, un manque de nourriture par suite d'un développement normal progressief de la situation mondiale. Il y a cependant plusieurs indices d'un changement considérable dans la consommation, ainsi que dans la production de matières alimentaires pendant les dernières décades.

Il est donc probable—

1. Que dans plusieurs pays la consommation de carbohydrates par tête de la population a diminuée, tandis que la consommation de protéiques a augmentée et que des changements ont également eu lieu dans la consommation de diverses espèces de graisses animales et végétales.

Indices de cette probabilité :

(a) La diminution du travail musculaire exigé en conséquence de l'emploi étendu de machines;

(*b*) L'augmentation de la partie de la population qui s'occupe principalement du travail intellectuel;

(*c*) L'augmentation générale de la production des matières alimentaires.

2. Que la production de céréales utilisées pour la consommation directe de l'homme (surtout le froment) a moins augmentée que la production de denrées alimentaires animales, et de produits de laiterie, de sucre, de légumes et d'huiles végétales.

Bien que des études différentes aient été entreprises dans le domaine de ce problème, la Commission pour les Pays-Bas est d'avis qu'il n'y a pas assez de faits disponibles pour donner une idée exacte de la situation réelle.

C'est pour cette raison que la Commission propose à l'Union Internationale pour l'étude scientifique des problèmes de la Population de stimuler les Commissions Nationales des Pays à étudier les changements qui se sont présentés dans la production et la consommation des denrées alimentaires depuis 1900.

THE WORK OF THE SWEDISH NATIONAL COMMITTEE

By Dr. S. D. WICKSELL

(*Sweden*)

THE Swedish National Committee was, as I think has already been stated in the *Bulletin*, constituted in the autumn of 1928. The Committee now has about seventy-five members, with a President, a Vice-President, and a Secretary and Treasurer as its officers. At the side of this *Presidium* is placed a Council of eleven members chosen as representatives of the divers fields of research which are of particular importance for the investigation of Population Problems.

Now, in Sweden, there is very little chance for a committee of this type, and with practically no funds at its disposal, to take up research work of a co-operative nature. The only thing that the Committee has been able to do, as a body, is to approach the authorities in order to exert an influence on the official statistical output of the country, in particular the Census. Thus the National Committee has as one of its first acts laid before the Royal Government a Memorandum on the Census of 1930, recommending along general lines several important additions to and extensions of the Census programme, and also requesting the Government to appoint a special commission to prepare that programme in co-operation with the Central Statistical Bureau. I am glad to say that this request was met with approval, and that several members of the National Committee have been appointed also on this official commission. I am also glad to say that as the result of the work of this commission the programme of the 1930 Census has been enlarged and specified particularly concerning sizes of families, occupations, and educational standing. The attempt made at the 1920 Census to combine the Census with an inventation of the income-tax declarations will be taken up again at the 1930 Census, it is hoped with still better results than last time, the year 1930 being a less abnormal economic year than 1920. I know I am not exaggerating when I say that as regards official population statistics, the possibilities for important research work is in Sweden extraordinarily favourable. It is not only that we have this well-known, unbroken record of regular Censuses and vital statistical registrations through more than 180 years. It is also a fact that in Sweden the possibilities of co-ordinating the Census data and the data concerning the births, deaths, and marriages, as well as the migrations, will in the next years be, as I believe, more promising than in any other country. Direct investigations into mortality, nuptiality, and fertility will be possible with a division according to occupation and social standing, income and wealth, and, as I hope, also according to educational standing. The members of the National Committee are eagerly awaiting the results of the 1930 Census, and there is no doubt that, if the funds can be found for extending Dr. Edin's identification work to a greater part or to the whole of the population, most striking and important results will come out of the next few years of Swedish vital statistics.

Of the demographic work at present carried out independently by members of the National Committee, I shall only mention the following. Dr. Edin is, as you already have heard, continuing his important researches into differential fertility in Stockholm and Gothenburg. He is also concluding some genealogical-historical researches for a few parishes in the Province Westmanland, which he has been working on for many years. Dr. Linders is continuing his researches on the demography of the clergy and of the medical profession, and also working in the field of anthropometry. Dr. Dahlberg is doing anthropometrical and demographical research work concerning twins and concerning the mentally deranged. Professor Myrdal is preparing an extensive study of the inner migrations. For my own part I may mention that my work at the Statistical Institute of the University of Lund has been carried out along two different lines. In the first place I have taken up the formal theory of population in a general way. More as a numerical check on the theory than as a separate investigation, I have worked out quite a number of population forecasts for Sweden and Norway, according to different sets of hypothetical trends of natality, fertility, and mortality. On the other side I have for many years been investigating into the geographical and regional distribution of the demographic elements in my country. A few papers on this subject were published some years ago, and some new ones are now in preparation.

REPORT ON THE STUDIES OF DR. J. SANDERS:*
THE WORK OF THE DUTCH NATIONAL COMMITTEE

By Dr. G. P. FRETS
(*Holland*)

WITH the collaboration of the Population Section in the town of Rotterdam, and of various enterprises, nearly 25,000 forms have so far been filled in. These forms state names and addresses of individuals, religious denomination, and profession of parents and children, year of birth and death of parents and children, and year of marriage. Thanks to the courtesy of the Director of the Municipal Statistical Office of Amsterdam, punching-cards showing the information were sorted in different ways with the help of machines, thus presenting the falling birth-rate from various aspects. Before the punching and the sorting of the cards, the Director of the Amsterdam Bureau assisted in drawing up the schedules. This work is, from a statistical point of view, very difficult and valuable, and no less important than the mechanical work.

In the first place, the birth-rate was examined for the various professions, which to this end was divided into seven groups, viz.:

(*a*) Members of higher intellectual professions, such as members of the South Navigation Society, notaries, lawyers, physicians, clergymen.

(*b*) Higher grade officials and their equivalents.

(*c*) Middle-class individuals, mostly shopkeepers.

(*d*) Artisans,† including members of an office staff, draughtsmen, painters, carpenters.

(*e*) Skilled labourers, including commercial travellers, messengers, bricklayers, tram-conductors, etc., policemen, cooks, dock-workers in permanent service.

* Published by Martinus Nijhoff, The Hague: "The Declining Birth-rate of Rotterdam," by Dr. J. Sanders.

† In his book Dr. Sanders distinguishes "skilled labourers" from "practised labourers." These terms are here rendered as "artisans" and "skilled labourers" in order to approximate more closely to familiar English terms.

(f) Unskilled labourers, inclusive of temporarily employed workmen, dock-workers, ship-breakers, and porters.

(g) Finally, a group of individuals not classified under any calling or profession, but selected because they adhere to birth-control doctrines, i.e. the members of the Rotterdam branch of the Neo-Malthusian League.

The figures calculated are the numbers of children born in each family up till January 1, 1929. The lowest figure appears in the officials, i.e. second group. For 100 families of this type there are 228 children. In families of the higher intellectual group, 249; in the skilled artisans' group, 280; in the skilled labourers' group, 318; in the shopkeepers' group, 318; in the unskilled labourers' group, 373; and in the Neo-Malthusian group, 170. One should be careful, however, not to jump to conclusions. It is wrong to say that the Neo-Malthusians have the smallest number of children, for the majority of them are younger people, who were married after the War. These marriages have not yet exhausted their fertility; children may still be born in these families. The comparatively low birth-rate of skilled labourers is due to the fact that they include tram-conductors and policemen. If these were not included, the number of births would be the same as for the unskilled labourers, 373. In 100 physicians' families there are 232 children, in 100 families of clergymen there are 355.

As for the different religions, members of the Reformed (Calvinist) Church have the greatest number of children, i.e. 409 per 100 families; Roman Catholics have 367; members of the Dutch Reformed Church, 325; Jews, 272.

As the numbers in the social groups do not correspond to the numbers in the religious groups, it is desirable to calculate the numbers of children with regard to the parents' religion and profession. It then appears that in all the seven occupational groups mentioned, members of the Reformed (Calvinist) Church have the greatest number of children; the Roman Catholics follow next; and finally the members of the Dutch Reformed Church.

It is just as important to know when the marriage was contracted, for in the course of the last fifty years the birth-rate has fallen regularly. Marriages which were contracted forty years ago have on the whole produced more children than marriages contracted after the

War. For this reason the marriage years have been grouped for six periods, viz.:

(*a*) Before 1879	(*d*) 1904–1913
(*b*) 1879–1893	(*e*) 1914–1918
(*c*) 1894–1903	(*f*) 1919–1928

When the families belonging to these periods are divided according to the seven professional groups, we find that with regard to all professional groups there has been a regular and almost equal fall of the birth-rate in the last fifty years. Among the labourers the fall was not any less noticeable than among the higher intellectual group and the officials, but we also find that originally there was a great difference between the numbers of births in the various professional groups. Supposing the number of children per 100 families of the higher intellectual group married between 1879 and 1893 to be 100, then this number was 110 for the officials married during the same period, 173 for the shop-keepers, 163 for the skilled artisans, 191 for the skilled labourers, and 203 for the unskilled labourers. With regard to marriages of later years these differences become smaller, and numbers approach a same level. Thus the corresponding numbers with regard to the marriages con-tracted between 1914 and 1918, i.e. marriages which for the greater part have, from the fertility point of view, come to an end, were 100 for the higher intellectual group, 86 for the officials, 99 for the shop-keepers, 117 for the skilled artisans, 114 for the skilled labourers, 116 for the unskilled labourers, 106 for the Neo-Malthusians. With regard to the marriages in the latest period, these differences are smaller still, but it should be borne in mind that these marriages have not yet, from the fertility point of view, come to an end.

So we find that Neo-Malthusians have not a smaller number of children than the others.

When we classify the families in these various marriage periods according to the religious denomination groups, we find also that for all these denominations, without a single exception, the fall in the birth-rate is about the same, and that in all the periods the members of the Reformed (Calvinist) Church have the greatest number of children. With regard to the marriages contracted between 1879 and 1893, the members of the Dutch Reformed Church had more children than the Roman Catholics. In the following years it is just the reverse, however, and this has remained so until now.

All this shows, according to the author, that in spite of the more or less vigorous opposition and exhortation of the pastors of the various religious groups, the fall in the birth-rate has steadily gone on.

The length of the marriage naturally has a great influence on the number of children. Generally speaking, there will be fewer children in a family that has existed five years than in one that has existed ten years. When we consider the number of children per 100 families of the same length of duration in the above periods in which the marriages were contracted, we find that marriages of shorter duration, but contracted in a later period, have produced fewer children than the marriages which were contracted in an earlier period. This is a phenomenon of regular occurrence, and it proves that birth control was practised immediately at the beginning of married life. In the course of the last fifty years births have been spaced at longer intervals, and the first birth has tended to be postponed to a longer interval after the wedding-day.

A study has also been made of the number of children alive on January 1, 1915, with regard to marriages contracted before that date, as well as of the number of children alive with regard to marriages contracted after January 1, 1918. These investigations showed that with marriages of equal duration, in families founded previously to 1915, there were more children alive than in families founded after 1917. This conclusion is of great importance. Budge, Roesle, and others, have asserted that the falling rate of infant mortality is the principal reason of the fall in the birth-rate. If this were true, there would not be a decrease in the number of children alive.

The above statements prove, however, that with regard to surviving children, the decrease is just as considerable as the decrease in the birth-rate.

The conclusions of the author are the following: So far the investigations have shown already that in all classes of society the number of children has decreased considerably, and even more among the working classes than in the higher ones. They show also that the decrease has been the same for all religious denominations, in spite of all endeavours to prevent the fall of the birth-rate.

REPORT ON THE ACTIVITIES OF THE BELGIAN SOCIETY FOR THE SCIENTIFIC STUDY OF POPULATION PROBLEMS

By M. EUGÈNE DUPRÉEL

SINCE it was constituted the Belgian Society has promoted three lines of research:

1. The first and principal objective has been *Research into the Living Conditions of Large Families in Belgium*. As the writer of this report I was privileged to present and to comment on its first conclusions in the Second Session, June 16th.

2. The second objective of our programme is an inquiry into the demographic effects of *family allowances*. The Society has been in communication with the Ministries of Industry, Works, and Social Insurance, as well as with the State Insurance Department of Brabant. From one source or another we have received the following information:

    (*a*) The system of family allowances has been in force for too short a time for it to be possible to appreciate its effects.

    (*b*) Documentary particulars received to date have neglected the demographic aspect of the problem of family allowances, but we are assured that in the two institutions consulted this consideration will receive attention in future.

3. The compilation of a Bibliography on the problems of *Differential Fertility* in Belgium forms the third objective in the programme of the Society. This work is being carried out.

I wish to call your attention, as relevant to our work, to the recent study by Professor Baudhuin, Secretary of the Society, on *The Future of the Belgian Population*, of which a few copies are available for collaborators.

RAPPORT SUR LES TRAVAUX DE L'ASSOCIATION BELGE POUR L'ÉTUDE SCIENTIFIQUE DES PROBLÈMES DE LA POPULATION

Par M. EUGÈNE DUPRÉEL

DEPUIS sa constitution, l'association belge a retenu trois ordres de recherches:

1. C'est d'abord, et au principal, *l'Enquête sur les conditions de vie des familles nombreuses en Belgique*, dont l'auteur de ce rapport a eu l'honneur, dans la séance du 16 juin, d'exposer et de commenter les premiers résultats.

2. Le second point du programme est une enquête sur les effets démographiques des *allocations familiales*. L'association s'est adressée au Ministère de l'Industrie, du Travail et de la Prévoyance sociale, ainsi qu'à la Caisse de compensation du Brabant. De part et d'autre elle a reçu les informations suivantes:

   (*a*) Le système des allocations familiales est en vigueur depuis trop peu de temps pour qu'il soit possible d'en constater les effets.

   (*b*) La documentation recueillie jusqu'ici négligeait l'aspect démographique du problème des allocations familiales; mais on s'attachera désormais, dans les deux institutions consultées, à prendre ce point en considération.

3. La constitution d'une bibliographie du problème de *la reproduction différentielle* pour la Belgique est le troisième point du programme de l'Association. Ce travail est en cours d'exécution.

Je signale aussi, comme se rattachant à nos travaux, l'étude récente de M. le professeur Baudhuin, secrétaire de l'association, sur *l'Avenir de la Population belge*, dont un certain nombre d'exemplaires est mis à la disposition des assistants.

CLOSING ADDRESS BY THE CHAIRMAN OF THE BRITISH POPULATION COMMITTEE

CLOSING ADDRESS BY THE CHAIRMAN OF THE BRITISH
POPULATION COMMITTEE

SIR BERNARD MALLET said he would like to express the gratitude of the British Committee to the delegates, especially those from foreign countries, who had attended the Assembly, and to say how greatly the attendance of so many men of great distinction in their own line had been appreciated. He was very glad to hear that the papers had been found to be of interest, and he looked forward to the publication of those papers.

It was proposed to send out within a few weeks a short résumé of the principal results of the Assembly, such as the alteration in the Statutes and a few remarks on finance, and the full minutes would appear later; a full report of the Proceedings containing the scientific papers would be published. This volume should be of great interest, and he hoped that it would be widely read; it should contribute to increase the reputation of the Union.

With regard to Dr. Dublin's offer from America of the substantial contribution to the finance of the Union, he hoped that all members would make that offer widely known. It ought not to be impossible to raise a thousand pounds a year for three years in the whole of the rest of the world. Sir Bernard Mallet said he would consult with the President as soon as possible and see what could be done in Great Britain in the way of getting some substantial contributions to the Union. Times were so bad that he did not feel too hopeful; it largely depended upon getting hold of two or three rich men interested in the subject. It would mean personal application and personal effort, but something might be done by publishing a letter in the leading journals of each country, stating that this offer had been made and emphasizing the importance of trying to match it.

For his own part, Sir Bernard Mallet expressed the great pleasure it had been to him to attend the Assembly and to meet and make so many friends.

DISCOURS DE CLÔTURE PRONONCÉ PAR LE PRÉSIDENT DU COMITÉ BRITANNIQUE DE LA POPULATION

SIR BERNARD MALLET dit qu'il voudrait exprimer la gratitude du Comité Britannique aux délégués, particulièrement ceux des pays étrangers, qui avaient assisté à l'Assemblée, et dire combien avait été appréciée la présence d'un si grand nombre de personnes jouissant d'une haute distinction dans leurs propres spécialités. Il était très heureux d'apprendre que les rapports avaient été dignes d'intérêt et il pensait d'avance au plaisir de les lire publiés.

On avait l'intention d'envoyer dans un délai de quelques semaines un bref résumé des principaux résultats de l'Assemblée, tels que les modifications aux Statuts et quelques remarques sur la situation financière; le procès-verbal complet paraîtrait plus tard; un compte-rendu complet des Travaux, contenant les rapports scientifiques, serait publié. Ce volume serait d'un grand intérêt et l'orateur espéra qu'il serait lu par un public nombreux; il contribuerait sans aucune doute à accroître la réputation de l'Union.

Au sujet de l'offre américaine faite par le Dr. Dublin d'une contribution substantielle aux ressources de l'Union, il espéra que tous les membres feraient connaître cette offre aussi largement que possible. Il ne devrait pas être impossible de se procurer mille livres par an pendant trois ans dans le reste du monde. Sir Bernard Mallet dit qu'il conférerait dès que possible avec le Président pour examiner ce qui pourrait être fait en Grande-Bretagne en vue d'obtenir quelques contributions substantielles à l'Union. Les temps étaient si durs qu'il n'avait pas un espoir excessif; ce qui serait le plus utile serait de toucher deux ou trois personnes riches s'intéressant au sujet. Cela demanderait des démarches et des efforts personnels. Mais il pourrait être profitable de publier une lettre dans les principaux journaux de chaque pays, annonçant que cette offre avait été faite et insistant sur l'importance d'un effort pour obtenir des offres analogues.

Pour sa propre part, Sir Bernard Mallet exprima le grand plaisir qu'il avait eu à assister à l'Assemblée et à y rencontrer ses Amis et à y faire tant de nouvelles connaissances.

INDEX